# JUST
# INTERVENTION

*Carnegie Council on Ethics and International Affairs series*
JOEL ROSENTHAL, series editor

# JUST INTERVENTION

## ANTHONY F. LANG JR., EDITOR

Georgetown University Press,Washington, D.C.

Georgetown University Press
© 2003 by Georgetown University Press. All rights reserved.

Printed in the United States of America.
10 9 8 7 6 5 4 3 2 1     2003

This book is printed on acid-free paper meeting the requirements of the American National Standard for Permanence in Paper for Printed Library Materials.


Library of Congress Cataloging-in-Publication Data

Just Intervention / Anthony F. Lang, Jr., editor.
    p. cm. — (Carnegie Council on Ethics and International Affairs)
Includes bibliographical references and index.
    ISBN 0-87840-341-8 (pbk. : alk. paper)
    1. Humanitarian intervention. I. Lang, Anthony F., 1968– II. Series:
Carnegie Council on Ethics and International Affairs (Series)
    KZ6369.J87 2003
    341.5'84—dc21

                                                        2003006944

# Contents

# Acknowledgments

This book resulted first and foremost from the hard work of Joel Rosenthal, the president of the Carnegie Council on Ethics and International Affairs and the former editor of its journal, *Ethics & International Affairs*. Joel played the primary role in generating much of the literature in the journal on the topic of humanitarian intervention and, hence, much of the material in this book. Moreover, his work at the Carnegie Council for almost twenty years in putting together workshops and conferences on the themes discussed here has vastly increased our ability to think critically about the moral norms underlying humanitarian intervention. As the editor of this volume, I owe a personal debt of gratitude to Joel for making it a reality; as a scholar, I, like many others, owe a much greater debt to him for creating the space where this literature could develop.

A number of other people at the Carnegie Council have played an important role in creating this volume. Deborah Washburn, formerly the council's director of publications, helped initiate the process through which the volume came about. Paige Arthur, the former managing editor of *Ethics & International Affairs*, helped evaluate a number of the essays that make up the volume's chapters, including some of the newly commissioned ones. Christian Barry, the current editor of the journal, brought a rigor and professionalism to the entire journal process. Not only that, Christian has helped sharpen my own thinking on these issues and many others. Assistance at the council has also come from Janice Gabucan, Vivek Nayar, Lydia Tomitova, and Yesim Yemni in bringing the volume to fruition.

# INTRODUCTION

# Humanitarian Intervention— Definitions and Debates

## Anthony F. Lang Jr.

Humanitarian intervention was poised to be one of the central topics of debate among policymakers, scholars, and activists before September 11, 2001. But after that day's terrorist attacks and the military response to them, debates about sovereignty, human rights, and intervention suddenly took on different meanings. Partisans to old debates refocused their energies on terrorism, asymmetric warfare, and nation building.

Debates over humanitarian intervention may have been eclipsed by the war on terrorism, but the dilemmas that it generated have not disappeared. Indeed, if we look beyond the shallow "lessons of Somalia," the questions that generated the debates of the 1990s remain central to international affairs. Should sovereignty prevent outside agents from interfering in the affairs of a state? What moral weight should we give to sovereignty and sovereign borders? Do humanitarian "emergencies" justify the use of military force? Can military force be used for actions other than waging war? Can a humanitarian intervention be in the "national interest"? More fundamentally, should military force be used to save lives or protect rights? Should we kill in order to save?

This volume provides some answers to these and related questions. During the past twenty years, the Carnegie Council on Ethics and International Affairs has been exploring these questions through its publications and programs. Articles on this topic have appeared primarily in the council's journal, *Ethics & International Affairs*, and also in other council publications, including *Human Rights Dialogue* and its annual Morgenthau lectures. The council has also been addressing these themes in its conferences and workshops, although only a portion of that work can be represented in this volume. The selections included here—including five newly commissioned essays—represent the most important and enduring attempts to explore questions of humanitarian intervention.

Why another book on humanitarian intervention? This volume makes its distinct contribution by focusing on ethics and moral argument. Studies of the ethics of humanitarian intervention can be divided into two types: descriptive and normative. Descriptive ethics explains the particular moral beliefs and ideas that guide decisions to intervene.[1] Normative ethics provides the tools for evaluating the practices and outcomes that constitute humanitarian intervention.[2] This volume, like much of the work of the Carnegie Council, falls more into the latter category than the former, providing policymakers, activists, citizens, and scholars alike with new ways of evaluating humanitarian action. Rather than a single approach, the goal of this volume is to provide a range of different evaluative approaches to the study of humanitarian intervention.

Providing this range of evaluations should not be seen as an exercise in metaphysics with no relevance to the practical dilemmas faced by policymakers and activists. Rather, the authors of the chapters below recognize that those who make the difficult decisions surrounding humanitarian action must take into account political realities, strategic considerations, and the resistance of leaders to having the sovereignty of their state violated. Nor should these restraints to intervention be seen as evil attempts to block the efforts of good humanitarians. Rather, the restraints of sovereignty and the structures of international law that support those restraints serve a moral purpose: the protection of a community inside clearly defined borders.[3] Here arises a dilemma, not one between amoral politicians and moralistic humanitarians, but one between competing moral claims about the nature of responsibility and political community. Thus to make the claim that an intervention is necessary to save lives (often a true statement of fact) does not settle the moral question of humanitarian intervention.

## DEFINITIONS

The contention over the meaning of such terms as "humanitarian intervention" suggests both the difficulty and importance of definitions. In fact, in trying to define this particular term, two issues arise. First, there is no clearly defined understanding of the term. Second, any definition contains within it certain normative assumptions. Indeed, not only does humanitarian intervention have a normative dimension to it, the concept of intervention itself is inherently normative. James Rosenau argues that intervention should be defined on the basis of its "observable characteristics" that would allow the concept to be "operationalized" for future research.[4] This approach, however, ignores the fact that intervention presupposes a series of normative structures that cannot be observed. To seek to define "intervention" without engaging in some mode of normative analysis ignores central features of the action itself.

These normative structures become clearer when we turn to international legal definitions. Louis Henkin has pointed out that almost any action undertaken by one state in its relations with another could be considered a form of intervention. No single rule or definition has become the norm in international legal discourse, perhaps because, as Henkin notes, many states do not want to limit their ability to engage in such actions.[5] The closest to a definition that Henkin provides is a "violation of a state's sovereignty," suggesting that intervention should be understood primarily as a violation of a normative structure. In other words, the legal definition of intervention is inherently ethical. As Henkin notes, most international legal definitions give a negative valence to this definition, allowing it only under specially defined circumstances.

"Humanitarian" intervention raises even further difficulties in definition. In being prefaced by an adjective with an explicitly positive valence, humanitarian intervention is imbued with moral meaning. Some have highlighted the fact that this concept privileges the motives of the intervenors in the definition, a problematic assumption if one wishes to create a definition for purposes of further investigation (i.e., how does one determine motives?). In chapter 11 of this volume, Nicholas Wheeler explores this issue in some detail, arguing that "Making the primacy of motives the defining test of a legitimate humanitarian intervention excludes cases in which states act for nonhumanitarian reasons but produce a positive humanitarian outcome." In his book *Saving Strangers*, Wheeler demonstrates that some of the most important humanitarian interventions have been undertaken by states that had very mixed motives in their decision to act.[6] As Michael Walzer has suggested when considering the value of unilateral versus multilateral interventions:

> Political motivations are always mixed, whether the actors are one or many. A pure moral will doesn't exist in political life, and it shouldn't be necessary to pretend that kind of purity. The leaders of states have a right, indeed, they have an obligation, to consider the interests of their own people, even when they are acting to help other people.[7]

Clearly, an understanding of an agent's motives is important to defining an intervention as humanitarian. But it should not be the sole criterion. Rather, a mix of motives, means, and outcomes must all play a role in determining if an intervention is humanitarian or otherwise.

Moreover, in light of these cautions and debates, one might ask whether debates about definitions serve any purpose. Does it matter how we define intervention or humanitarian intervention? It matters a great deal, especially when it comes to the evaluation of these actions. How we assess the use of military force requires that we have a clear understanding of the purpose behind that action. In domestic law, involuntary manslaughter and premeditated murder have two very distinct definitions, even though they both entail the death of one person at the hands of another. The penalties and moral evaluations a community imposes on the agent in these two cases depends very much on how the actions are defined. Similarly, if a state defines its ordering of tanks across a border as launching a war, it will be evaluated very differently than if it defines that action as the beginning of a humanitarian intervention.

Finally, in light of the fact that an intervention can only be understood in the context of motives, means, and ends, moral evaluations of intervention must address not only the initial decision to intervene but also the entire process of an intervention. In other words, understanding and evaluating humanitarian interventions requires historically grounded descriptions of contexts, decisions, and outcomes. Indeed, one might argue that evaluations of intervention are never truly complete, because new information about a decision and about results will continue to appear months and years after tanks and troops cross a border.[8]

## DEBATES

Defining humanitarian intervention points us toward the contrasting positions that surround the practice of intervention. Although these contrasting positions have been mapped onto American political debates since the end of the cold war, conflicts over obligations and restraints on the use of military force are not new. In chapter 1 of this volume, Terry Nardin suggests that intervention can be usefully understood not just in the context of violating sovereignty and protecting human rights—the predominant debates of the late twentieth century—but also in the context of older debates about rectifying wrongs and protecting the innocent.

This framework, which overlaps with the just war tradition but does not parallel it directly, leads us back to medieval debates about communal society and obligations of rulers. In chapter 2, Nicholas Onuf moves these debates to the Enlightenment period and debates between classical liberals and republicans, in which contrasting notions of international society also framed the obligations of those who had the power to use force.

This domestic political debate over Somalia framed much of the discourse on the moral imperative of intervention during the first half of the 1990s. Partisans fell into rather predictable positions, with conservative realists railing against humanitarian intervention and liberal idealists pushing to expand it as a tool of U.S. foreign policy. This debate became a political one in the aftermath of the Somali intervention. The administration of George H. W. Bush decided to intervene in Somalia in November 1992, after losing the election to Bill Clinton. Accounts of the decision suggest that Bush was influenced by news reports from the summer of 1992 that described a population being starved by power-hungry warlords.[9]

The Clinton administration took over the mission in January 1993, explicitly called for nation building in March 1993, and launched a hunt for Mohammed Aideed, one of the warlords, in September 1993. When these changes led to the tragic deaths of U.S. soldiers in an October 1993 firefight, former Bush administration officials and other Republicans blamed the Democrats for pursuing idealistic ends with no concern for the national interests of the United States.[10] In fact, however, evidence indicates that the Bush administration's policies assumed that the United States would be engaged in Somalia on a longer-term basis, suggesting that an evaluation of the outcomes in Somalia should not be laid simply at the feet of the Clinton administration.[11]

These divisions hardened as the United States became more engaged in Bosnia-Herzegovina. Traditional liberals, concerned that there was to be a repeat of the Holocaust, urged a more expansive use of U.S. military force to prevent the large-scale slaughter of Muslims in the former Yugoslavia. The coercive bombing in Kosovo further complicated the issues, for it was not framed as an attempt to save a starving population by sending in troops but rather as an attempt to coerce a recalcitrant leader through threats and uses of airpower.

Debates in the scholarly community have reflected some of these political positions but have not mapped them directly. The contrast between a recent series of articles in *Orbis* and one in *Dissent* reflects the spectrum of thinking on the political and strategic utility of intervention. Led by Alexander Haig, the contributors to a recent *Orbis* roundtable on intervention challenge the norm that intervention is always the right use of U.S. military force.[12] Alternatively, the articles in a recent edition of *Dissent* focus on the humanitarian emergencies and human rights violations that require a military response.[13]

Nor have academic journals been the only place for this debate. Nongovernmental organizations and international organizations have also undertaken studies and constituted working groups to establish criteria for intervention, often with explicitly moral principles at the core of their investigations. In chapter 5, Thomas Weiss explores the challenges faced by nongovernmental organizations such as the International Committee of the Red Cross in developing an ethos that balances competing moral claims. One of the most important of these reports has come from a group organized by the Canadian Foreign Ministry, which issued *The Responsibility to Protect.* This report seeks to reframe the debate on intervention by moving the discourse from one of "the right to intervene" to that of a "responsibility to protect." This shift is an attempt to generate more of an awareness of the responsibility to protect that should obligate all states to come to the aid of those facing situations of dire emergency.[14]

The chapters of this volume reflect some of these debates, but at levels removed from direct policy debate. In chapter 6, Thomas Weiss and Amir Pasic examine the role of the UN in the former Yugoslavia, whereas in chapters 7, 8, and 9, Richard Caplan, Martin Cook, and Julie Mertus, respectively, raise important questions about the use of force in Kosovo. In chapter 10, Michael Barnett explores the ways in which international organizations, specifically the United Nations, may be just as hesitant as states to use force because of bureaucratic inertia. In the case of Rwanda, which Barnett explores and with which he was involved as a fellow at the United Nations, the lack of a UN response to the rapidly worsening genocide led to a failure to adequately respond to the situation.

An entirely different set of debates arises from the different frameworks that give rise to moral principles. For many in the world, religious traditions provide a starting point for the formulation of moral values and ethical frameworks. To understand the principles that do or do not lend support to decisions to intervene requires a grounding in religious texts and assumptions about the nature of the human person and the relationship between divine commands and political communities. In the U.S. context, these debates have been overshadowed by more political and philosophical principles, although religious institutions continue to play a role in laying out justifications for the use of force in certain contexts. The Catholic Church and many mainline Protestant churches in the United States, for example, continue to issue statements on the use of force. In chapter 4 of this volume, Sohail Hashmi lays out some Islamic principles that might guide decisions to intervene. Although there is no single institutional Islamic authority that can provide insights on these questions, Hashmi demonstrates that careful attention to sacred scriptures and interpretive debates in a religious tradition can yield important insights on how a religious believer can formulate principles that can guide the use of force to save human lives.

A different starting point for evaluating humanitarian intervention is international law. Traditionally, international lawyers have looked with great skepticism on humanitarian interventions, because it violates one of the core principles of that tradition, state sovereignty. Indeed, the legal prohibitions on intervention have often put international legal scholars in the quandary of wishing to support human rights without the enforcement capacity of military force.

Some of the most heated debates on the issue of humanitarian intervention have pitted international lawyers against nongovernmental organization activists who see where force can be used to prevent suffering and protect rights. In chapter 3 of this volume, Simon Chesterman, an international lawyer who has worked with many in the nongovernmental organization community, presents an international legal perspective on humanitarian intervention. His conclusions, which are skeptical about the misuse of force, raise important cautions for those prepared to intervene across sovereign borders.

These debates suggest that there do not yet exist clear answers about moral obligations and restraints on the use of military force for humanitarian purposes. The lack of agreement about how to evaluate these actions, however, does not mean the task of which this book is a small part should be halted. Rather, moral evaluation is a process, one that reflects changing circumstances and different communities of interpreters. The conversation about whether or not we have an obligation to aid those in need or to respect political boundaries—essentially moral questions—must continue. Simply listening to the conversation will edify us all.

## NOTES

1. For a good example of this approach, see Martha Finnemore, "Constructing Norms of Humanitarian Intervention," in *The Culture of National Security: Norms and Identity in World Politics*, ed. Peter Katzenstein (New York: Columbia University Press, 1996).

2. For a good example of this approach, see International Commission on Intervention and State Sovereignty, *The Responsibility to Protect* (Ottawa: International Development Research Center, 2001).

3. See chapter 3 of this volume by Simon Chesterman for a defense of international legal restrictions on sovereignty. Also see Michael Walzer's defense of the "statist" paradigm in

*Just and Unjust Wars* (New York: Basic Books, 1992), 86–108. For a more recent articulation of this point, see his "The Argument about Humanitarian Intervention" in *The New Killing Fields: Massacre and the Politics of Intervention*, ed. Nicolaus Mills and Kira Brunner (New York: Basic Books, 2002).

4. See James Rosenau, "Intervention as a Scientific Concept," *Journal of Conflict Resolution* 13(2) (1969): 149–71.

5. Louis Henkin et al., *International Law: Cases and Materials*, 3d ed. (Minneapolis: West Publishing Co., 1993), 868–70.

6. Nicholas Wheeler, *Saving Strangers: Humanitarian Intervention in International Society* (Oxford: Oxford University Press, 2002).

7. Michael Walzer, "The Argument about Humanitarian Intervention," in *The New Killing Fields: Massacre and the Politics of Intervention*, ed. Nicolaus Mills and Kira Brunner (New York: Basic Books, 2002), 26.

8. I make this point in my own work on intervention; see Anthony F. Lang, Jr., *Agency and Ethics: The Politics of Military Intervention* (Albany: State University of New York Press, 2002), 25–26.

9. See John L. Hirsch and Robert A. Oakley, *Somalia and Operation Restore Hope: Reflections on Peacemaking and Peacekeeping* (Washington, D.C.: United States Institute for Peace, 1995) for an account of decision making in the George H. W. Bush and Clinton administrations on Somalia.

10. See, e.g., John Bolton, "Wrong Turn in Somalia," *Foreign Affairs* 73 (1994): 56–66; and Michael Mandlebaum, "Foreign Policy as Social Work," *Foreign Affairs* 75 (1996): 16.

11. See Lang, *Agency and Ethics*, 155–78, for more details on the shared responsibility of the two administrations for the outcome in Somalia.

12. Alexander Haig et al., "A Decade of Humanitarian Intervention," *Orbis* 45 (fall 2001): 495–578.

13. Nicolaus Mills et al., "The New Killing Fields," *Dissent* (winter 2002): 21–124.

14. International Commission on Intervention and State Sovereignty, *Responsibility to Protect*.

# PART I
# ISSUES

ONE

# The Moral Basis for Humanitarian Intervention

Terry Nardin

*If one person is able to save another and does not save him, he transgresses the commandment, Neither shalt thou stand idly by the blood of thy neighbor.*

—Maimonides, *Mishneh Torah*, XI

*To those for whom the greatest threat to the future of international order is the use of force in the absence of a Security Council mandate, one might say: leave Kosovo aside for a moment, and think about Rwanda. Imagine for one moment that, in those dark days and hours leading up to the genocide, there had been a coalition of states ready and willing to act in defense of the Tutsi population, but the Council had refused or delayed giving the green light. Should such a coalition then have stood idly by while the horror unfolded?*

—UN secretary-general Kofi Annan,
Annual Report to the General Assembly, September 20, 1999

Humanitarian intervention is usually discussed as an exception to the non-intervention principle. According to this principle, states are forbidden to exercise their authority, and certainly to use force, within the jurisdiction of other states. The principle finds firm support in the UN Charter, which permits a state to defend itself from attack but forbids the use of armed force against the territorial integrity or political independence of other states. Taken literally, these provisions prohibit armed intervention, including intervention to protect human rights. And in general, humanitarian intervention finds scant support in modern international law.

There is, however, a much older tradition in which the use of force is justified not only in self-defense but also to punish wrongs and protect the innocent. This tradition is in some tension with modern international law and especially with the UN Charter. It holds that armed intervention is permissible to enforce standards of civilized conduct when rulers violate those standards, and it finds expression today in the widely held opinion that states, acting unilaterally or collectively, are justified in enforcing respect for human rights. It is this enduring tradition, not current international law, that best explains the moral basis for humanitarian intervention.

My strategy in this chapter is to relocate discussion of humanitarian intervention, moving it out of the familiar discourse of sovereignty and self-defense and into the discourse of rectifying wrongs and protecting the innocent. I do this in two ways. First, I examine arguments made in early modern Europe for using armed force to uphold natural law. I want to understand how what we now call humanitarian intervention was conceived by moralists, theologians, and philosophers writing about international relations before the emergence of modern international law. My aim is not to read current concerns back into a period that might not have shared them but rather to see whether earlier ideas about the use of force to protect people from injuries inflicted or tolerated by their own governors might illuminate current debates.

Second, I consider how humanitarian intervention is justified within a powerful reformulation of natural law worked out by philosophers influenced by Immanuel Kant. This post-Kantian version of natural law, which I follow Alan Donagan in calling "common morality," suggests why humanitarian intervention remains morally defensible despite modern efforts to make it illegal.[1]

## HUMANITARIAN INTERVENTION IN EARLY MODERN NATURAL LAW

In twentieth-century international law, a just war is above all a war of self-defense. But sixteenth- and seventeenth-century European moralists justified war as a way to uphold law and protect rights, of which self-defense was only one. Rulers, these moralists argued, have a right and sometimes a duty to enforce certain laws beyond their realms. Some of these belong to the "law of nations" (*ius gentium*), understood not as international law but as general principles of law recognized in many different communities. This law of nations is an inductively established body of norms common to all or most peoples.

But the most important class of universally enforceable laws is "natural law," understood as comprising precepts that can be known by reason and are binding on all rational beings. What the law of nations and natural law have in common is that each identifies principles more general than the often-idiosyncratic norms of particular communities. And in many respects, their principles are similar, though there are glaring exceptions. Slavery, for example, was long regarded as permitted by the law of nations, simply because it was widely practiced. But slavery cannot be defended as permissible under natural law, though many have, mistakenly, so defended it. The right to enforce these laws was understood to justify rulers in punishing moral wrongdoing and defending the innocent, wherever such action was needed.

The medieval literature on just war, like that of modern times, is concerned with wrongs done by one community to another. When Aquinas suggests that a "just cause" is required for resorting to war, he is thinking of situations in which one community acts to punish another. "Those who are attacked," he says, "should be attacked because they deserve it on account of some fault."[2] And he goes on to quote Augustine, for whom a just war is one that "avenges wrongs"—for example, when a state "has to be punished for refusing to make amends for the wrongs inflicted by its subjects or to restore what it has unjustly seized."[3]

To get to the idea of humanitarian intervention, we must shift our attention from wrongs done by one community to another to those done by a government to its own subjects, either directly or by permitting mistreatment. And if the justification of war is to prevent or punish wrongdoing, it is not hard to make this shift. Thomas More accomplishes it effortlessly when he reports that the Utopians go to war only "to protect their own land, to drive invading armies from the territories of their friends, or to liberate an oppressed people, in the name of humanity, from tyranny and servitude."[4] In the absence of a norm of nonintervention, no special justification for humanitarian intervention is needed. Even those who treat "the liberation of an oppressed people" as needing further justification will have an easier time making their case if the core justification for war is to "avenge wrongs."

One kind of oppression that medieval moralists saw as justifying intervention was the mistreatment of Christians in non-Christian ("infidel") kingdoms. Some realized that this one-sided concern could be generalized to include situations in which infidels injure one another, and even situations in which Christians injure infidels. In medieval discourse, the question of whether a Christian ruler might properly use force to protect the victims in these situations was eventually framed as a question of whether the pope, as the recognized universal authority, should intervene. Because the pope was responsible for seeing that all human beings obey God's laws, he could punish violations by anyone, infidel or Christian. Papal intervention, here, meant that the pope would authorize princes to intervene, just as UN intervention means that states are authorized to use armed force under its mandate.

A key figure in this discussion, on whom many sixteenth- and seventeenth-century moralists relied, is the thirteenth-century canon lawyer Sinibaldo Fieschi, who wrote authoritatively as Pope Innocent IV on relations between the papacy and non-Christian societies. The immediate context of Innocent's discussion was the Crusades, which raised the issue of whether it is morally justifiable for Christians to invade lands ruled by non-Christian princes. He argued that infidels, being rational creatures, are capable of making their own decisions, including forming civil societies and choosing rulers. Furthermore, infidels cannot be forcibly converted. But because the gospel is addressed to everyone, the pope must be concerned with infidel as well as Christian souls. And all people are under the jurisdiction of natural law.

Putting these arguments together, Innocent concludes that the pope has authority to act when infidels violate natural law. This might happen if infidel rulers violate this law, or if infidel subjects violate it and their rulers do not prevent or punish them. So, for example, if infidels practice idolatry or sodomy, which Innocent thinks are forbidden by natural law, Christians are justified in punishing them. Christians can also seek to promote the spiritual good of infidels by preaching the gospel among them. And should infidels interfere with Christian missionaries, their right to preach can be defended by armed force. Finally, force can be used to prevent persecution of Christians in infidel kingdoms. In short, the pope can intervene in any community to enforce natural law. Innocent IV, no naïf in these matters, knew that Christian rulers would twist these principles to justify the conquest of infidel societies. He therefore insisted that Christians could wage war against infidels to enforce natural law only with papal authorization.[5]

These principles were applied three centuries later by Francisco de Vitoria to the Spanish conquest of America. This brutal conquest was the subject of a long-running debate concerning the rights and conduct of the conquerors. But there was a new element in this debate, for Europeans saw the indigenous inhabitants not only as infidels but also as barbarians, that is, as uncivilized, even subhuman. These barbarians were distinguished from civilized peoples by their cannibalism and rituals of human sacrifice, practices that Europeans often invoked to justify subjecting them to Spanish rule.

Drawing explicitly upon Innocent IV, Vitoria considers whether cannibalism and human sacrifice provide grounds for the conquest. He argues that although natural law prohibits these acts, this does not necessarily justify war against those who practice them. Other crimes—adultery, sodomy, and theft, for example—also contravene natural law, but one cannot justly wage war against countries in which these crimes occur. "Surely," he writes, "it would be strange that fornication should be winked at in Christian society, but used as an excuse for conquering the lands of unbelievers!"[6] If armed intervention is a permissible response to cannibalism and human sacrifice, it must be because these crimes are especially evil. In such cases, outsiders are justified in defending the victims, even if they have not invited such assistance.

Like modern defenders of humanitarian intervention, Vitoria insists that a war to protect the innocent must be strictly limited. If the Spaniards wage war to suppress crimes against natural law, they cannot lawfully continue the war once it has achieved its goal, nor can they seize the property of the Indians or overthrow their governments. In other words, a lawful intervention cannot, without additional justification, become a lawful conquest. Moreover, if Europeans do, for whatever reason, come to rule the Indians, they must govern them for their own good.[7]

Some defenders of the conquest held that because the Indians were subhuman "brutes," it was lawful to hunt and kill them at will. Others argued that the barbarians, though human, were intellectually deficient and culturally primitive. These "brutish men" were what Aristotle had called "natural slaves"—human beings possessing enough reason to follow commands but not enough to assume responsibility for their own affairs. They were, moreover, slaves without masters, an anomaly for which the Spanish conquest seemed an obvious remedy. Vitoria rejects these claims. The Indians are not natural slaves. Even though their beliefs and conduct are strange and offensive, they have cities, laws, governments, and property, and in this respect are no different from other human beings. But even if the Indians were incapable of governing their own affairs, this would hardly justify killing, enslaving, or expropriating them. Like that of children, madmen, or the senile, their incapacity calls for paternal care.

Another defender of Indian rights, the missionary priest Bartolomé de las Casas, argues that the Spaniards were not justified in harming many to rescue a few. Such injury is disproportionate and, when its victims are innocent, inherently immoral. "In those provinces where unbelievers eat human flesh and sacrifice innocent persons, only a few persons commit these crimes, whereas innumerable persons . . . do not participate in these acts in any way."[8] The conquistadors wage war on the pretext of freeing the innocent, but they annihilate thousands of innocents. Luis de Molina, Domingo De Soto, and other contemporary critics of the conquest make similar points.

The Protestant Hugo Grotius is a key figure in debates over intervention to uphold natural law. The international morality he defends is one that permits such intervention but does not demand it. Grotius's "thin" or minimal morality requires human beings to refrain from injuring one another but does not require that they help one another. The basis for this morality, which he expounds in an unpublished early work, is self-preservation. Because the desire for self-preservation is inherent in their nature, human beings cannot be blamed for acting on it. And if they have a right to preserve themselves, they must also have the right to acquire the things needed for life and to defend their lives and possessions.[9]

These presocial rights, which are the foundation of natural law, in Grotius's view are enjoyed not only by natural persons but also by artificial persons, such as states, that coexist in a condition of nature. In such a condition, the first imperative is self-preservation. And because it rests on self-preservation, the law that governs this condition, the law of nature, is a law that prescribes mutual forbearance, not beneficence. Natural law requires only that we leave one another alone; it does not demand that we assist or protect one another. But we may assist or protect one another. It would contravene the teaching of Christ, Grotius argues, to say that Christians have nothing in common with non-Christians, for the injunction to love one's neighbor means that a Christian must love every human being. It follows that "the protection of infidels from injury (even from injury by Christians) is never unjust."[10] He concludes that the Dutch East India Company might justly wage war on the Portuguese for seeking to prevent the sultan of Johore from trading with the Dutch.[11] This conclusion may cause us to raise an eyebrow with respect to Grotius's motives, but it does not undermine his argument that justice may require forcibly protecting the rights of anyone who is the victim of unjust coercion.

In a subsequent work, Grotius asks whether a sovereign can rightly wage war to punish violations of natural law that do not affect him or his subjects. His answer is that sovereigns have the right to punish any acts that "excessively violate the law of nature or of nations in regard to any persons whatsoever." He invokes Innocent IV against those who argue that punishment is a civil power and therefore that a government has no right to wage war to defend persons over whom it has no legal jurisdiction.

If we accept this view, Grotius argues, no sovereign would be able to punish another for harming him or his subjects. The right to punish is based not on civil power but on the law of nature, which existed before there were civil societies. Therefore, wars are justly waged on those who "sin against nature" by engaging in cannibalism, piracy, and other barbaric practices. "Regarding such barbarians, wild beasts rather than men, one may rightly say . . . that war against them was sanctioned by nature; and . . . that the most just war is against savage beasts, the next against men who are like beasts."[12] Because Grotius does not distinguish between bestial men and bestial societies, sentences such as these justify punitive wars that go far beyond humanitarian intervention, narrowly defined. They point to deep worries about the threat that such societies pose to civilization itself, as Europeans understood it.

According to the new understanding of international relations that was emerging along with the idea of the sovereign state, any government has the right to enforce natural law against any other government that is guilty of violating it. In the "state of nature" postulated by Grotius and other seventeenth-century natural law theorists, there is no enforcing power superior to that of the sovereign of each state. Because in the state of nature unpunished violations of natural law by one sovereign harm every other sovereign by undermining natural law, any sovereign can punish such violations. A sovereign is even justified in punishing crimes that another commits against his own subjects, provided the offense is "very atrocious and very evident."[13] This general "right of punishment" owned by every sovereign in the international state of nature therefore justifies humanitarian intervention, at least in some situations.

The nonintervention principle, which became more and more important in international law during the eighteenth and nineteenth centuries, can be understood as a reaction against the view that every state has a right to enforce natural law. The chief objection to this doctrine was made by Samuel Pufendorf in works published during the 1670s. "We are not to imagine," Pufendorf writes, "that every man, even they who live in the liberty of nature, has a right to correct and punish with war any person who has done another an injury," for it is "contrary to the natural equality of mankind for a man to force himself upon the world for a judge and decider of controversies. . . . Any man might make war upon any man upon such a pretense."[14]

Nevertheless, according to Pufendorf, any person may justly assist any victim of oppression who invites assistance. "Kinship alone"—the mere fact of common humanity—"may suffice for us to go to the defense of an oppressed party who makes a plea for assistance, so far as we conveniently may."[15] For Pufendorf, to come to the aid of the oppressed is not only a right but in some cases a duty. It is, however, an "imperfect duty"—not a specific obligation like that prescribed by a contract but a duty of beneficence to be performed insofar as it can be performed without disproportionate inconvenience. The proviso that the victim must have invited assistance cannot, however, bear the weight Pufendorf gives it in distinguishing justifiable humanitarian intervention from unjustifiable interference by a sovereign who has usurped the office of judge over other sovereigns. Morally speaking, it is the act of oppression, not a request for assistance, that justifies an intervention.

The natural law argument for humanitarian intervention continued to erode during the eighteenth and nineteenth centuries as the view that international law is "positive law" based on the will of states emerged. The enlightenment philosopher Christian Wolff and his popularizer, Emmerich de Vattel, are among the last to treat international law as part of natural law (i.e., as belonging in effect to morality rather than to positive law), and both dismiss the classic argument justifying humanitarian intervention. According to Wolff, "A punitive war is not allowed against a nation for the reason that it is very wicked, or violates dreadfully the law of nature, or offends against God." And he explicitly asserts the principle of nonintervention, even when a sovereign abuses his subjects.[16] Vattel agrees, though he adds a qualification: If "by his insupportable tyranny" a prince "brings on a national revolt against him," any foreign power "may rightfully give assistance to an oppressed people who ask for its aid."[17] But in the absence of armed rebellion, intervention must be condemned; to say that one nation can use force to punish another for grave moral abuses is to open the door to war motivated by religious zealotry or economic ambition.[18]

Here we have a new principle, added to Pufendorf's requirement that the victims of oppression must request outside assistance: They must mount their own armed resistance. By the middle of the nineteenth century, this principle was being used to argue against humanitarian intervention. In his essay "A Few Words on Non-intervention, " J. S. Mill argues that the subjects of an oppressive ruler must win their own freedom, without outside assistance, and they must suffer the consequences if their struggle is unsuccessful. Not even bloody repression can justify armed intervention by foreign powers, for were such intervention permissible, the idea of "self-determination," which Mill thinks is basic to political community, would be meaningless.[19]

Though he is a moralist, not an international lawyer, Mill perfectly articulates the view of humanitarian intervention we find in mainstream nineteenth-century international law. W. E. Hall, the author of a standard English work on international law at the end of that century, treats humanitarian intervention under the heading "Interventions in Restraint of Wrongdoing," a precise title, morally speaking. He argues that tyrannical oppression by a government of its own subjects, including religious persecution or massacres and brutality in a civil war, has nothing to do with relations between states. And he insists that we must not confuse outraged public opinion with the requirements of law. Some commentators, he writes, hold that states can lawfully intervene "to put an end to crimes and slaughter," but in the absence of consensus on this point, their judgment is not law.[20] If there is any legal basis for humanitarian intervention, it must rest not on principles of international morality but on agreement among states to recognize such principles as law. Hall here invokes the doctrine—a keystone of legal positivism—that international law is enacted by the joint will of sovereign states. Just as legislation is the criterion of law within each state, so agreement between states is the criterion of international law. The age of natural law had come to an end.

## COMMON MORALITY AND THE DUTY TO PROTECT

Though banished from the realm of positive law, natural law did not simply disappear. It continued to march under the banner of morality. To distinguish this latter-day natural law, stripped of its religious and legal connotations, from the mores of particular communities, we may speak of a "common morality" binding on all human beings. Common morality assumes that human beings are thinking, choosing agents, and that everyone has an equal right to think and choose. It therefore requires us to recognize the inherent capacity of each person to make choices of his or her own. The foundation of common morality, then, is the principle that each person must respect the agency of every other. This is Kant's "principle of respect."[21] The more specific precepts of common morality are interpretations of this basic principle.

We must distinguish common morality from the mores of particular communities. Its principles constitute a common moral world in which human beings have rights not as members of this or that community but as members of the human community. Common morality rests neither on positive law nor on custom. It is, rather, the product of critical reflection on laws and customs, and in this sense may be said to be known by "reason." Its principles provide a standard "by which everybody ought to live, no matter what the mores of his neighbors might be."[22]

The principles of common morality—such as those that prohibit murder and deliberate harm to innocents and teach friendship, cooperation, and fairness—are basic to civilized life and are in fact recognized in most communities and traditions. This broad recognition is of immense practical importance, for it means that in appealing to common morality the moralist is appealing to principles whose authority has already been granted, implicitly if not explicitly, by a great many people. There are certainly people who do not belong to the common moral world, but one should not underestimate the degree to which its principles are generally acknowledged.[23] It is important to emphasize, however, that although the principles of common morality may be "common" in the sense that they are recognized in different communities, their validity does not depend on such recognition. They are required by a conception of the person and of what is owed to persons, not by convention. Common morality is a critical morality possessing wider authority than the moral practices of particular communities, and for this reason it provides a standard by which to criticize these practices. Like the idea of human rights, the idea of common morality is opposed to communitarian ethical theories that ground moral duties on custom and consent.

The relevance of common morality to humanitarian intervention should by now be apparent. Humanitarian intervention is a response to grave human rights violations, and the most basic human rights are universal moral rights—rights, in other words, that rest on the principles of common morality. There are, then, good reasons for grounding the ethics of humanitarian intervention in common morality and not in particular religious or national moralities, or even in international law, which rests on custom and agreement, not moral reasoning.

Unlike some ethical traditions, common morality does not regulate every aspect of life. In any situation, there is always a wide range of morally permissible responses, and common morality is for the most part unconcerned with choosing among them. Common morality is a minimal morality, and for this reason it must be distinguished from religious and other traditions that make a broad range of concerns a matter of moral duty.[24] It regulates the choices we make as rational agents, not as adherents of this or that tradition. But precisely because it rests on a view of human beings as rational agents, common morality permits us considerable freedom to choose as we will. It imagines a human community in which individuals pursue their own self-chosen ends, and it seeks to regulate this pursuit so that the actions of one do not unjustly interfere with the actions of others.

Common morality forbids us to use other human beings coercively to achieve our ends. Using force, without good reason, violates the principle of respect. This explains not only why murder and slavery are wrong but also why self-defense is morally justifiable. But common morality does not limit the use of force to self-defense. It also permits us to defend the rights of others when those rights are threatened. We are therefore justified in using force to thwart violence against other persons, provided those persons are morally "innocent"—that is, not themselves engaged in unjust violence. Using force to resist those who attack the innocent does not violate the attackers' rights as free persons because they have, by their own actions, lost the moral right to act as they choose. It is even permitted to kill attackers, if necessary, to protect their victims. We are justified in using as much force as is needed to thwart the attack, but not more—bearing in mind that precise calculations about such matters are impossible.[25]

Though derived ultimately from the principle of respect, the right to use force to defend the innocent from violence rests more immediately on the idea of beneficence, which is the idea that human beings should support one another in appropriate ways. To respect other human beings as rational agents means not only that we must not interfere with their freedom but also that we should assist them in achieving their ends. Common morality is at its core a morality of constraint, but its precepts are not limited to those that constrain us. It also asks us to advance the well-being of others—by being cooperative, helpful, charitable, and the like—in ways that are morally permissible and not disproportionately costly. In other words, in helping others we are forbidden to do wrong for their sake and we are not required to do more than we can reasonably afford.

Given the principle of beneficence, common morality may require us to act when others are in danger of serious injury, whether by accident or as victims of wrongdoing. This requirement is expressed in the parable of the Good Samaritan (Luke 10:29–37) and, more pointedly, in the divine command that you must not stand idly by when lives are in danger (Leviticus 19:16). The principle of beneficence, which this command invokes, leaves us free to decide how to promote the well-being of others. Nevertheless, if we are able to provide immediate assistance to someone who needs it, we should provide that assistance. And this implies that we must not allow anyone to be harmed by violence if we can reasonably prevent it. In short, assuming that the costs are not too high, it is "not merely permissible but a duty to employ force against the violent if their victims cannot otherwise be protected."[26] This is the fundamental principle underlying humanitarian intervention.

The principle addresses three aspects of the decision to act on behalf of persons threatened by violence. First, we must ask under what circumstances such action is morally called for. Who should be protected (who is my "neighbor"), and from which harms? Second, who should intervene? Who is the "thou" who is forbidden to stand idly by when another is in danger? And third, what must we do to avoid the charge that we are standing idly by? And what must we not do—what constraints, in other words, must we observe in providing aid?

We can use these questions to illuminate the morality of humanitarian intervention. But in doing so, we must remember that principles alone cannot determine complex foreign policy decisions. Moral principles can provide broad goals to guide deliberation, and they prescribe constraints on what choices can be made. But they cannot more precisely determine those goals and choices. Humanitarian action may require anything from ending a massacre to rebuilding a society whose institutions have failed. Deciding which of several morally permissible courses of action to pursue in a particular situation demands judgment and prudence, but this task belongs to politics, not moral philosophy.

## When Is Humanitarian Intervention Permissible?

For Maimonides, the biblical injunction is to "save" another, and the implication is that the victim's life is endangered. If humanitarian intervention means acting to protect human rights, many such rights besides the right to life might be threatened, including rights against torture, arbitrary detention, and racial discrimination. But usually only the gravest violations, such as genocide and ethnic cleansing, are held to justify armed intervention. Such acts affect the lives of many people and the fate of entire communities. In the classic phrase, they "shock the conscience of humankind."

It is consistent with common morality to argue that humanitarian intervention is justified, in principle, in a wide range of situations, but that practical considerations usually override this justification.[27] Yet one can also justify limiting intervention to the gravest abuses by invoking considerations that arise from the aims of civil association. The state as a coercive institution is morally justifiable because, in principle, it enables human beings to fulfill their potentialities by living together according to common rules. Once a state has been established, however, its citizens must obey the laws it adopts for this purpose, assuming these laws are not substantially unjust. And a substantially just state is entitled to respect by other states, which are morally barred from interfering with its government.

The nonintervention principle is therefore basic to relations between states. It is not a mere custom of the international system. There are moral reasons why a state must be recognized as having rights, in particular the right that outsiders respect its independence and boundaries. But the same principles that justify the nonintervention principle justify exceptions to the principle. If a government seriously violates the moral rights of those it governs, others may defend those rights, using force if necessary. The nonintervention principle is not a shield behind which an unjust state can hide while it violates the moral rights of its subjects. Such violations, if serious enough, permit forcible humanitarian intervention and may even demand it. But respect for the rights of a political community requires that those violations be truly grave.

Christian tradition holds explicitly that all human beings are "neighbors." Vitoria, for example, writes that "the barbarians are all our neighbors, and therefore anyone, and especially princes, may defend them from . . . tyranny and oppression."[28] Common morality, also, holds every human being is in principle my neighbor and therefore entitled to assistance, though practically speaking I may be limited to helping those with whom I am connected in some way. It follows that humanitarian intervention is governed by the same principles of nondiscrimination that govern all conduct. It would, for example, be discriminatory in a way that deserves moral condemnation if Western governments acted to redress gross violations of human rights in Europe but remained indifferent to equivalent or graver harms suffered by Africans. To be sure, Europeans today do not necessarily have the same duty to intervene in Africa as in Europe, for there may be special obligations or practical constraints that distinguish the situations. But the case must be made carefully. No people can be arbitrarily excluded from humanitarian concern in ways that amount to prejudicial discrimination.

## Who Should Intervene?

Humanitarian intervention is traditionally defined as the use of force by states to protect human rights. This definition presumes that states should do the intervening. It is sometimes argued that the traditional definition is obsolete because humanitarian intervention is increasingly a matter of collective action under UN auspices, not action undertaken by states acting on their own authority.[29]

However, to say that humanitarian intervention should be collective is simply to offer a different answer to the question of who should intervene. The moral principle is general: *You* shall not stand idly by, whoever you are, if you can provide effective assistance at reasonable cost and without neglecting other duties. There are practical reasons for suggesting that the international community should authorize humanitarian interventions. Such interventions may, for example, be more likely than unilateral actions to benefit from collective wisdom and to gain wide support.[30] But to insist on such authorization is to presume a degree of justice and effectiveness at the supranational level that the world has not yet achieved.

There are, however, moral reasons why states should adhere to international law and therefore why unilateral intervention should be condemned if international law forbids it. It is regrettable that NATO's decision to intervene in Kosovo had to be made outside the framework of the United Nations and in a manner not explicitly provided for by its own charter, which requires its members to defend one another if attacked, but says nothing about intervention or peacekeeping that is unrelated to collective defense. But if unilateral intervention is illegal and procedures exist for collective action, and yet the international community as a whole is unable to act effectively, must individual states also "stand idly by"? As UN secretary-general Kofi Annan implies in discussing the world's failure to act in Rwanda, to say "yes" is to repudiate common morality.

Some moralists argue that only a government that respects human rights is entitled to intervene to protect human rights.[31] There are reasons for favoring such a requirement in many cases, but the principle is not part of common morality. A murderer is not forbidden to save a drowning child. The objectionable character of the Vietnamese government in 1979 does not mean that its intervention in Cambodia, which ended the genocide there, was morally wrong.[32]

## What Means of Protection Are Called For?

Common morality prescribes that we must not stand idly by when human lives are threatened, but this is a very broad injunction. As we have seen, coercive action is not immoral if it is aimed at those who are themselves acting immorally, and provided we do not pursue good ends by immoral means. Clearly, this means that forces conducting humanitarian interventions must comply with the laws of war, as these laws are understood both in the just war tradition and in international law. It means in particular that such forces must respect the principle of noncombatant immunity, which is that innocent persons may not be directly attacked either as an end or as a means to an end, and that the costs of indirect injury must not be unfairly distributed.[33]

The responses we might choose are not limited to those requiring military force. War is an extreme remedy. The label "humanitarian intervention" is sometimes applied to transnational charitable efforts to relieve human suffering as well as to forcible interventions to protect human rights. Those who see armed intervention as a kind of just war sometimes protest that using a common label muddies the waters by linking modes of international assistance that raise different issues and should be handled in different ways. Common morality certainly recognizes as morally relevant the distinction between coercive and noncoercive assistance. But it also prescribes assisting fellow human beings in any effective and morally permissible manner. It therefore allows a wide range of responses to situations in which lives are endangered, while recognizing that responses involving the use of force require additional justification. It also reminds us that military action cannot be assumed to be effective and that the only force that is morally justifiable is the minimum necessary to accomplish its purpose.

In considering what to do, an intervening state is not barred from considering the costs and from deciding not to act if those costs are too high. Although beneficence is a duty, it is what moralists sometimes call an imperfect duty. Like an individual person, a state is not obligated to intervene at great cost to itself. Risking all to save others may be praiseworthy, even saintly, but common morality does not demand it.[34] But if no country can be asked to seriously harm its own interests to assist another, what can we reasonably ask it to do? If I save someone's life, I am not supposed to have taken on a long-term obligation to care for that person.

However, the injunction to "save" my neighbor, if my neighbor is a community, might entail continued involvement. Armed intervention to halt a massacre is likely to be only the first of many measures needed to restore order to a chaotic society and prevent subsequent massacres. If prevention is important, the challenge for humanitarian policy is to move from responding to humanitarian crises to forestalling them. And if common morality requires civil association and the rule of law, a policy of progressively strengthening civil institutions at the international level may itself be morally required, as Kant long ago argued in "Perpetual Peace."[35] It is perhaps no coincidence that the greatest theorist of common morality was also concerned with the conditions of a just and peaceful international order.

In sum, common morality suggests that humanitarian intervention is justifiable under three conditions. First, it must be an extraordinary remedy, chosen in response to grave human rights abuses that cannot be ended by diplomatic means. This limitation recognizes that the legal rights of states cannot be lightly set aside, and that military intervention is an uncertain remedy, which has great costs of its own.

Second, interventions should be approved by a recognized international authority acting in accordance with reasonably just international laws. But if such an authority does not exist or is substantially unjust or ineffective, either in general or in a given situation, states may act without its approval. Whether the United Nations is a just and effective international authority is a judgment that those contemplating intervention will have to make—and defend.

Third, any intervention must be conducted by effective and morally permissible means. It must respect domestic and international laws unless there is good reason to override them because they are manifestly unjust or because the relevant governments or international authorities are ineffective. But above all, those who intervene must respect the moral laws that forbid harming innocent people as a means to an end and that require a fair distribution of risk (by prescribing attention to considerations of "proportionality" and "due care") between the intervening forces and those they aim to assist.

Decisions about whether and how to intervene will always involve a wide range of contingencies, for states have no duty to intervene unless they can do so successfully and at reasonable cost to themselves and to others. It follows that selectivity in the choice of occasions for intervention is both inevitable and potentially justifiable.

These conclusions are neither novel nor especially controversial. This should be taken as an encouraging sign, for it suggests that the contribution of common morality to the debate over humanitarian intervention is to help us clarify the rational foundation of views whose cogency is already widely acknowledged. Its contribution is to indicate, from the standpoint of a carefully articulated and intellectually powerful position, where, morally speaking, arguments over particular interventions can and cannot go.

## CONCLUSION

I began by briefly contrasting two traditions of thought on humanitarian intervention. One, embedded in modern international law and the UN Charter, sees intervention as inherently problematic, given the importance the law attaches to preserving the political independence and territorial integrity of states. The other, which belongs to the tradition of natural law or common morality, sees humanitarian intervention as an expression of the basic moral duty to protect the innocent from violence. The tension between them raises the question of how we can reconcile the complex institutional duties prescribed by international law with the more primitive, noninstitutional, duties of common morality. Common morality achieves its reconciliation by requiring that we respect institutions established through the free exercise of human capacities—the family, property, the state, and international law—provided these institutions are reasonably effective and just.

The problem of humanitarian intervention, then, is analogous to the problem of political obligation. The question "Are citizens morally obligated to obey the laws of the civil society in which they live?" becomes "Are states obligated to obey the law of international society?" Precisely how ineffective or unjust the relevant laws and institutions must be before states are entitled to override the nonintervention principle or to ignore the UN Charter is a practical question to which no general answer can be given. But it is helpful to see that this is the right question to ask in debating humanitarian intervention. Moral guidance can be obtained neither by asserting existing law, as if its authority were unquestionable, nor by asserting moral principles, as if in obeying humanitarian imperatives no attention need be given to respecting laws, but only by giving careful attention to the claims of each in the particular situations to which the international community is called to respond.

As I have emphasized, common morality does not prescribe answers to many of the practical questions raised by particular interventions, except within very wide limits. It has little to say about whether acts of beneficence, and therefore humanitarian interventions, should be unilateral or collective, beyond requiring that collective procedures be respected, where they exist and are not ineffective or unjust. Although it forbids us to deny any human being the status of neighbor, it leaves us wide latitude in deciding whom we can assist, by what means we can assist them, and how much assistance we can provide. What common morality does provide is a way of viewing the ethics of humanitarian intervention that is rooted in a widely shared and rationally defensible conception of human dignity, and which for these reasons is relatively independent of the contingencies of particular situations. It follows that the moral principles underlying humanitarian intervention do not need to be rethought "in the post–cold war world" or "after Kosovo." These principles have been known for centuries, if not millennia. They will acquire new meanings in each new situation to which they are applied, and because this requires judgment, they will often be misapplied. But the principles themselves will not soon be replaced.

## NOTES

Earlier versions of this chapter were presented at the Travers Ethics Conference, held at the University of California, Berkeley, in December 1999; at a symposium sponsored by the Center for Global Peace and Conflict Studies at the University of California, Irvine, in May 2000; at the annual meeting of the International Studies Association in February 2001; and at conferences hosted by the Center for European Studies and the Carr Center for Human Rights Policy at Harvard University in January and September 2001. The author is grateful to the participants in these events and to the editors and reviewers of *Ethics & International Affairs* for helpful criticism and advice.

1. Alan Donagan, *The Theory of Morality* (Chicago: University of Chicago Press, 1977; reprinted with corrections, 1979).
2. Saint Thomas Aquinas, *Summary of Theology* II–II, Q. 40, a. 1, in *On Law, Morality, and Politics*, ed. William P. Baumgarth and Richard J. Regan, S.J. (Indianapolis: Hackett Publishing Company, 1988), 221.
3. Augustine, *Questions on the Heptateuch* 6.10, quoted by Aquinas, *On Law, Morality and Politics*, 221.
4. Thomas More, *Utopia* (1516), ed. George M. Logan and Robert M. Adams (Cambridge: Cambridge University Press, 1989), 87–88.
5. James Muldoon, *Popes, Lawyers, and Infidels: The Church and the Non-Christian World 1250–1550* (Philadelphia: University of Pennsylvania Press, 1979), 10–11, 12.
6. Francisco de Vitoria, "On Dietary Laws, or Self-Restraint" (1537), in *Political Writings*, ed. Anthony Pagden and Jeremy Lawrance (Cambridge: Cambridge University Press, 1991), 230.
7. Vitoria, "On Dietary Laws," 225–26; and Vitoria, "On the American Indians" (1539), in *Political Writings*, ed. Pagden and Lawrance, 288.
8. Bartolomé de las Casas, *In Defense of the Indians* (1552), trans. Stafford Poole (DeKalb: Northern Illinois University Press, 1992), 207.
9. Hugo Grotius, *De jure praedae* (1604), published in English as *Commentary on the Law of Prize and Booty*, trans. Gwladys L. Williams (Oxford: Clarendon Press, 1950), 10.
10. Grotius, *De jure praedae*, 315.
11. Richard Tuck, *The Rights of War and Peace: Political Thought and the International Order from Grotius to Kant* (Oxford: Oxford University Press, 1999), 93–94.
12. Hugo Grotius, *De jure belli ac pacis* (1625), *On the Law of War and Peace*, 1646 edition trans. Francis W. Kelsey (Oxford: Oxford University Press, 1925), 504–6.

13. Grotius, *De jure belli ac pacis,* 508.

14. Samuel von Pufendorf, *Of the Law of Nature and Nations* (1672), trans. C. H. Oldfather and W. A. Oldfather (Oxford: Clarendon Press, 1934), 847. I have modernized the spelling and punctuation.

15. Samuel von Pufendorf, *On the Duty of Man and Citizen,* ed. James Tully (Cambridge: Cambridge University Press, 1991), 170.

16. Christian von Wolff, *The Law of Nations Treated According to a Scientific Method* (1748), trans. Joseph D. Drake (Oxford: Oxford University Press, 1934), section 637; sections 258 and 1011.

17. Emmerich de Vattel, *The Law of Nations, or Principles of Natural Law Applied to the Conduct and Affairs of Nations and Sovereigns* (1758), trans. Charles G. Fenwick (Washington, D.C.: Carnegie Institution, 1916), 131; see also 340.

18. de Vattel, *Law of Nations,* 116.

19. J. S. Mill, *Dissertations and Discussions,* 2d ed. (London: Longmans, 1867), vol. 3, 153–78. The essay was first published in 1859.

20. William Edward Hall, *A Treatise on International Law,* 6th ed. (Oxford: Oxford University Press, 1909), 284, 287–88.

21. Immanuel Kant, *Foundations of the Metaphysics of Morals* (1785), trans. Lewis White Beck (Indianapolis: Bobbs-Merrill, 1959), 66–67.

22. Donagan, *Theory of Morality,* 1. My sketch of common morality draws freely on Donagan and on Michael Walzer, *Just and Unjust Wars* (New York: Basic Books, 1977). On the connection between the arguments of these works, see Joseph Boyle, "Casuistry and the Boundaries of the Moral World," *Ethics & International Affairs* 11 (1997): 83–98.

23. Two recent and especially cogent explorations of the relationship between universal and communal moral views are Amartya Sen, "Human Rights and Asian Values," Sixteenth Morgenthau Memorial Lecture on Ethics and Foreign Policy (New York: Carnegie Council on Ethics and International Affairs, 1997); and Michael Walzer, "Universalism and Jewish Values," Twentieth Morgenthau Memorial Lecture on Ethics and Foreign Policy (New York: Carnegie Council on Ethics and International Affairs, 2001).

24. Grotius offers a statement of this distinction in Christian tradition when he writes that in the "holy law" of the New Testament, "a greater degree of moral perfection is enjoined upon us than the law of nature . . . would require" (*Law of War and Peace,* 27).

25. Donagan, *Theory of Morality,* 85–87.

26. Donagan, *Theory of Morality,* 86.

27. Jerome Slater and Terry Nardin, "Nonintervention and Human Rights," *Journal of Politics* 48 (1986): 86–96.

28. Vitoria, "On the American Indians," 288.

29. For criticism of the traditional definition, see Oliver Ramsbotham and Tom Woodhouse, *Humanitarian Intervention in Contemporary Conflict* (Cambridge: Polity Press, 1996), 113–14.

30. Stephen A. Garrett, *Doing Good and Doing Well: An Examination of Humanitarian Intervention* (Westport, Conn.: Praeger, 1999), chap. 7.

31. Fernando R. Tesón, *A Philosophy of International Law* (Boulder, Colo.: Westview Press, 1998), 59.

32. Nicholas J. Wheeler, *Saving Strangers: Humanitarian Intervention in International Society* (Oxford: Oxford University Press, 2001), 110.

33. Walzer provides a clear explanation of the principle of discrimination, and related ideas like double effect and due care, in *Just and Unjust Wars,* 151–59.

34. Walzer, in his preface to the third edition of *Just and Unjust Wars* (2000), agrees that intervention is an "imperfect duty," but he is bitter about it: "the massacres go on, and every country that is able to stop them decides that it has more urgent tasks" (p. xiii).
35. Immanuel Kant, *Political Writings*, 2d edition, ed. Hans Reiss (Cambridge: Cambridge University Press, 1991).

# TWO

# Normative Frameworks for Humanitarian Intervention

## Nicholas Onuf

In recent years, millions of people have experienced great hardship, injury and loss—not least, loss of life—in circumstances that have been politically charged and well publicized. War can cause suffering on this scale, and we can count the many wars that have done so. Indeed, we might wish to say that any great calamity that some people inflict on other people is war. Yet we only say this for a rhetorical flourish, because the term "war" refers generally to a situation in which two parties knowingly choose courses of action that will cause great suffering on both sides. Few instances of massive human suffering in recent years fit this general description. People suffer on a scale that we associate with war but not as parties to war.

That war has the properties it does is an institutional fact of the modern world. Several centuries ago, people in Western Europe began to put their traditional ways of life behind them. In doing so, they began to see themselves and their world as modern. Change is an institutional fact of the modern world, and the global reach of the modern world today is one of its consequences.

Institutional facts always have normative implications. In the instance of war, at least some of these implications are so formal and extensive that we know them as the law of war—a body of rules said to be authored by and binding on states. These rules are predicated on the assumption that governments do not conduct war against their own people unless the people have themselves organized for war. Yet governments and other organizations have made a mockery of this assumption. How then are we to think about one-party wars, bring our normative resources to bear on them, and prevent them from happening?

What can we do? When we see massive suffering, we can intervene on humanitarian grounds. Most of us would say that the victims have been denied their human rights. Whether we invoke the body of rules that tell us what these rights are and how they operate, or refashion the law of war to include these rights, we take advantage of one obvious normative resource, but not the only one or perhaps even the best one.

The burden of this chapter is to show that we have other such resources available to us. We are only able to appreciate what these resources are by standing back and locating them within the largely implicit normative frameworks that we draw upon to make moral sense of the world that we have made for ourselves. On first look, we see two frameworks, which give liberalism and socialism their moral content. On second look, we can see the outlines of an older, more encompassing framework— one that is rich in history but recessive today. It has long given republicanism its moral content, and it presents us even now with normative resources that we may too easily overlook when we are confronted with massive human suffering.

## CONSTRUCTING FRAMEWORKS

Who is this "we"? What do we mean by "our world"? After all, one can speak of the modern world, of the whole world, and of many worlds, in the same breath.[1] We know that these variant terms are imprecise and ambiguously related but evocative. It is these very properties that make such terms so suitable for our rhetorical needs. When we wish to be more precise, few terms come to mind. The term "civilization" is even more evocative than "world," more laden with affective resonance. Samuel Huntington's alarm over the "clash of civilizations" offers a notorious example.[2] Joining these terms—civilized world, world civilization— compounds the rhetorical effect with no gain in precision, and perhaps some loss.

An alternative term is "paradigm." Although hardly free of ambiguity, its use by scholars in many fields suggests a core meaning sufficiently precise to orient their goals and projects in some larger context. A paradigm provides a coherently articulated set of goals, standards, and activities to anyone willing to accept them as a set. Adopting a paradigm supplies a firm but not completely fixed relation between one's goals and projects and those of anyone else who has adopted the same paradigm. The term implies a reasonable division of labor, a basis for evaluating one's own and others' activities, and a sense of belonging and achievement.

In the usual conception, observers take their paradigms to be about the world as an objective reality. This world has a discernibly coherent structure. Within paradigms, progress means an ever closer fit between the world under study and the contents of the paradigm. When competing paradigms offer accounts of the world that are either incomplete or incompatible, a new, more inclusive paradigm that better fits the world signifies a higher order of progress.

Missing from this standard conception is any sense that some paradigms fit the world as well as they do because they make the world what it is—they contribute at least some of the structure that they tell us to look for. Our world is a world of our making, but not entirely. There are as many worlds as there are paradigms of this sort, but none of these worlds is unrelated to any other.[3] To distinguish these paradigms from the ones that observers believe to be simply, or merely, about the world, we might follow Sheldon Wolin by calling them "operative" paradigms.[4]

Operative paradigms constitute worlds within worlds, ways of life within the form of life common to the human species. The modern world is distinctively a world of its own because it is an operative paradigm of remarkable power, coherence, and durability—the very properties that we typically attribute to a civilization. Yet this world is hardly uniform across its structure because too many of us have had a hand, or a say, in its making. It is also less coherent than we would like to believe.[5] We can identify its distinctive features only in the most general of terms. According to Anthony Giddens, the distinguishing feature of the modern world is the degree to which we whose world it is think and talk about ourselves, our world, and the ways in which we and our conceptions of the world relate to each other. "The reflexivity of modern life consists in the fact that social practices are constantly examined and reformed in light of the incoming information about those very practices, thus constitutively altering their character."[6]

We might say that modern reflexivity is heightened paradigm awareness, which is systematically applied to the modern world as an operative paradigm. Correlative features of modernity are a sharp discrimination between subjective and objective states (my world, the world), an instrumental disposition toward the objects of the world, and a religiously freighted belief that the human species is uniquely favored in its ability to reflect on the world, to form goals and plans, and to change the world by carrying them out.

The modern world acquired its distinctive features over the course of two or three centuries; epochal thinking has made a world of an epoch.[7] In the story that we tell (about, to) ourselves, we (here meaning our forebears in northwestern Europe) put tradition behind us (by 1800, or perhaps earlier), but only after two or three centuries of sustained effort.[8] Success has meant a dynamic, expanding modern world; the contest between traditional and modern ways continues into the present. Our world has become the whole world, and whatever happens in it is, at least in principle, our business. Of course, this epochal story is conveniently simple, self-serving, and morally complacent.

## NORMATIVE COMPLEXITY IN THE MODERN WORLD

Because paradigms provide standards by which to form goals, develop plans, and evaluate conduct, they are always normative frameworks. As a normative framework, modernity resists generalization along the lines indicated just above. The struggle against tradition is not a simple story of universal truths, systematic thinking, and beneficial consequences prevailing over ignorance, superstition, and benighted practices. Nor is it a simple story of hubris and greed running roughshod over nature and imposing an artificial, homogeneous culture of consumption on a gullible planet. The normative complexity of the modern world, with its discord, indignities, debilities, disasters, and despoliation, suggests a selective appreciation of the past and its moral legacy, superabundant standards, mismatched means and ends, and the disjuncture of intentions and consequences. In such a situation, we have to surmise that several operative paradigms variously compete and converge to give modernity its distinctive character.[9]

The early modern world saw the advent of three paradigms operating on a scale sufficient to have the effects just indicated. For present purposes, we might call them normative frameworks, thereby limiting the task of describing their descent, distinctive features, and current relevance. Here given familiar labels—republican, liberal, and socialist—they are rarely discussed in a way that makes them normative frameworks in the first instance.[10] Instead, they are typically identified as socioeconomic and political theories, ideologies, or institutional frameworks, which in practice are subject to the vicissitudes of history. Although it may be fair to say that the republican framework is, politically speaking, recessive and the socialist framework in disarray, it is hardly appropriate to say that the liberal framework has come to define the modern world for all intents and purposes—and least of all for my purposes in this chapter.[11]

## The Republican Framework

Early modern thinkers focused on human nature and the human condition. These earnest discussions epitomized modern reflexivity. They also constituted a philosophical anthropology anchored in the art and literature of Classical civilization. Among early modern republican authors as different as Nicollò Machiavelli and Hugo Grotius, it is Grotius to whom we must turn to appreciate republicanism as a normative framework.[12]

"Man is, to be sure, an animal," Grotius observed in 1625, "but an animal of a superior kind, much farther removed from all other animals than the different kind of animals are from one another; evidence may be found in the many traits peculiar to the human species. But among the many traits characteristic of man is an impelling desire for society, that is, for the social life."[13] There is nothing novel in this claim. Grotius immediately signaled his Classical allegiances: "This social trend the Stoics called 'sociability'"; and quoting Marcus Aurelius in a footnote, "we were born for fellowship."[14]

The Stoic emphasis on *societas*, or fellowship, set the tone for the republican normative framework for another century and a half. For Thomas Hobbes even to raise questions about the framework prompted Samuel Pufendorf's point-by-point refutation.[15] Society is the "natural state of man," Pufendorf wrote in 1672, "instituted and sanctioned by nature herself without any human intervention"—this is the law of nature, binding on everyone "endowed with reason," just as Grotius had said.[16] Fellowship entails fellow feeling—"a phrase of this present time" Hobbes called it in Leviathan (1651)—and fellow feeling, or sympathy, is a natural feature of the human experience.[17] A century later, Adam Smith put a natural disposition toward fellow feeling at the center of his *Theory of Moral Sentiments* (1759).[18] Smith, who was indebted no less than Pufendorf to Stoic thought, relied less overtly on natural law for normative support.

We should be clear on what natural sociability entails. We need each other to flourish, and to flourish is to be able to act on our plans and achieve our goals individually. This is as much Hobbes's position as it is the position of Grotius, Pufendorf, and Smith. A Stoic goes on to say that we should strive for self-sufficiency, even if we can never achieve it fully. An Aristotelian goes on to say that we should orient ourselves to the common good to achieve collective self-sufficiency. Both imply that our plans and goals can never be simply our own.

Aristotle's conception of the good life as a life lived not just in common with others but also in mutual support and assistance forms the normative foundation for republicanism in all its variety. If society—the polis—is our natural condition, then each of us owes the rest such aid as nature causes them to need and equips us to provide. Nevertheless, we cannot infer a condition of equality from this familiar equation of abilities and needs. Doing what nature has equipped each of us to do best takes care of most needs collectively but unevenly. Extraordinary need calls for assistance directed specifically to that need.

We cannot find in Aristotle and his republican followers a general duty to come to the aid of others because need is not itself generalizable. Instead, we find them commending a disposition to respond to others' needs. To be thus disposed is a virtue and not a rule of conduct. Stoic thought simultaneously recommended that we individually strive for self-sufficiency and we collectively imagine our social arrangements on the largest scale.[19] The problem here is that universal duties, whether Stoic or Kantian, are too abstract to guide conduct in most situations. Aristotle at least offered two rules—so informal that they are never described as such—to help us know when to act on the disposition to give others our help, and most republicans took these two rules for granted.

First, our assistance to others should not disrupt the natural order of the household writ large; men rank over women, and masters over slaves, for good reasons. Second, the polis as an association of households is naturally self-sufficient; assistance beyond its confines defeats the point. Even Cicero, a Stoic of enormous importance to early modern writers, accepted these normative qualifications on virtuous conduct. As he expressed it, "There are indeed several degrees of fellowship among men," running from familial to universal.[20] With each comes privileges and duties appropriate to social life on that scale.

The small size of early modern republics meant that each member knew everyone else's social position. Visitors could expect to benefit from the rule of hospitality. Beyond this, considerations of status and honor shaped everyone's response to anyone else's need. The church, always sensitive to these considerations, made charity a duty and coordinated the niceties of giving and receiving. By definition, there were no unaccounted needs. As an institutional innovation, confederal arrangements could make small republics less vulnerable to imperial neighbors, but they did so without altering the conception of need as local and the response to it as paternal.

## The Liberal Framework

The liberal paradigm grew out of the republican one. Yet the family resemblance is deceptive. As normative frameworks, both start with moral persons. Nevertheless, liberalism stresses abilities and achievements over needs and differences. Objective individual rights prevail over subjective duties to one's fellows. Thus we find Grotius following his Stoic claim of natural sociability with an analysis of *jus*—the justness of an act or, more familiarly, right. *Jus* is a property of any moral person (*qualitas moralis personae*) forming aptitudes and faculties. Grotius further divided aptitudes and faculties into powers, titles, and contractual rights.[21]

The Grotian emphasis on natural rights is necessary but not sufficient for the development of the liberal paradigm. After all, natural law consists of rights and duties, each entailing the other. The moral person is a social being, perhaps an individual human being, perhaps a corporate being such as a guild. Only gradually did some early modern writers reconceive the person as a being whose right to autonomy took precedence over the encumbrances of society.

The key here is the Hobbesian claim that a corporate being is a moral person (in his terms, a "civil person") only to the extent that the natural persons composing it have empowered some agent to act on their behalf.[22] Preeminently, nations meet this requirement because sovereign agents act for them. To say that these nations are sovereign is to claim for them rights and duties in their relations and thus to acknowledge that they are subject to a branch of the law of nature called the law of nations.[23] The natural society of nations formed a liberal world before there were liberal societies.

In theory, liberal society consists of natural persons—individual human beings—who have aptitudes and faculties—abilities—that come close to making them self-sufficient. In this respect they are substantially equal, even if particular abilities are normally, not equally, distributed. Initially, they need society to allow them to develop and employ their abilities to good effect, and society does this by protecting what is rightfully theirs by nature. Faculties translate into rights; holders of the same rights are formal equals.

In John Locke's definitive analysis (chapter 5, "Of Property," *Second Treatise of Government*, 1690), faculties translate into property, whether considered on their own or applied to whatever else nature makes available for the satisfaction of human needs. "Though the earth, and all inferior Creatures be common to all Men, yet every Man has a Property in his own Person. This no Body has any Right to but himself. The Labour of his Body, and the Work of his Hands, we may say, are properly his."[24] On Locke's account, we flourish in society because we, as "proprietors" of our faculties and whatever we produce by using our faculties, are free to exchange and combine what we rightfully own as we see fit.[25]

Locke foreshadowed the liberal faith in the division of labor as the answer to human need. Smith made it the central tenet of *The Wealth of Nations* (1776). He postulated a natural human "propensity" to engage in exchange as the basis of specialized productive activity.[26] In a "well-governed society," the division of labor produces "universal opulence which extends to the lowest ranks of the people."[27] Clearly, his well-governed society is one in which government interferes as little as possible in natural operation.

For liberals, the division of labor takes care of most needs through its multiplicative productive powers and distributive dynamics. If people could count on minimal security for themselves and their property and institutional remedies to infringements on their rights, they would have few if any needs that doing what they do best would not fulfill. Insofar as this is not literally true, liberals could always fall back on the republican normative framework and its institutionalized response to human need in its many manifestations. Doing so routinely has blurred the boundaries of operative paradigms.

## The Socialist Framework

If the liberal paradigm emphasizes abilities over needs, the socialist paradigm reverses the equation. Needs become the primary normative focus, and the common good calls for a comprehensive assessment of what we need and how institutions should be designed to provide for these needs. Socialists believe that, intentions aside, the strong will victimize the weak if circumstances permit. Yet this is not their starting point. Liberal competition increases the neediness already implicit in the human condition. Some of us are weaker and thus needier than others, but all of us are weaker, and needier, than we realize.

Among early modern writers, Pufendorf most clearly articulated the starting point for the socialist paradigm of endemic neediness and comprehensive institutional design.[28] Consider his general sense of the human condition: "It is clear that man is an animal extremely desirous of his own preservation, in himself exposed to want, unable to exist without the help of his fellow-creatures, fitted in a remarkable way to contribute to the common good, and yet at all times malicious, petulant, and easily irritated, as well as quick and powerful to do injury."[29] Our circumstances are even more miserable than Hobbes reckoned; they are so dire that we must assist each other simply to survive. Among these circumstances, none are more compelling than those of our birth. We are completely vulnerable and utterly dependent: "scarcely any other animal is attended from birth with such weakness [*imbecillitas*]."[30]

We enter the world helpless, and we never fully outgrow our dependence on others. Furthermore, the immediate source of help is the family into which we are born, and so it has always been. Pufendorf insisted that nature supplies paternal authority (*patria potesta*) in the degree necessary for parental support.[31] If the household organized around paternal power is the primary vehicle for meeting our needs, then the family writ large is the model for all other social arrangements whose purpose is to meet needs exceeding the family's capacities. Endemic neediness calls for rationalized authority; just as parents care for their children, watchful guardians of the common good care for their civil wards.

Although the liberal paradigm has something of a British flavor, the socialist paradigm has a German one deriving from conditions in Central Europe. Throughout the eighteenth century, German teachers and writers developed a science of administration—*Cameral-Wissenschaft*—for the promotion of public order and well-being. As Keith Tribe has pointed out, "concepts such as wealth, liberty, need, and happiness" were "linked in a chain of meaning which is founded on the economy as a constitutive moment." In linking them, one finds an imperative to regulate human conduct. Yet "this process of regulation cannot be conceived in terms of state intervention in the economy, for state and economy have no independent existence—or put another way, they are the same thing."[32]

The social context, whether household, agrarian estate, or kingdom, provides rationalized paternal authority with a comprehensive response to every conceivable need and eliminates any possible threat to the statuses and privileges ordering society. This is modern thinking in defense of the old regime, or possibly in aid of its perfection. And this is G. W. F. Hegel when he linked civil society to the "system of needs" in *Elements of the Philosophy of Right* (1821).[33] Some nineteenth-century socialists saw planning and regulation as the answer to the many deficiencies of modernity, and some saw paternal authority as an artifact of the old regime. Either way, they suffered the charge of utopianism, whether from liberals or their own kind. In practice, a broad conception of need fostered the limitless extension of rationalized authority, and with it the collision of paradigms for which the twentieth century would pay so dearly.

## FRAMING HUMANITARIAN INTERVENTION

In 1758, Emmerich de Vattel presented his many readers with an elegant and accessible exposition of the republican normative framework. Supporting it are two general laws of nature. "The first general law, which is to be found in the very end of the society of nations, is that each Nation should contribute as far as it can to the happiness and advancement of other Nations." Vattel's first law makes mutual assistance a duty among nations limited only by the duties that any nation's leaders have to their own people. "Since Nations are free and independent of each other as men are by nature," Vattel went on to say, it is a "general law of their society that each Nation should be left to the Peaceful enjoyment of that liberty which belongs to it by nature."[34] The second law of nature establishes the principle of nonintervention in the relations of sovereign nations.

There are five things to notice about Vattel's formulation. First, it hews to the early modern standard in ascribing normative properties to nature. Second, it presumes that people are both free by nature and needy in many ways; as such, they choose to subject themselves to public authority and its normal operations for the common good; as a consequence, they live in societies that are also nations. Third, it takes for granted the existence of a society of nations; by implication, the society of nations is a world that nature has set apart with a normative framework of its own. Fourth, it follows Stoic thought in holding that nations owe each other assistance in principle, as if need itself were a generalizable condition. Fifth, it nevertheless makes nonintervention a practical feature of the normative framework that nature grants to the society of free and independent nations, and this makes the society of nations a world unlike any other—a liberal world.

Vattel seems not to have been troubled by the apparent tension between the requirements of mutual aid and nonintervention. There is, of course, no problem if needy nations request assistance and other nations respond accordingly, or if nations offer assistance that other nations freely accept. The problem comes when nations refuse pleas for help, or when nations insist that other nations, or their societies, or some people or institutions in those societies, need help that those nations, represented by their public authorities, refuse to countenance. The principle of nonintervention enjoins nations—as public authorities and as societies—to refrain from unwanted assistance, and the absence of any generalizable conception of need prevents nations from invoking the principle of mutual aid to override the principle of nonintervention. If nations are to intervene, they must offer grounds for doing so that are at once situationally specific and normatively powerful.

Vattel's liberal way of thinking separates what goes on between nations—their intercourse is by choice and thus not interventionary—and within nations. Civil war and insurgency lead the list of concerns that nations may have about what goes on elsewhere. Public authorities are free to suppress civil disturbances within their nations. A prolonged civil war might threaten the peace and order of Europe, but even in this case intervention is not to be undertaken lightly. The liberal world that Vattel helped to create saw interventionary conduct, surely enough, but it also saw a concerted effort by intervening nations (we can now call them states without risking anachronism) to provide a plausible rationale for their conduct.

George Canning, who became Britain's foreign minister in 1822, offered just such a rationale in 1818 at the beginning of a new era in material prosperity, social reform and, for Britain, world leadership. In Canning's words, intervention is appropriate only "in great emergencies and then with commanding force."[35] Urgent need warrants a concentrated response, one that is immediate, focused, and temporary. Even for liberals, a disastrous situation in another state justifies whatever means the intervening state's government deems necessary to overcome the resistance offered by the other state's government. A coercive response is unquestionably acceptable, and coordination with other governments is desirable.

Although civil wars have humanitarian implications, foreign governments are reluctant to view these situations as emergencies until the actions of other governments prompt them to do so. At least in the first instance, Canning's emergencies were more likely to be framed as diplomatic crises than as humanitarian disasters. Conversely, humanitarian concerns are likely to well up from a society, without particular relation to a government's position on these matters or indeed for the normative framework of a world defined in liberal terms. We need only take a quick look at the best-known instance of humanitarian intervention in Canning's era to see these dynamics at work. Here is a concise description from a leading twentieth-century international legal treatise: "Great Britain, France and Russia intervened in 1827 in the struggle between revolutionary Greece and Turkey when public opinion reacted with horror to the cruelties committed during the struggle."[36]

And here is a slightly fuller account.[37] Unruly Greeks rose up against the Ottoman Empire in 1821. Both sides committed atrocities, Greek Christians first when they massacred thousands of Moslem Turks in the Peloponnesus, and Turks most notoriously when they massacred perhaps 100,000 Greeks on and from the island of Chios. Governments could hardly ignore these events, which brought the sultan and the tsar almost to war in 1822. Although great-power diplomacy kept the peace, hundreds of progressive Europeans, many of them admirers of Hellas, went to fight in Greece but accomplished nothing; a frustrated Lord Byron died there in 1824. The war dragged on, outside support faded, and the empire held together. The Turks resisted diplomatic efforts to give Greece autonomy within the empire until allied naval forces defeated them in 1827. Russia went to war against the Turks in 1828, and Greece became fully independent in 1830.

Even this spare account makes it clear that the Greek insurgency severely strained the public order of Europe. The diplomatic response was episodic and ineffectual; local peoples acted without restraint; shocked outsiders responded nobly but to no avail; forcible intervention by governments bore almost no connection to the incidence and magnitude of local violence. If we go by Canning's liberal formula, there was no humanitarian intervention, despite the later claims of international legal treatises.

The republican normative framework casts quite different light on the whole affair. Modern Europeans took pride in their civilization and nourishment from their faith. They knew their debt to the ancients. In a world of status, they believed that human beings possess a common status requiring them not to be treated like animals. Human dignity is a natural and thus universal state of affairs, and the common good is a civilizational responsibility, however attenuated. They knew that there are as many ways of acknowledging worth and doing good as there are occasions of need. Greece offered an instance of conspicuous need; conscientious Europeans responded by sending material assistance and freedom fighters, and by mobilizing public opinion and pressuring governments to redefine a diplomatic morass as a humanitarian disaster.

Years of carnage, war, failed initiatives, duplicity, and stalemate in Greece point to the weaknesses and limitations of the republican paradigm as a normative framework. Yet there were also successes—humanitarian interventions that worked—primarily involving Britain during this time of transition to liberal societies in a liberal world. One striking success was the emancipation of slaves throughout the empire.[38] Less successful, though hardly futile, were the British government's persistent efforts to extirpate the international slave trade. Though condoned by Aristotle, Grotius, and Locke, slavery had become a principled issue for Enlightenment writers. In Britain, dissident religious groups agitated against slavery; courts freed Britain's few slaves in the 1770s.

Thereafter, antislavery sentiments grew rapidly, with Caribbean slavery their focus. In 1807, Parliament stopped slave trading in the empire, and on Britain's lead the Congress of Vienna condemned the international slave trade. Millions of people petitioned Parliament to end slavery in the empire, which it did in the 1830s. Ending the slave trade on the high seas took longer because some other states refused to become parties to relevant treaties. In a liberal international society, the slave trade was a matter of states' rights.

By contrast, no one saw the battle over slavery as a matter of human rights in the societies where it was practiced. Indeed, the historical treatment of slaves as property complicated the issue for liberals, and liberal predilections in the United States did nothing to spare it from an agonizing sectional confrontation over slavery, constitutional crisis, and civil war. For progressive intellectuals and evangelical Christians (often the same people), slavery was odious and intolerable. Its very existence translated into an urgent need, a humanitarian emergency, to which diverse moral and institutional resources could be directed. Governments constituted an arena for action, a target, and an institutional resource for use at home, across the empire, and against other governments.

We can see the same pattern with *sati*, which is the Hindu practice of widow burning.[39] For the British public, this reprehensible practice was not a human rights issue but a matter of honor and a mark against civilization. That *sati* took place within the empire made humanitarian intervention easier and all the more imperative. William Bentinck—utilitarian, evangelical Christian, and governor general in Calcutta—abolished it by decree in 1828.

The 1820s and 1830s stand as a high point in the modern response to distressing situations and odious practices in distant places. Thereafter, specifically liberal features of international society embodied in the principles of sovereignty, non-intervention, and national self-determination rapidly undermined the relevance of the republican normative framework.[40] Uneven development in liberal societies pointed to unmet human needs and unrealized human capabilities. Meanwhile, utilitarian ideas, awesome feats of engineering, and compounding material achievements served to dampen normative awareness, whether socialist or liberal, or to subordinate it to grandiose claims about human possibilities. The last decades of the century witnessed the rise of two such claims that reverberate even today.

One was social Darwinism. On scientific authority, social Darwinists claimed for themselves and their bourgeois compatriots superior abilities so as to justify their inordinate privilege and the right to rule. They invoked a new, allegedly scientific conception of nature—of natural history—to free the liberal paradigm from anything resembling normative constraints of any kind. Racist, sexist, and culturally smug, they were at their best capable of republican-style paternalism; such was "the white man's burden." At their worst, they despised human weakness.

In theory, social Darwinists could sound like republicans. In practice, they supported to an egregious extreme the liberal presumption that anything goes. Their new science of nature alienated large numbers of Christians, for whom modern skepticism was deeply disturbing and enduring status arrangements a source of comfort. That utilitarians and evangelical Christians could come together in the popular reform movements of the 1820s and 1830s seems so odd today is but one indication of the Darwinist impact on the way that we in the modern world think about our world.

The second, no less grandiose claim about human possibilities focused on needs rather than abilities. Needs are the great equalizer in the human condition; institutionalized inequalities exacerbate endemic neediness; the systematic elimination of such inequalities is the first stage in dealing with endemic neediness and not just an eventual consequence of doing so. This is utopian socialism. Some early versions suggest a nostalgic longing for premodern social arrangements. Invoking science in support of a systematic response to human need made later versions no less utopian and perhaps more so.

An abstractly humanitarian objective and reliance on the authority of science had the effect of freeing the socialist paradigm from normative constraints. Utopian socialists—sworn enemies of other social arrangements and dedicated to the necessity of planning for all needs—insisted on their need to rule and inevitably succumbed to the corruptions of privilege. At their best, they construed religious conviction as ignorance, dismissed conventional ethics, and treated spiritual needs with indifference; many people responded with the same hostility that believing Christians felt for Darwinist science. At their worst, socialists butchered and brutalized vast numbers of people for utopian ends.

Utopian socialists matched social Darwinists in taking the operative paradigms of liberalism and socialism to normatively disabling extremes. They mirrored each other in many ways, and they were jointly responsible for the institutional machinery and human catastrophes identified with Lenin, Stalin, Hitler, and Mao. All four combined a Darwinist conception of struggle, fitness, and desert with a utopian commitment to planning for every need in all possible detail. They shared a longing for "total revolution" (Friedrich Schiller's term, taken over by Karl Marx), a totalizing vision of modernity, and an abiding faith in instrumental powers of science.[41] Intervention is the standard, not the exception. If humanity is to fulfill its potential, then it must endure what amounts to a permanent state of emergency, complete with mass internment, concentration camps, and extermination programs.

A common faith in mastery through science spans the modern experience from the utopian left to the Darwinist right. At both ends of the spectrum, we find a ruthless disposition to act on principle with maximum efficiency and minimal emotional involvement. It is tempting to blame this disposition on the rapid rise of positivism in science, law, and society after 1800. Early moderns held a normative view of nature. Positivists took a detached, instrumental stance toward nature, which they held to consist of discrete, measurable things and their causal relations. Yet faith in science and positivist predilections inspired a good many moderns in the nineteenth and twentieth centuries to act on limited objectives and humane sentiments, and it helped them achieve remarkable successes ranging from the organization of productive activity to the provision of public health and safety.

The instrumental methods and successes of positivist modernity nourished liberal and socialist paradigms in ways that have brought them closer together without making everyone into ruthless ideologues. In this collusion of paradigms, liberal-minded positivists have used their skills to organize activities on a large scale, thereby drawing on many people's diverse abilities and rewarding them accordingly. Welfare-oriented positivists have used theirs to find solutions to needs defined as problems—for example, health, nutrition, and sanitation problems—thereby enabling many more people to use their abilities productively. The extraordinary growth in organizational and problem-solving activities has occasioned their progressive differentiation along functional lines. Aristotle based his conception of social life on the differentiation of activities necessary to the functioning of the whole. The same conception informs the division of labor upon which the liberal paradigm is predicated. As positivism's necessary complement, functional differentiation is a striking feature of modernity—modern societies and modern international society.

In the modern world, unleashed abilities and undeniable needs stand in complementary opposition, as do paradigm preferences and practices. Functional differentiation mediates their complex relations. It also permits piecemeal intervention, not by institutions as such, but by so-called problem-solving technicians. Being carefully calibrated, such intervention is said to comport with individual rights when it produces the desired results. Cumulatively, functionally rationalized intervention threatens the delicate balance between paradigms. This threat has become a leading source of tension in modern social life.

Early on, positivist premises, functional differentiation, and the perception of need eventuated in a solution to a problem—an urgent humanitarian problem—for which the republican normative framework had no meaningful institutional response. The problem was that wounded soldiers needed to be removed from the battlefield to be helped, and the solution took form as the International Committee of the Red Cross.[42] This response constituted humanitarian intervention in functional garb—a specialized nongovernmental activity institutionally situated in international society by multilateral treaty. Over the decades, its success has generated a functional domain populated by a host of public and private institutions designed to respond to humanitarian emergencies.

Typically, natural disasters are the proximate cause of these emergencies. Appalled by the human suffering, large numbers of people from distant places contribute resources to relief organizations, many of them religious, to help bring the situation under control. Normally, local populations welcome the assistance, even if their governments worry about compromised sovereignty and the inevitable criticism that they were ill prepared. In the past decade, people have started to see governments as the direct cause of human suffering on a scale recalling utopian-Darwinist calamities of the recent past. Because they are both humanitarian emergencies and sociopolitical crises, beleaguered functional specialists are calling them complex emergencies.[43] As emergencies that are out of control, they subject governments to a great deal of public attention and make some sort of unwelcome intervention inevitable.

Meanwhile, the legal framework for Red Cross intervention continued its well-known path of development as a humanitarian counterpart to the more broadly regulative law of war. These two bodies of law, which are only vaguely differentiated functionally, have now merged into a single regime that the International Court of Justice has advised us to call "international humanitarian law."[44] As Theodor Meron has suggested, this development "reflects the influence of the human rights movement."[45] Human rights advocacy—a movement of gathering momentum, gigantic proportions, and global significance—marks liberalism as the ascendant normative framework for the modern world.

By liberal standards, international humanitarian law is massively interventionary. The modern distinction between a world of states, and states as worlds in their own right, has lost some of its normative power, although how much is hard to say. States are no longer the sole proprietors of their own domains, and the legal order is no longer theirs except in name.[46] Under the new dispensation, governments are more likely to be objects than agents of intervention. Emergencies once overrode the presumption that governments would not intervene in each other's affairs except on rare occasions. Now, notorious human rights violations trigger intervention. Acting on behalf of those whose rights have been violated are any number of institutions equipped with legal expertise, a vast liberal literature on the link between human rights and humanitarian intervention, and even the support of important public officials.

For example, consider this statement by the then–secretary-general of the United Nations, Javier Pérez de Cuellar, in 1991: "We need not impale ourselves on the horns of a dilemma between respect for sovereignty and the protection of human rights. . . . What is involved is not the right of intervention but the collective obligation of states to bring relief and redress in human rights emergencies."[47] Cuellar's statement shows that in today's world, liberal terms, such as human rights and the right of intervention, suffuse all discussion of responding to humanitarian disasters. At the same time, any observer can see that these disasters constitute emergencies. The problem is that emergencies compel immediate action. Yet the appropriate institutional response to the violation of rights is necessarily cumbersome and slow.

There are several reasons why the institutional machinery associated with human rights is so unresponsive in emergency situations. First and most obviously, the liberal world continues to give international society room to play out its own liberal dynamics. As a practical result, the institutional machinery that governments have authorized for the protection of human rights greatly favors states over their nationals; in effect, states rights trump individual rights. Second, the available machinery tends to define the protection of human rights as a matter of anticipating and preventing their violation by persuading governments to change their practices, and not a matter of providing effective remedies to individuals whose rights have been violated. Third, liberal institutional machinery always provides for third-party adjudication whenever one party claims that another has violated its rights. The procedural rigor, evidentiary requirements, and legal expertise necessary to insure fairness in these situations restricts institutional access and makes the process lengthy, combative, and often inconclusive.

It would seem that "relief and redress" are substantially incompatible goals undermining the very possibility of an effective institutional response to so-called human rights emergencies. Urgent need calls for an immediate response. Insofar as the normative framework for such a response is liberal, then it is imperative to see the situation as an emergency. As such, it is analogous to a natural disaster that demands a quick fix and not a fastidious concern for anyone's rights.

Urgent moral need—for example, widow burning or the genital mutilation of young women—represents a special case. In such situations, liberals are reluctant to intervene directly, and their governments resist doing so even indirectly, for there is no actual emergency. The republican framework, with its emphasis on the common good, may seem to be more relevant. Yet from Aristotle on, republicans have tended to conceptualize the common good in reference to the small worlds of their immediate experience. Thus they are characteristically reluctant to intervene where the need is physically and socially distant. Only by making universal claims about civilizational values can we who live in a very big, modern world think about humanitarian intervention far from home.[48] Although anyone who appreciates the rich normative resources of modernity can argue the case for intervention where there is urgent moral need, it was easier to do so in 1828 than it is today.

## NOTES

The author is grateful to Tony Lang for the opportunity to write this chapter, to Wayne Sandholtz for an earlier opportunity to order his thoughts on the subject, and to François Debrix, Harry Gould, Sandra Keowen, Christopher Rudolph, and Daniel Whelan for their help.

1. See R. B. J. Walker's important book, *One World, Many Worlds: Struggle for a Just World Peace* (Boulder, Colo.: Lynne Rienner, 1988).

2. Samuel P. Huntington, *The Clash of Civilizations and the Remaking of World Order* (New York: Simon & Schuster, 1996).

3. I advance this claim and address its many conceptual implications in *World of Our Making: Rules and Rule in Social Theory and International Relations* (Columbia: University of South Carolina Press, 1989).

4. Sheldon Wolin, "Paradigms and Political Theories," in *Paradigms and Revolutions*, ed. Gary Gutting (Notre Dame, Ind.: University of Notre Dame Press, 1980); Onuf, *World of Our Making*, 14–23.

5. On the modern belief that modernity forms, or should be made into, "a coherent and integrated whole," see Bernard Yack, *The Fetishism of Modernities: Epochal Self-Consciousness in Contemporary Social and Political Thought* (Notre Dame, Ind.: University of Notre Dame Press, 1997), 4 and throughout.

6. Anthony Giddens, *The Consequences of Modernity* (Stanford, Calif.: Stanford University Press, 1990), 36–45, at 38.

7. Yack, *Fetishism of Modernities*, 17–25.

8. This is a broadly Weberian rendition of the story. See Giddens, *Consequences of Modernity*, 3–6, 17–21; Yack, *Fetishism of Modernity*, 30–36; and Nicholas Onuf, *The Republican Legacy of International Thought* (Cambridge: Cambridge University Press, 1998), 18–23.

9. I have deliberately excluded consideration of paradigms operating to give other worlds their distinctive features, and thus the thorny question of whether, or to what extent, our modern paradigms might have drawn from them, or should do so. Nor do I consider whether any complex and lasting world will produce similar versions of the same few paradigms. But see *World of Our Making*, chap. 3, where I suggest that an affirmative answer to the latter question does not mean that cultures, as I call them there, will develop similar features.

10. In *World of Our Making*, 17–22, I also identified three operative paradigms, there labeled *liberalism, Marxism*, and (again following Wolin) *political society*, but in that book I emphasized different features than I do here.

11. See Francis Fukuyama, *The End of History and the Last Man* (New York: Free Press, 1991), for an egregious example of this practice.

12. See Onuf, *Republican Legacy*, chap. 2, on Machiavellian and Grotian versions of the republican paradigm, there styled Atlantic republicanism and Continental republicanism.

13. Hugo Grotius, *De jure belli ac pacis libris tres*, trans. Francis W. Kelsey (Oxford: Oxford University Press, 1925), "Prolegomena," § 6, p. 11.

14. Grotius, *De jure belli ac pacis*. In the Kelsey translation, *affectus socialis* is rendered "sociableness"; "sociality" is also often used.

15. Samuel Pufendorf, *De jure naturae et gentium libri octo*, trans. C. H. Oldfather and W. A. Oldfather (Oxford: Clarendon Press, 1934), I: II, 154–78.

16. Pufendorf, *De jure naturae*, I, II, § 11, 175. Grotius, *De jure belli ac pacis*, "Prolegomena," §§ 7–10, 11–3.

17. Thomas Hobbes, *Leviathan*, ed. C. B. Macpherson (Harmondsworth, U.K.: Penguin Books, 1968), I: VI: 126.

18. Adam Smith, *The Theory of Moral Sentiments*, ed. D. D. Raphael and A. L. Macfie (Oxford: Clarendon Press, 1976), I: I: i, §§ 3–5, 10.

19. Here see Martha Nussbaum's helpful discussion of Stoicism in relation to compassion. Nussbaum, *Upheavals of Thought: The Intelligence of Emotions* (Cambridge: Cambridge University Press, 2001), 356–86.

20. Cicero, *On Duties*, trans. Margaret Atkins (Cambridge: Cambridge University Press, 1991), I: § 53: 22, and see Onuf, *Republican Legacy*, 49–55. Recent discussions of communitarian and cosmopolitan values reflect the continuing relevance of contrary tendencies in republican thought: family, humanity; small world, big world. Chris Brown, *International Relations Theory: New Normative Approaches* (New York: Columbia University Press, 1992).

21. Grotius, *De jure belli ac pacis*, I, iv–v: 35–36.

22. Thomas Hobbes, *On the Citizen*, trans. Richard Tuck and Michael Silverthorne (Cambridge: Cambridge University Press, 1998), V, § 11: 73. See also Hanna Finchel Pitkin, *The Concept of Representation* (Berkeley: University of California Press, 1967) and David Runciman, *Pluralism and the Personality of the State* (Cambridge: Cambridge University Press, 1997).

23. I trace this development in Onuf, *Republican Legacy*, 58–81.

24. John Locke, *The Second Treatise of Government*, II, v, § 27, in Locke, *Two Treatises of Government*, ed. Peter Laslett (Cambridge: Cambridge University Press, 1988), 287–88; his emphasis.

25. See John Locke, *The First Treatise of Government*, I, IX, § 92, p. 209, and *Second Treatise*, II, v, § 44, p. 298, for the term *proprietor*; also see C. B. Macpherson's well-known dis-

cussion of its implications, *The Political Theory of Possessive Individualism* (Oxford: Oxford University Press, 1962).

26. Adam Smith, *An Inquiry into the Nature and Causes of the Wealth of Nations*, ed. R. H. Campbell and A. S. Skinner (Oxford: Clarendon Press, 1976), I, II, §§ 1–2; I: 25–27.
27. Smith, *Wealth of Nations*, I, I, § 10, 22.
28. Although the term *socialist* seems highly anachronistic in an early modern context, some eighteenth-century writers used it specifically to describe Pufendorf. Istvan Hont, "The Language of Sociability and Commerce: Samuel Pufendorf and the Theoretical Foundations of the 'Four Stages Theory'," in *The Languages of Political Theory in Early-Modern Europe*, ed. Anthony Pagden (Cambridge: Cambridge University Press, 1987), 253.
29. Pufendorf, *De jure naturae et gentium*, II, III, § 15, 207–8.
30. Samuel Pufendorf, *On the Duty of Man and Citizen* (1673), trans. Michael Silverstone (Cambridge: Cambridge University Press, 1991), I, III, 3, p. 33. Also see II, I, § 4, 115–16.
31. Pufendorf, *Duty of Man*, II, III, §§ 1–2, 124.
32. Keith Tribe, *Strategies of Economic Order: German Economic Discourse, 1750–1950* (Cambridge: Cambridge University Press, 1995), 12. See generally 8–31 and, for more detail, Tribe, *Strategies of Economic Order: The Reformation of German Economic Discourse 1750–1840* (Cambridge: Cambridge University Press, 1988), 19–118.
33. G. W. F. Hegel, *Elements of the Philosophy of Right*, trans. H. B. Nisbet (Cambridge: Cambridge University Press, 1991), III, II, §§ 182–256, 220–74. Illustratively: "For the *poor*, the universal authority [*Macht*] takes over the role of the family with regard not only to their immediate deficiencies, but also to the disposition of laziness, viciousness, and the other vices to which their predicament and sense of wrong give rise"; § 241, 265, emphasis in translation.
34. Emmerich de Vattel, *The Law of Nations or the Principles of Natural Law Applied to the Conduct and to the Affairs of Nations and of Sovereigns*, trans. Charles G. Fenwick (Washington: Carnegie Institution, 1916), Introduction, §§13, 15, 6.
35. Quoted in Charles Webster, *The Foreign Policy of Castlereagh 1812–1815*, 2d ed. (London: G. Bell, 1934), 147; and R. J. Vincent, *Nonintervention and International Order* (Princeton, N.J.: Princeton University Press, 1974), 82.
36. L. Oppenheim, *International Law: A Treatise*, vol. I, *Peace*, 8th edition, ed. H. Lauterpacht (New York: David McKay, 1955), 312–13. Canning died in 1827.
37. Among my sources are George Finlay, *A History of Greece from Its Conquest by the Romans to the Present Time B.C. 146 to A.D. 1864, Vol. VI, The Greek Revolution. Part I, A.D. 1821–1827* (New York: AMS Press, 1970, reprinting ed. of 1877), 96–438; William Saint Clair, *That Greece Might Still Be Free: The Philhellenes in the War of Independence* (London: Oxford University Press, 1972); Yannis Stivachtis, *The Enlargement of International Society: Culture versus Anarchy and Greece's Entry into International Society* (New York: Saint Martin's Press, 1998), 112–86.
38. Here I draw on David Brion Davis, *The Problem of Slavery in Western Culture* (Ithaca, N.Y.: Cornell University Press, 1966), 291–445; Thomas Bender, ed., *The Antislavery Debate: Capitalism and Abolitionism as a Problem in Historical Interpretation* (Berkeley: University of California Press, 1992); Andrew Porter, "Trusteeship, Anti-Slavery and Humanitarianism," in *The Oxford History of the British Empire, Vol. III, The Nineteenth Century*, ed. Andrew Porter (Oxford: Oxford University Press, 1999).
39. But see V. N. Datta, *Sati: A Historical, Social and Philosophical Enquiry into the Hindu Rite of Widow Burning* (Riverdale, Md.: Riverdale, 1988); Jörg Fisch, *Tödliche Rituale,*

*Die indische Witwenverbrennung und andere Formen der Totenfolge* (Frankfurt: Campus Verlag, 1998), 213–328; Lata Mani, *Contentious Traditions: The Debate on Sati in Colonial India* (Berkeley: University of California Press, 1998). As for Bentinck, see John Rosselli, *Lord William Bentinck: The Making of a Liberal Imperialist 1744–1839* (Berkeley: University of California Press, 1974).

40. This is made clear in John Stuart Mill's essay, "A Few Words on Non-Intervention" (1859). The essay is found in Mill's *Dissertation and Discussions: Political, Philosophical, and Historical*, vol. 3 (Boston: William V. Spencer, 1864).

41. "The longing for total revolution develops out of reflection on the obstacles to overcoming the dehumanizing spirit of modern society." Bernard Yack, *The Longing for Total Revolution: The Philosophic Sources of Social Discontent from Rousseau to Marx and Nietzsche* (Berkeley: University of California Press, 1992), 9.

42. For an overview, see David P. Forsythe, *Humanitarian Politics: The International Committee of the Red Cross* (Baltimore: Johns Hopkins University Press, 1977), 1–56.

43. Office for the Coordination of Humanitarian Affairs, *OCHA Orientation Handbook on Complex Emergencies* (New York: United Nations, 1999), 2–3; U.S. Department of State, "Interagency Review of U.S. Government Civilian Humanitarian & Transition Programs," Washington, D.C., January 2000, 3, 6–8.

44. *Advisory Opinion on the Legality of the Threat or Use of Nuclear Weapons,* § 75, reprinted in *International Legal Materials,* 35, no. 4 (July 1996): 827.

45. Theodor Meron, "The Humanization of Humanitarian Law," *American Journal of International Law,* 94, no. 2 (April 2000): 239.

46. See, e.g., Thomas G. Weiss and Jarat Chopra's assessment, "Sovereignty under Siege: From Intervention to Humanitarian Space," in *Beyond Westphalia? State Sovereignty and International Intervention,* ed. Gene M. Lyons and Michael Mastanduno (Baltimore: Johns Hopkins University Press, 1995).

47. Javier Pérez de Cuellar, *Report on the Work of the Organization,* UN document A/46/1, September 6, 1991, 10; quoted, 111.

48. See the further discussion of small worlds and universal claims in my "Everyday Ethics in International Relations," in *Ethics in International Relations,* ed. Hakan Seckinelgin and Hideaki Shinoda (London: Palgrave, 2001).

THREE

# Hard Cases Make Bad Law: Law, Ethics, and Politics in Humanitarian Intervention

## Simon Chesterman

Three months after NATO concluded its seventy-eight-day campaign over Kosovo, UN secretary-general Kofi Annan submitted his annual report to the United Nations General Assembly. Referring to debates over the legality of the Kosovo campaign, he presented the dilemma in stark terms:

> To those for whom the greatest threat to the future of international order is the use of force in the absence of a Security Council mandate, one might ask—not in the context of Kosovo—but in the context of Rwanda: If, in those dark days and hours leading up to the genocide, a coalition of States had been prepared to act in defense of the Tutsi population, but did not receive prompt Council authorization, should such a coalition have stood aside and allowed the horror to unfold?[1]

The hypothetical neatly captured the ethical problem as many of the acting states sought to present it: Could international law truly prevent such "humanitarian" intervention?

Ironically, this was not the dilemma in the context of Rwanda. Rather than international law restraining a state from acting in defense of the Tutsi population, the problem in 1994 was that no state wanted to intervene at all. When France, hardly a disinterested actor, decided to intervene, its decision was swiftly approved in a UN Security Council resolution (though reference was made to "impartiality," a two-month time limit and five abstentions suggested wariness about France's motivation).[2]

The capriciousness of state interest is a theme that runs throughout the troubled history of humanitarian intervention. Although much ink has been spilled on the question of the legality of using military force to defend human rights, it is difficult to point to actual cases that demonstrate the significance of international law on this issue. States do not appear to have refrained from acting in situations like Rwanda (or Kosovo) simply from fear of legal sanction. Nor, however, do any of the incidents frequently touted as examples of "genuine" humanitarian intervention correspond to the principled articulation of such a doctrine by legal scholars.[3]

What, then, is the relevance of international law here? This chapter will attempt to answer this question by examining the legal status of humanitarian intervention. The next section will consider "traditional" international law and arguments that seek to assert a right of humanitarian intervention. This will be followed by an examination of how states dealt with the apparent contravention of such traditional norms in relation to Kosovo, and the impact this has had on subsequent military actions in East Timor and Afghanistan.

Of particular interest here is the relative importance of ethics and international law in the actual decision-making process of states. From a legal perspective, the question of whether the law may be violated is not itself susceptible to legal regulation. For the ethicist, running beneath the discussion here is the basic question of whether international law itself demands obedience. If international law per se is suspect, states (or other actors) might be justified in disregarding it, or at least the more offensive of its provisions. A problem confronting one who would argue such a position is the absence of any situations in which the dilemma has been posed in these terms.

It is difficult to point to a case in which international law alone has prevented a state from otherwise acting to protect a foreign population at risk. And in those incidents usually marshaled as "best cases," factors other than concern for the population were paramount. (An important—but discrete—area of ethical inquiry is whether states and other actors have an *obligation* to act to protect populations at risk. Such action could, of course, take many forms other than military intervention.[4])

Can ethical demands trump such legal structures? The answer, however unsatisfactory, will be that the question is so unlikely to arise in practice as to be of questionable value answering in theory.

## HUMANITARIAN INTERVENTION AND INTERNATIONAL LAW

The status of humanitarian intervention in international law is, on the face of it, quite simple. The UN Charter clearly prohibits the use of force. The renunciation of war must be counted among the greatest achievements of international law in the twentieth century; that this was also the bloodiest of centuries is a sober warning as to the limits of law's power to constrain the behavior of states.[5]

The passage agreed to by states at the San Francisco conference of 1945 where the United Nations was founded was broad in its scope:

All Members shall refrain in their international relations from the threat or use of force against the territorial integrity or political independence of any state, or in any other manner inconsistent with the Purposes of the United Nations.[6]

The prohibition was tempered by only two exceptions. First, the UN Charter preserved the "inherent right of individual or collective self-defense."[7] Second, the newly established Security Council was granted the power to authorize enforcement actions under Chapter VII. Although this latter species of military action is sometimes considered in the same breath as unilateral humanitarian intervention, council authorization changes the legal questions to which such action gives rise.[8]

Both exceptions provide examples of the inexorable expansion of certain legal rights. Self-defense, for example, has been invoked in ever wider circumstances to justify military actions such as a preemptive strike against a country's nuclear program and in "response" to a failed assassination attempt in a foreign country.[9] It also provided the initial basis for the United States's extensive military actions in Afghanistan in late 2001. Security Council authorizations have expanded even further, permitting actions in Somalia and Haiti that would never have been contemplated by the founders of the United Nations in 1945.[10] Nevertheless, neither exception encompasses humanitarian intervention, which entails the threat or use of armed force in the absence of a Security Council authorization or an invitation from the recognized government, with the object of protecting human rights.[11]

A third, possible, exception concerns the role of the General Assembly. Interestingly, it first arose at a time when it was feared that a Russian veto would block a resolution authorizing intervention. For some months in 1950, the representative of the USSR boycotted the Security Council for continuing UN recognition of the recently defeated Kuomintang regime in China. In his absence, three resolutions were passed that, in effect, authorized the United States to lead a military operation against North Korea under the UN flag. The return of the Soviet delegate precluded any further council involvement.[12]

At the initiative of Western states, the General Assembly adopted the *Uniting for Peace* resolution, which allowed the assembly to recommend collective measures in situations where the veto prevented the Security Council from fulfilling its primary responsibility to maintain international peace and security. In the case of a breach of the peace or act of aggression, the measures available would include the use of armed force.[13] Whether the General Assembly could legally do more than authorize peacekeeping is questionable.[14]

Nonetheless, a resolution was passed recommending that all states lend every assistance to the UN action in Korea;[15] it was used again in the Suez crisis in 1956,[16] and in the Congo in 1960.[17] The procedure has subsequently fallen into disuse, however. In particular, it appears not to have been seriously contemplated during the Kosovo crisis—reportedly due to fears that NATO would have been unable to muster the necessary two-thirds majority from the member states.[18]

At first glance, then, traditional international law does not allow for humanitarian intervention. There have, however, been many attempts to locate a foundation for humanitarian intervention within this body of law. These have tended to follow two strategies: limiting the scope of the prohibition against the use of force, or arguing that a new customary norm has created an additional exception to the prohibition.

The UN Charter prohibits the use of force "against the territorial integrity or political independence of any state, or in any other manner inconsistent with the Purposes of the United Nations." It has sometimes been argued that certain uses of force might not contravene this provision. For example, it has been argued that the U.S. invasion of Panama in 1989 was consistent with the UN Charter because "the United States did not intend to, and has not, colonialized [sic], annexed or incorporated Panama."[19] As Oscar Schachter has observed, this demands an Orwellian construction of the terms "territorial integrity" and "political independence."[20] It also runs counter to various statements by the General Assembly[21] and the International Court of Justice[22] concerning the meaning of nonintervention, as well as the Security Council's practice of condemning and declaring illegal unauthorized uses of force even when it is "temporary."[23] This is consistent with the drafting history of the provision, which, as the U.S. delegate to the San Francisco conference (among others) emphasized, left "no loopholes."[24]

Is it possible, however, that a new norm might have developed to create a separate right of humanitarian intervention? Customary international law allows for the creation of such norms through the evolution of consistent and widespread state practice,[25] when accompanied by the necessary *opinio juris*—the belief that a practice is legally obligatory.[26] Some writers have argued that there is evidence of such state practice and *opinio juris*, typically pointing to India's action to stop the slaughter in East Pakistan in 1971, Tanzania's actions against Idi Amin in neighboring Uganda in 1978–79, and Vietnam's intervention in Kampuchea (later Cambodia) in 1978–79. In none of these cases, however, were humanitarian concerns invoked as a justification for the use of force. Rather, self-defense was the primary justification offered in each case, with humanitarian (and other) justifications being, at best, secondary considerations.[27]

Such justifications are important, as they may provide evidence of change in the law. As the International Court of Justice has observed:

> The significance for the Court of cases of State conduct *prima facie* inconsistent with the principle of non-intervention lies in the nature of the ground offered as justification. Reliance by a State on a novel right or an unprecedented exception to the principle might, if shared in principle by other States, tend towards a modification of customary international law.[28]

That states continued to rely on traditional justifications—most notably self-defense—undermines arguments that the law has changed.

The international response to each incident is also instructive. In relation to India's action (which led to the creation of Bangladesh), a Soviet veto prevented a United States–sponsored resolution calling for a cease-fire and the immediate withdrawal of armed forces.[29] Tanzania's actions were broadly tolerated, and the new regime in Kampala was swiftly recognized, but states that voiced support for the action typically confined their comments to the question of self-defense.[30] Vietnam's successful ouster of the murderous regime of Pol Pot, by contrast, was met with positive hostility. France's representative, for example, stated that

> the notion that because a régime is detestable foreign intervention is justified and forcible overthrow is legitimate is extremely dangerous. That could ultimately jeopardize the very maintenance of international law and order and make the continued existence of various régimes dependent on the judgment of their neighbors.[31]

Similar statements were made by the United Kingdom[32] and Portugal,[33] among others.[34] Once again, only a Soviet veto prevented a resolution calling upon the foreign troops to withdraw;[35] Pol Pot's delegate continued to be recognized as the legitimate representative of Kampuchea at the United Nations until 1990.[36] Even if one includes these three "best cases" as evidence of state practice, the absence of accompanying *opinio juris* fatally undermines claims that they marked a change in the law.[37]

More recent examples of allegedly humanitarian intervention without explicit Security Council authorization, such as the no-fly zones in protection of the Kurds in northern Iraq and NATO's intervention in Kosovo, raise slightly different questions.[38] Acting states have often claimed that their actions have been "in support of" Security Council resolutions, though in each case it is clear that the Council did not decide to authorize the use of force.[39] Indeed, it is ironic that states began to claim the need to act when the Security Council faltered in precisely the same decade that the council's activities expanded so greatly. At a time when there was a far stronger argument that paralysis of the UN system demanded self-help, the International Court of Justice considered and rejected arguments that "present defects in international organization" could justify an independent right of intervention.[40]

Interestingly, despite the efforts by some legal scholars to argue for the existence of a right of humanitarian intervention, states themselves have continued to prove very reluctant to embrace such a right—even in defense of their own actions.[41] This is particularly true in the case of NATO's intervention in Kosovo. This reluctance appears to have stemmed in part from recognition that such a legal argument is dubious, but also that if any such right were embraced, it might well be used by other states in other situations.

In October 1998, Germany referred to NATO's threats against the Federal Republic of Yugoslavia as an instance of "humanitarian intervention," which is unusual among NATO states. The Bundestag affirmed its support for the NATO—provided that it was made clear that this was not a precedent for further action.[42] This desire to avoid setting a precedent was reflected in subsequent statements by NATO officials. U.S. secretary of state Madeleine Albright later stressed that the air strikes were a "unique situation *sui generis* in the region of the Balkans," concluding that it was important "not to overdraw the various lessons that come out of it."[43] U.K. prime minister Tony Blair, who had earlier suggested that such interventions might become more routine,[44] subsequently retreated from this position, emphasizing the exceptional nature of the air campaign.[45] This was consistent with the more sophisticated U.K. statements on the legal issues.[46]

This trend continued in the proceedings brought by Yugoslavia against ten NATO members before the International Court of Justice. In hearings on provisional measures, Belgium presented the most elaborate legal justification for the action, relying variously on Security Council resolutions, a doctrine of humanitarian intervention, as compatible with Article 2(4) of the UN Charter or based on historical precedent, and the argument of necessity. The United States also emphasized the importance of Security Council resolutions, and, together with four other delegations (Germany, the Netherlands, Spain, and the United Kingdom), made reference to the existence of a "humanitarian catastrophe."[47] Four delegations did not offer any clear legal justification (Canada, France, Italy, and Portugal). The phrase "humanitarian catastrophe" recalls the doctrine of humanitarian intervention, but some care appears to have been taken to avoid invoking the doctrine by name. The formulation was first used by the United Kingdom as one of a number of justifications for the no-fly zones over Iraq, but no legal pedigree had been established beyond this.[48] (The court ruled against Yugoslavia for technical reasons concerning its jurisdiction, but remains seized of eight of the ten cases originally brought. It did not discuss the merits of the case.[49])

Such reticence to embrace a clear legal position was repeated in two major commissions that investigated the question of humanitarian intervention. The Kosovo Commission, headed by Richard Goldstone, concluded somewhat confusingly (from an international legal perspective) that NATO's Kosovo intervention was "illegal but legitimate."[50] The International Commission on Intervention and State Sovereignty, chaired by Gareth Evans and Mohamed Sahnoun, acknowledged that, as a matter of "political reality," it would be impossible to find a consensus around any set of proposals for military intervention that acknowledged the validity of any intervention not authorized by the Security Council or the General Assembly:[51]

> But that may still leave circumstances when the Security Council fails to discharge what this Commission would regard as its responsibility to protect, in a conscience-shocking situation crying out for action. It is a real question in these circumstances where lies the most harm: in the damage to international order if the Security Council is bypassed or in the damage to that order if human beings are slaughtered while the Security Council stands by.[52]

What is a lawyer to make of all this? It seems fairly clear that there is no positive right of humanitarian intervention. Nor, however, does it appear that a coherent principle is emerging to create such a right. Rather, the arguments as presented tend to focus on the nonapplication of international law to particular incidents. The next section will explore the implications of such an approach to international law, and where it might lead.

## THE EXCEPTION AND THE RULE

James Rubin provides a graphic illustration of the debates between NATO capitals on the question of the legality of the Kosovo intervention:

> There was a series of strained telephone calls between Albright and Cook, in which he cited problems "with our lawyers" over using force in the absence of U.N. endorsement. "Get new lawyers," she suggested. But with a push from Prime Minister Tony Blair, the British finally agreed that U.N. Security Council approval was not legally required.[53]

Such equivocation about the role of international law in decision-making processes is hardly new; the history of international law is to some extent a struggle to raise law above the status of being merely one foreign policy justification among others. As is indicated above, however, most of the acting states appear to have taken some care to present the Kosovo intervention as an exception rather than a rule.

This approach to humanitarian intervention is not new. Various scholars have attempted to explain the apparent inconsistency by reference to national legal systems. Ian Brownlie, for example, has likened this approach to the manner in which some legal systems deal with the question of euthanasia:

> In such a case the possibility of abuse is recognized by the legal policy (that the activity is classified as unlawful) but . . . in very clear cases the law allows mitigation. The father who smothers his severely abnormal child after several years of devoted attention may not be sent to prison, but he is not immune from prosecution and punishment. In international relations a difficulty arises in that "a discretion not to prosecute" is exercisable by States collectively and by organs of the United Nations, and in the context of *practice* of States, mitigation and acceptance in principle are not always easy to distinguish. However, the euthanasia parallel is useful since it indicates that moderation is allowed for in social systems even when the principle remains firm. Moderation in application does not display a legislative intent to cancel the principle so applied.[54]

Obviously, as the demand for any such violation of an established norm increases, so the need for legal regulation of the "exception" becomes more important. This seems to be occurring in the case of euthanasia, as medical advances have increased the discretion of doctors in making end-of-life decisions. In many jurisdictions, continued reliance on the possibility of a homicide charge is now seen as an inadequate legal response to the ethical challenges posed by euthanasia.[55] In relation to humanitarian intervention, however, such demand remains low, and it is widely recognized that legal regulation of any "exception" is unlikely in the short term.[56]

For this reason, an alternative analogy is sometimes used: that of a person acting to prevent domestic violence in circumstances where the police are unwilling or unable to act.[57] The analogy is appealing because it appears to capture the moral dilemma facing an intervenor, but it is of limited value because such acts are typically understood in the context of the existing authority structures. An individual in most legal systems may defend another person against attack and, in certain circumstances, may exercise a limited power of arrest. In the context of humanitarian intervention, this analogy merely begs the question of its legality.

The better view, then, appears to be that humanitarian intervention is illegal but that the international community may, on a case-by-case basis, tolerate the wrong. In such a situation, claims that an intervention was "humanitarian" should be seen not as a legal justification but as a plea in mitigation. Such an approach has the merits of a basis in international law. In the *Corfu Channel Case*, the United Kingdom claimed that an intervention in Albanian territorial waters was justified on the basis that nobody else was prepared to deal with the threat of mines planted in an international strait. The International Court of Justice rejected this argument in unequivocal terms,[58] but it held that a declaration of illegality was itself a sufficient remedy for the wrong.[59]

Similarly, after Israel abducted Adolf Eichmann from Argentina to face criminal charges, Argentina lodged a complaint with the Security Council. The council passed a resolution stating that the sovereignty of Argentina had been infringed and requesting Israel to make "appropriate reparation." Nevertheless, "mindful" of the concern that Eichmann be brought to justice, the council clearly implied that "appropriate reparation" would not involve his physical return to Argentina.[60] The governments of Israel and Argentina subsequently issued a joint communiqué resolving to "view as settled the incident which was caused in the wake of the action of citizens of Israel, which violated the basic rights of the State of Argentina."[61]

This is also broadly consistent with current state practice. During the Kosovo intervention, some suggested that the action threatened the stability of the international order—in particular the relevance of the Security Council as the UN Charter body with primary responsibility for international peace and security.[62] In fact, the Security Council became integral to resolving the dispute (despite the bombing of the embassy of one permanent member by another). In Resolution 1244 (1999), the Security Council, acting under Chapter VII, welcomed Yugoslavia's acceptance of the principles set out in the May 6, 1999, meeting of Group of Eight foreign ministers, authorized member states, and "relevant international organizations" (*sc.* NATO) to establish an international security presence in Kosovo. The resolution, passed within hours of the suspension of bombing, was prefaced with a half-hearted endorsement of the role of the council:

> *Bearing in mind* the purposes and principles of the Charter of the United Nations, and the primary responsibility of the Security Council for the maintenance of international peace and security . . .[63]

More important, Resolution 1244 (1999) reaffirmed the commitment "of all Member States to the sovereignty and territorial integrity of the Federal Republic of Yugoslavia,"[64] even as it called for "substantial autonomy" for Kosovo. The tension between these provisions has left the province in a legal limbo ever since.[65]

Subsequent military action in East Timor affirmed more clearly the continued role of the Security Council, with authorization being a condition precedent for the

Australian-led UN Sanctioned International Force in East Timor (INTERFET) action. (This authorization, in turn, depended on Indonesia's consent to the operation.)[66] Though it was presented at the time as evidence that the international community was prepared to engage in Kosovo-style interventions outside Europe, the political and legal conditions in which the intervention took place were utterly different. The view that they were comparable reflected the troubling assumption that, when nations face a humanitarian crisis with a military dimension, there is a choice between doing something and doing nothing. That "something" means the application of military force.[67]

This narrow view has been challenged by UN secretary-general Kofi Annan, who stressed that "it is important to define intervention as broadly as possible, to include actions along a wide continuum from the most pacific to the most coercive."[68] Similarly, the International Commission on Intervention and State Sovereignty has sought to turn this policy question on its head. Rather than examining at length the right to intervene, it focuses on the states' responsibility to protect vulnerable populations at risk from civil wars, insurgencies, state repression, and state collapse.[69]

Implicit in many arguments for a right of humanitarian intervention is the suggestion that international law currently prevents interventions that should take place. This is simply not true. Interventions do not take place because states choose not to undertake them. On the contrary, states have frequently intervened for a great many reasons, some of them more humanitarian than others. For those who would seek to establish a law or a general ethical principle to govern humanitarian intervention, a central question must be whether it could work in practice. Do any of the incidents commonly marshaled as examples of humanitarian intervention provide a model that should be followed in future? Should Kosovo, for example, be a model for future negotiations with brutal regimes? If so, why were the terms presented to Serbia at Rambouillet more onerous than those offered after a seventy-eight–day bombing campaign?[70]

Returning to Kofi Annan's analogy quoted at the beginning of this article, it is not Kosovo but the problem of Rwanda that is confronting human rights today. Put differently, the problem is not the legitimacy of humanitarian intervention but the overwhelming prevalence of inhumanitarian nonintervention.[71]

## CONCLUSION

Following the September 11, 2001, terrorist attacks on New York and Washington, D.C., the United States swiftly sought and received UN Security Council endorsement of its position that action taken in self-defense against "those responsible for aiding, supporting or harboring the perpetrators, organizers and sponsors of these acts" was justified.[72] Self-defense does not require any form of authorization (though measures taken should be "immediately reported" to the council). The United Nations' immediate involvement in the crisis, however, was widely seen as a welcome counterpoint to the unilateralist impulses of the George W. Bush administration.[73]

Nevertheless, the decision to seek Security Council approval also reflected a troubling trend throughout the 1990s. Military action under its auspices has taken place only when it was in the national interests of a state that was prepared to act, thus placing the council in danger of becoming what Richard Falk has described as a "law-laundering service."[74] Such an approach downgrades the importance of authorization to the point where it may be seen as a policy justification rather than a matter of legal significance. A consequence of this approach is that, when authorization is not forthcoming, a state or group of states will feel less restrained from acting unilaterally. This represents a fundamental challenge to the international order established at the conclusion of World War II, in which the interests of the powerful would be balanced through the exercise (real or threatened) of the veto.[75]

In the context of humanitarian intervention, it was widely hoped that such a departure from "traditional" conceptions of sovereignty and international law would privilege ethics over states' rights. In fact, as we have seen, humanitarian intervention has long had a troubled relationship with the question of national interest. Many attempts by scholars to formulate a doctrine of humanitarian intervention require that an acting state be disinterested (or "relatively disinterested").[76] By contrast, in one of the few articulations of such a doctrine by a political leader, Prime Minister Blair proposed his own criterion of whether "we" had national interests involved.[77]

The September 11 attacks have reduced the probability of "humanitarian" interventions in the short term, but they raise the troubling prospect of more extensive military adventures being undertaken without clear legal justification. President Bush's reference to an "axis of evil" in his 2002 State of the Union speech,[78] in particular, suggested a preparedness to use ethical arguments (and absolute ethical statements) as a substitute for legal—or, it might be argued, rational—justification.

All such developments should be treated with great caution. A right of humanitarian intervention depends on acceptance of the premise that humanitarian ends justify military means. As the history of this doctrine shows, the ends are never so clear and the means are rarely so closely bound to them. In a situation where no such ideal exists and Kosovo presents an imperfect model, it is better to hold that humanitarian intervention remains both illegal and morally suspect. Nevertheless, arguments can be made on a case-by-case basis that, given an imperfect world, international order may yet survive the wrong.

## NOTES

Thanks to Robert Dann for his comments on an earlier draft of this chapter; the responsibility for the final text remains with the author alone.

1. "The Secretary-General Presents His Annual Report to the General Assembly, UN Doc SG/SM/7136-GA/9596, 20 September 1999." This and other speeches on intervention have been collected in Kofi Annan, *The Question of Intervention: Statements by the Secretary-General* (New York: United Nations Department of Public Information, 1999).

2. See Simon Chesterman, *Just War or Just Peace? Humanitarian Intervention and International Law* (Oxford: Oxford University Press, 2001), 144–47.

3. See, generally, Sean D. Murphy, *Humanitarian Intervention: The United Nations in an Evolving World Order* (Philadelphia: University of Pennsylvania Press, 1996), 83–281; Nicholas Wheeler, *Saving Strangers: Humanitarian Intervention in International Society* (Oxford: Oxford University Press, 2000); Chesterman, *Just War or Just Peace?* Other examples sometimes cited include Belgian intervention in the Congo (Léopoldville) (1960), Belgian and U.S. intervention in the Congo (1964), U.S. intervention in the Dominican Republic (1965), Israeli intervention in Uganda (the Entebbe Operation) (1976), Belgian and French intervention in Zaire (1978), French intervention in the Central African Empire and later Republic (1979), U.S. intervention in Grenada, (1983), and U.S. intervention in Panama (1989–90).

4. See, e.g., International Commission on Intervention and State Sovereignty, *The Responsibility to Protect* (Ottawa: International Development Research Center, 2001).

5. See, generally, Ian Brownlie, *International Law and the Use of Force by States* (Oxford: Clarendon Press, 1963).

6. United Nations Charter, Article 2(4).

7. United Nations Charter, Article 51.

8. See, generally, Chesterman, *Just War or Just Peace?*, 112–218.

9. Chesterman, *Just War or Just Peace?*, 205–6.

10. See Chesterman, *Just War or Just Peace?*, 112–62.

11. On the question of invitation, see Georg Nolte, *Eingreifen auf Einladung—Zur völkerrechtlichen Zulässigkeit des Einsatzes fremder Truppen im internen Konflikt auf Einladung der Regierung* [Intervention upon Invitation: Use of Force by Foreign Troops in Internal Conflicts at the Invitation of a Government under International Law (English Summary)] (Berlin: Springer Verlag, 1999); David Wippman, "Pro-Democratic Intervention by Invitation," in *Democratic Governance and International Law*, ed. Gregory H. Fox and Brad R. Roth (Cambridge: Cambridge University Press, 2000); and Brad R. Roth, "The Illegality of "Pro-Democratic" Invasion Pacts," in *Democratic Governance and International Law.*

12. See Anjali V. Patil, *The UN Veto in World Affairs 1946–1990: A Complete Record and Case Histories of the Security Council's Veto* (London: Mansell, 1992), 189–96.

13. UN General Assembly, GA Res 377A(V) (1950).

14. The International Court of Justice (ICJ) has stated that the Charter allows the General Assembly to *recommend* peacekeeping operations at the request, or with the consent, of the state(s) concerned, but that this is limited by the requirement that any question on which "action" (here understood to mean enforcement action within the meaning of Chapter VII) is required be referred to the Security Council; *Certain Expenses Case* [1962] ICJ Reports 151, 164–65. The Court decided the case by adopting a principle of "institutional effectiveness" and held that "when the Organization takes action which warrants the assertion that it was appropriate for the fulfilment of one of the stated purposes of the United Nations, the presumption is that such action is not *ultra vires* the Organization": *Certain Expenses Case* [1962] ICJ Reports 151, 168. See Ian Brownlie, *Principles of Public International Law*, 5th ed. (Oxford: Clarendon Press, 1998), 700–701.

15. UN General Assembly, GA Res 498(V) (1951).

16. UN General Assembly, GA Res 997(ES-I) (1956); GA Res 1000(ES-I) (1956).

17. UN Security Council, SC Res 157 (1960); UN General Assembly, GA Res 1474(ES-IV) (1960). Also see Chesterman, *Just War or Just Peace?*, 118–19.

18. U.K. House of Commons, Foreign Affairs Committee, Fourth Report: Kosovo, Minutes of Evidence—vol. 2, HC 28-II, January 18, 2000.

    The "Uniting for Peace" procedure, which you are referring to, which originates in November 1950, would have, theoretically, opened the possibility for the Western powers to have gone to the General Assembly, which would have had to be a special session, in early 1999, and attempted to get a two-thirds majority there. I actually raised that issue in a meeting at Chatham House on the day Rambouillet initially failed, in February of 1999, and I suggested that might be one possible way out of the Security Council's obvious paralysis on the question of Kosovo. At that time, the Foreign Office took the view that this was very ill advised, and I was told that really it was not very helpful of me to have talked about this. Because I think they clearly took the view (a) that it was uncertain that they would get anything like the two-thirds majority which I believe is what is required under "Uniting for Peace," and (b) that the General Assembly is a somewhat cumbersome instrument, in that it does not meet continuously, it cannot continuously develop its policy, once you have got an agreement in the General Assembly you will be absolutely stuck with whatever that agreement is, and it is not the kind of flexible instrument that the Security Council is. Those, I think, were the arguments against going that route, I am not saying they were right, I think there was a serious case for trying that route, but that was the opinion at the time and the reason why it was not done. (www.parliament.the-stationery-office.co.uk/pa/cm199900/cmselect/cmfaff/28/0011806.htm Question 178 [Professor Adam Roberts])

19. Anthony D'Amato, "The Invasion of Panama Was a Lawful Response to Tyranny," *American Journal of International Law* 84 (1990): 520. Similarly, during the 1983 U.S. intervention in Grenada, its permanent representative to the United Nations, Jeanne Kirkpatrick, argued that references to the "purposes" of the United Nations provided "ample justification for the use of force in pursuit of other values also inscribed in the Charter—freedom, democracy, peace": (1983) 83(2081) *Department of State Bulletin* 74. See also W. Michael Reisman, "Coercion and Self-Determination: Construing Charter Art 2(4)," *American Journal of International Law* 78 (1984): 645; Fernando R. Tesón, *Humanitarian Intervention: An Inquiry into Law and Morality*, 2d ed. (Dobbs Ferry, N.Y.: Transnational Publishers, 1997), 150–62.

20. Oscar Schachter, "The Legality of Pro-Democratic Invasion," *American Journal of International Law* 78 (1984): 649.

21. See, e.g., UN General Assembly, "Declaration on Friendly Relations," GA Res 2625(XXV) (1970) (unanimous): "No State or group of States has the right to intervene, directly or indirectly, *for any reason whatever*, in the internal or external affairs of any other State"; "Every State has an inalienable right to choose its political, economic, social and cultural systems, *without interference in any form by another State*" (emphasis added). Cf. GA Res 45/150 (1990) (adopted 128-8-9): "the efforts of the international community to enhance the effectiveness of the principle of periodic and genuine elections should not call into question each State's sovereign right freely to choose and develop its political, social, economic and cultural systems, *whether or not they conform to the preferences of other States*" (emphasis added).

22. See *Corfu Channel Case* [1949] ICJ Reports 4 (International Court of Justice); *Nicaragua (Merits)* [1986] ICJ Reports 14; Chesterman, *Just War or Just Peace?*, 50–55.

23. See, e.g., UN Security Council, SC Res 332 (1973) (Israeli invasion of Lebanon); SC Res 455 (1979) (declaring temporary Rhodesian incursion into Zambia a violation of Zambia's territorial integrity); SC Res 545 (1983) (South Africa in Angola).

24. United Nations, Documents of the United Nations Conference on International Organization, San Francisco 1945, 21 vols. (New York: United Nations, 1945–55), vol. 6, 335. Also see Chesterman, *Just War or Just Peace?*, 47–53.

25. *Nicaragua (Merits)*, 98.

26. *Nicaragua (Merits)*, 109: "Either the States taking such action or other States in a position to react to it, must have behaved so that their conduct is 'evidence of a belief that this practice is rendered obligatory by the existence of a rule of law requiring it'" (quoting *North Sea Continental Shelf Cases* [1969] ICJ Reports 3, International Court of Justice).

27. Again, see generally Murphy, *Humanitarian Intervention*, 83–281; Wheeler, *Saving Strangers*; Chesterman, *Just War or Just Peace?* As was noted above, other examples sometimes cited include Belgian intervention in the Congo (Léopoldville) (1960), Belgian and U.S. intervention in the Congo (1964), U.S. intervention in the Dominican Republic (1965), Israeli intervention in Uganda (the Entebbe Operation) (1976), Belgian and French intervention in Zaire (1978), French intervention in the Central African Empire and later Republic (1979), U.S. intervention in Grenada, (1983), and U.S. intervention in Panama (1989–90).

28. *Nicaragua (Merits)*, 109.

29. The General Assembly later called upon India to conclude a cease-fire and withdraw its troops; [1971] *United Nations Yearbook* 146–48.

30. See, e.g., the statement of U.S. secretary of state Cyrus Vance: "Our position is very clear; there is a clear violation of Tanzania's frontier by Uganda. We support President Nyerere's position according to which Ugandan troops must withdraw immediately"; *Keesing's* (1979) 29669.

31. UN Document S/PV.2109 (1979) para 36 (France).

32. "Whatever is said about human rights in Kampuchea, it cannot excuse Viet Nam, whose own human rights record is deplorable, for violating the territorial integrity of Democratic Kampuchea"; S/PV.2110 (1979) para 65 (U.K.).

33. "There are no nor can there be any sociopolitical reasons that would justify the invasion of the territory of a sovereign State by the forces of another State"; S/PV.2110 (1979) para 26 (Portugal).

34. See S/PV.2109 (1979) para 10 (Kuwait), para 18 (Norway), para 20 (Czechoslovakia), para 50 (Bangladesh), para 59 (Bolivia), para 91 (Sudan); S/PV.2110 (1979) para 39 (Malaysia), paras 48-49 (Singapore, stating that "No other country has a right to topple the Government of Democratic Kampuchea, however badly that Government may have treated its people"), para 58 (New Zealand).

35. [1979] *United Nations Yearbook*, 275.

36. [1979] *United Nations Yearbook*, 292.

37. Some authors reject this understanding of international law. See Michael Byers and Simon Chesterman, "Changing the Rules about Rules? Unilateral Humanitarian Intervention and the Future of International Law," in *Humanitarian Intervention: Principles, Institutions and Change*, ed. J. L. Holzgrefe and Robert O. Keohane (Cambridge: Cambridge University Press, 2003).

38. For a discussion of the Nigeria-led actions by the Economic Community of West African States in Liberia and Sierra Leone, see Chesterman, *Just War or Just Peace?*, 134–37, 155–56.

39. UN Security Council, SC Res 688 (1991), which condemned the repression of the Iraqi civilian population in the wake of the Gulf War, was the first of the fourteen resolutions on Iraq *not* adopted under Chapter VII of the UN Charter (enabling the Security Council to authorize the use of force). SC Res 1199 (1998), which demanded action to improve the humanitarian situation in Kosovo, explicitly stated that, "should the concrete measures demanded in this resolution . . . not be taken, [the Council has decided to] consider further action and additional measures."

40. *Corfu Channel Case*, 35. See the quotation in n. 58 below.

41. But see Anthony Aust, legal counselor, British Foreign and Commonwealth Office, statement before House of Commons Foreign Affairs Committee, December 2, 1992, *Parliamentary Papers*, 1992–93, House of Commons, Paper 235-iii, p. 85, reprinted in (1992) *63 British YBIL*: 827. This was one of a number of rationales given for the no-fly zones in Iraq. See Chesterman, *Just War or Just Peace?*, 196–206.

42. Deutscher Bundestag, Plenarprotokoll 13/248, October 16, 1998, 23129; http://dip. bundestag.de/parfors/parfors.htm. Two weeks before the air campaign, Bruno Simma endorsed this position, noting that "only a thin red line separates NATO's action in Kosovo from international legality" but arguing that it should remain exceptional: Bruno Simma, "NATO, the UN and the Use of Force: Legal Aspects," *European Journal of International Law* 10 (1999): 22.

43. U.S. secretary of state Madeleine Albright, Press Conference with Russian Foreign Minister Igor Ivanov, Singapore, July 26, 1999; http://secretary.state.gov/www/statements/1999/990726b.html.

44. Colin Brown, "Blair's Vision of Global Police," *The Independent*, April 23, 1999.

45. See, e.g., U.K. Parliamentary Debates, Commons, April 26, 1999, col. 30 (Prime Minister Blair).

46. See, e.g., U.K. Parliamentary Debates, Lords, November 16, 1998, WA 140 (Baroness Symons); reaffirmed in U.K. Parliamentary Debates, Lords, May 6, 1999, col. 904 (Baroness Symons). Foreign Affairs Committee (United Kingdom), Fourth Report—Kosovo (May 23, 2000); www.fas.org, para 132 (concluding that "at the very least, the doctrine of humanitarian intervention has a tenuous basis in current international customary law, and that this renders NATO action legally questionable").

47. *Legality of Use of Force Case* (Provisional Measures) (International Court of Justice, 1999) pleadings of Belgium, May 10, 1999, 99/15 (uncorrected translation); pleadings of the United States, May 11, 1999, CR 99/24, para 1.7; pleadings of Germany, May 11, 1999, CR 99/18, para 1.3.1; pleadings of the Netherlands, May 11, 1999, CR 99/20, para 40; pleadings of Spain, May 11, 1999, CR 99/22, para 1; pleadings of the United Kingdom, May 11, 1999, CR 99/23, paras 17–18; pleadings of the United States, May 11, 1999, CR 99/24, para 1.7.

48. See Chesterman, *Just War or Just Peace?*, 196–206.

49. *Legality of Use of Force Case* (Provisional Measures) (International Court of Justice, 1999) order of June 2, 1999.

50. Independent International Commission on Kosovo, *The Kosovo Report* (Oxford: Independent International Commission on Kosovo, 2000), 4; www.kosovocommission.org.

51. On the question of General Assembly authorization, see notes 13–18 above. The Independent International Commission on Kosovo Report suggests that, although the General

Assembly lacks the power to direct that action be taken, a decision made by an overwhelming majority of member states "would provide a high degree of legitimacy for an intervention which subsequently took place"; International Commission on Intervention, *Responsibility to Protect*, 53.

52. International Commission on Intervention, *Responsibility to Protect*, 54–55.

53. James Rubin, "A Very Personal War: Countdown to a Very Personal War," *Financial Times*, September 30, 2000.

54. Ian Brownlie, "Thoughts on Kind-Hearted Gunmen," in *Humanitarian Intervention and the United Nations*, ed. Richard B. Lillich (Charlottesville: University Press of Virginia, 1973), 146 (emphasis in original). See also Lillich, *Humanitarian Intervention*, 117–21; Tom J. Farer, "A Paradigm of Legitimate Intervention," in *Enforcing Restraint: Collective Intervention in Internal Conflicts*, ed. Lori Fisler Damrosch (New York: Council on Foreign Relations Press, 1993), 327.

55. See Simon Chesterman, "Last Rights: Euthanasia, the Sanctity of Life and the Law in the Netherlands and the Northern Territory of Australia," *International and Comparative Law Quarterly* 47 (1998), and the sources there cited.

56. For a survey of attempts to codify a right of humanitarian intervention, see Chesterman, *Just War or Just Peace?*, 227–30.

57. See, e.g., Anthony D'Amato, "Nicaragua and International Law: The 'Academic' and the 'Real,'" *American Journal of International Law* 79 (1985): 660; Tesón, *Humanitarian Intervention*, 88.

58. *Corfu Channel Case*, 35: "The Court cannot accept this line of defense. The Court can only regard the alleged right of intervention as a policy of force, such as has, in the past, given rise to the most serious abuses and such as cannot, whatever be the present defects in international organization, find a place in international law."

59. *Corfu Channel Case*, 36.

60. UN Secretariat, S/4349 (1960); UN Security Council, SC Res 138 (1960).

61. Joint Communiqué of the Governments of Israel and Argentina, August 3, 1960, reprinted in 36 ILR 59. As the prohibition of the use of force is an obligation *erga omnes*, however, a simple waiver by the target State—particularly a waiver by a regime put in power by the intervening State, as in the case of the U.S. invasion of Panama in 1989— would not avoid the need to explain the action to the larger international community. See Simon Chesterman, "Rethinking Panama: International Law and the US Invasion of Panama, 1989," in *The Reality of International Law: Essays in Honour of Ian Brownlie*, ed. Guy S. Goodwin-Gill and Stefan A. Talmon (Oxford: Oxford University Press, 1999), 57.

62. See, e.g., Simon Chesterman and Michael Byers, "Has US Power Destroyed the UN?" *London Review of Books*, April 29, 1999.

63. UN Security Council, SC Res 1244 (1999), preamble.

64. UN Security Council, SC Res 1244 (1999), preamble.

65. See Simon Chesterman, "Elections Are What We Do," *World Today* 57 (11) (2001).

66. UN Security Council, SC Res 1264 (1999).

67. See Chesterman, *Just War or Just Peace?*, 219–36.

68. "Annual Report of the Secretary-General."

69. International Commission on Intervention, *Responsibility to Protect*. Also see Simon Chesterman and David M. Malone, "The Prevention–Intervention Dichotomy: Two Sides of the Same Coin?" in *From Civil Strife to Civil Society: Civil and Military Responsi-*

*bilities in Disrupted States*, ed. William Maley, Charles Sampford, and Ramesh Thakur (Tokyo: United Nations University Press, 2002).

70. Chesterman, *Just War or Just Peace?*, 224.
71. Cf. Shashi Tharoor and Sam Daws, "Humanitarian Intervention: Getting Past the Reefs," *World Policy Journal* 18(2) (2001).
72. UN Security Council, SC Res 1368 (2001).
73. See, e.g., Gerard Baker and James Kynge, "APEC Meeting: Leaders Condemn Terrorist Attacks," *Financial Times*, October 22, 2001.
74. Richard A. Falk, "The United Nations and the Rule of Law," *Transnational Law and Contemporary Problems* 4 (1994): 628.
75. For a useful discussion on the responsibilities that a veto-wielding power bears, see International Commission on Intervention, *Responsibility to Protect*, 51 (pointing the way toward a "code of conduct" for the use of the veto).
76. See, e.g., Jean-Pierre L. Fonteyne, "The Customary International Law Doctrine of Humanitarian Intervention: Its Current Validity under the UN Charter," *California Western International Law Journal* 4 (1974): 261; David J. Scheffer, "Toward a Modern Doctrine of Humanitarian Intervention," *University of Toledo Law Review* 23 (1992): 291; Chesterman, *Just War or Just Peace?*, 229.
77. Michael Evans, "Conflict Opens 'Way to New International Community': Blair's Mission," the *Times* (London), April 23, 1999. The five criteria were: Are we sure of our case? Have we exhausted all diplomatic options? Are there military options we can sensibly and prudently undertake? Are we prepared for the long term? And do we have national interests involved? Cf. Vaclav Havel's statements that NATO's intervention was "probably the first war that has not been waged in the name of 'national interests,' but rather in the name of principles and values"; Vaclav Havel, "Kosovo and the End of the Nation-State," *New York Review*, June 10, 1999, 6.
78. See www.whitehouse.gov.

FOUR

# Is There an Islamic Ethic of Humanitarian Intervention?

Sohail H. Hashmi

Humanitarian intervention in the contemporary Western discourse on international law and ethics has emerged as the exception that confirms the rule. Only in the case where the moral issues are starkly framed, only when the stakes of nonintervention are potentially catastrophic in human terms, only in the case of a regime that oppresses its own people to the point of genocide or massive violations of human rights is a violation of the rule of nonintervention in the internal affairs of a sovereign state deemed legitimate—and it is legitimated by the qualifying designation "humanitarian."

If framed in these terms, the problem of humanitarian intervention assumes quite a different dimension when considered from the perspective of Islamic theories of international behavior, both classical and modern. Indeed, the very factors that make intervention—humanitarian or otherwise—a problematic issue in the current discourse lose their relevance within the framework of Islamic theory. The reason is that the nation-state enjoys at best an ambiguous status in contemporary Islamic legal thought and virtually no standing in Islamic ethical thought. Rather, there persists to this day a strong tradition among Muslim theorists to invest moral standing not in the fifty-six or so Muslim-majority states but in the collective Muslim community, the *umma* referred to by the Qur'an. Therefore, there is an a priori assumption in Islamic thought for the legitimacy of humanitarian intervention in collective action that has to be disproved rather than proved. In other words, the burden of proof lies with those who would challenge the right of intervention on grounds of state sovereignty rather than on those who assert it.

This chapter has three objectives: first, to elaborate the problematic status of the nation-state in modern Islamic thought; second, to consider various arguments on when and how humanitarian intervention may be considered legitimate in an Islamic framework; and third, to look at practical measures that have been or may be undertaken by Muslim states to implement the ethical injunctions of intervention.

A consideration of Islamic approaches to humanitarian intervention is significant and necessary for a variety of reasons. First, on the theoretical level, international norms of humanitarian intervention are still far from being either fully elaborated or universally accepted. The concept is perhaps most problematic in developing countries, where any form of intervention is still strongly resisted due to the lingering legacy of Western imperialism. It is vital, therefore, that during this period of development, principles of humanitarian intervention be based on as truly a universal and cross-cultural consensus of fundamental human rights, and the legitimate means to enforce them, as possible.

Second, on a practical level, many of the most important "test cases" of humanitarian intervention have involved Muslims, as victims (as in Bosnia and Kosovo), as perpetrators (as in East Timor), or as both victims and perpetrators (as in Iraq and Somalia). These cases, however, are only the most publicized; numerous other human disasters involving large numbers of Muslims have occurred or are still unfolding with scarce international attention.[1] If humanitarian intervention is to become a viable instrument for the alleviation of severe human suffering, appropriate institutions must be created in the regions of the crises themselves for speedy relief and eventually for prevention.

## DEVELOPING AN INTERNATIONAL CONSENSUS ON HUMANITARIAN INTERVENTION

The 1991 Persian Gulf War was fought, at least "officially," to enforce the principle of territorial integrity of sovereign states. It ended—as wars are prone to confound expectations—by unleashing a debate on the contemporary relevance and value of the very principle of state sovereignty. The UN Security Council's decision in April 1991 to intervene in Iraqi Kurdistan for the humanitarian relief of people being massacred by their own state was indeed a significant departure from previous UN attitudes on the right of humanitarian intervention. For example, Michael Akehurst concluded in 1984 that the 1979 condemnation by the United Nations of Vietnam's unilateral incursion into Pol Pot's Cambodia reflected "a consensus among states in favor of treating humanitarian intervention as illegal."[2]

Thirteen years later, that consensus was challenged, if not totally reversed. In the aftermath of the Iraqi intervention, a UN Department of Humanitarian Affairs was created to coordinate more effectively the delivery of humanitarian assistance by the various UN agencies. Among the first tasks of this new department was to address the growing crisis in the Horn of Africa, which resulted in the adoption on April 24, 1992, of Security Council Resolution 751 establishing a small UN observer force in Somalia to assist in the delivery of relief supplies.

Simultaneous with UN actions in Somalia were Security Council resolutions providing for relief operations in the escalating conflict in Bosnia. Initial efforts aimed at maintaining the delivery of relief supplies into the capital of Sarajevo and other besieged parts of the country culminated in the adoption of Security Council Resolution 770 on August 13, 1992, authorizing the use of force to protect humanitarian operations. The language of this resolution is reminiscent of the earlier council resolutions authorizing humanitarian relief operations in northern Iraq. It is important to note, however, a major difference that separates the Bosnian case from traditional cases of humanitarian intervention: the intervention in Bosnia was at the request of, and not in opposition to, the national government.

Yet the Security Council's painfully slow responses to the crises in Somalia and Bosnia are stark testimony to the limited consensus on the principles of humanitarian intervention. They reflect the lack of agreement on either the criteria for declaring a crisis to be a humanitarian emergency or the appropriate means of intervention. The reason for this impasse is the apparent challenge that a right of humanitarian intervention—supported by military force if necessary—presents to the still sacrosanct notion of sovereignty, enshrined as the principle of noninterference in the domestic affairs of states under Article 2(7) of the UN Charter. As Richard N. Gardner points out, the Security Council was loath to establish a principle of military intervention on human rights grounds alone in the Iraqi intervention (and, it might be added, in both the Bosnian relief operations and the Somali intervention), justifying UN operations instead on the enforcement of "international peace and security" under Chapter VII of the UN Charter.[3]

Thus codification of a principle of humanitarian intervention will require nothing less than a thorough review of the meaning of state sovereignty as the fundamental principle of international society. This process must inevitably include a more systematic and critical review and resolution of what Jarat Chopra and Thomas Weiss have identified as the twin contradictions "running through the United Nations Charter": (1) sovereignty versus human rights and (2) peace versus justice.[4] The present bias in interpreting the charter to favor values of state sovereignty and peace—that is, order—is a vestige of the post–World War II Western realist tradition that produced the present UN system. However, in the aftermath of the cold war, the time is right to reassess this dominant interpretation of the charter and to reappraise the value of human rights and justice in the international system. Islamic thought, I would suggest, may make valuable contributions to this reappraisal.

Any discussion of "Islam" in the modern world must begin by emphasizing that most aspects of contemporary Islamic thought are in flux. This situation is particularly acute in the area of international relations, where the classical theory elaborated between the eighth and the thirteenth centuries C.E. has yet to evolve or be replaced by a coherent modern theory or even the foundations of such a theory.[5] Instead, what we find is that the Muslim world is still struggling to reconcile itself with the Western-originated and -dominated international system.

If Muslim practice is any indication, then the classical theory would have to be considered obsolete. The Muslim countries that emerged from the retreat of European colonialism have without exception acceded to the prevailing international legal regime. All of the Muslim states, for example, are members of the United Nations—and some, including Saudi Arabia (one of the most conservative Muslim states), are charter members.

Although the classical Islamic theory of world order is today clearly in disuse, it has not been entirely repudiated by the majority of Muslim states. Indeed, the Organization of the Islamic Conference (OIC) voted in 1980 to establish an International Islamic Law Commission "to devise ways and means to secure representation in order to put forward the Islamic point of view before the International Court of Justice and such other institutions of the United Nations when a question requiring the projection of Islamic views arises therein."[6]

This commission has yet to materialize, largely because the state elites that embraced the idea in principle realize that in practice there are interpretations of Islamic law that would open a Pandora's box of unexpected and undesired conclusions by jurists. Even if it does ever convene, its mandate does not ostensibly include—for obvious reasons—the one question that is perhaps central to modern Islamic discussions of political order: Simply, is the present international system, based upon the primacy of the sovereign, independent nation-state, compatible with Islamic law and, more important, with Islamic ethics? We will return to the OIC below, but it is necessary here to deal with this central question of the state—albeit briefly—before proceeding to the issue of humanitarian intervention.

## POLITICAL ORGANIZATION AND MORAL OBLIGATION IN ISLAMIC THOUGHT

Many students of the Christian and Islamic traditions have noted the different histories of each faith as a political community. Unlike the experience of Christianity, Islam did not evolve as a religious community apart from or in opposition to an established or hostile political order. Quite the opposite, Islamic civilization evolved from its formative phase very much as a political phenomenon, with politics thoroughly incorporated within and intrinsic to its moral order.

The Qur'an's approach to political organization is premised upon the common ontology of humanity, because all of creation is described as a unified whole with a single origin in the divine creator, a common purpose known only to that creator, and a common end. Thus all human beings are described in their origins as being *umma wahida* (one community), which, since that primordial state, have splintered according to their belief or disbelief in God or gods (Q. 2:213). Despite its fractured state, humanity is still fundamentally united in the Islamic view by virtue of its common beginnings and destiny. The Islamic ethical framework is premised on the universality of its principles.

The duty to realize these principles falls, of course, upon the Muslim community by virtue of its submission to the divine injunctions, that is, by virtue of its *islam*. Muslims form one *umma*, a single community, described by the Qur'an as the "me-

dian" community (2:143) and the "best" community (3:110), a community that
carries the moral obligation "to order the right and to forbid the wrong" (3:104,
110). Among the many things that the Qur'an enjoins upon the Muslim *umma* is
that it retain its unity and avoid internal dissension or division (3:103, 105).

Of course, this Qur'anic injunction—like many other political and ethical ideals—was never realized after the death of the prophet Muhammad in 632 C.E. The
most serious division and the earliest chronologically was the dispute on the
Prophet's legitimate successor, leading ultimately to the evolution of the Shi'i tradition apart from the Sunni majority. Sunni law developed subsequently by maintaining the fiction of the united community under a single head, the *khalifa* (caliph),
but with a number of *walis* (agents) for the caliph administering his different realms.
Even those jurists who attempted to reconcile theory with reality could never abjure
the moral primacy of the unified community, the *umma*.[7]

In analyzing the current Muslim literature on this subject, one is struck by the degree to which the fundamentals of the discourse have remained unchanged. Modern
approaches to the status of the nation-state in Islamic thought may be divided very
generally into three strands.

First, there is a quite diffuse *secular* school of Muslim theoreticians and politicians, whose members may be further subdivided into two groups. The first sub-
group, including figures such as 'Ali 'Abd al-Raziq and Taha Hussein in Egypt and
Sati' al-Husri in Syria, seek to operate within the framework of Islamic discourse.
Their position tends to crystallize around the contention that the Qur'an and *sunna*
(the example of the Prophet) do not stipulate any political theory or specific political
institutions and hence remove issues of political organization from the religious
sphere. As a result, the concept of the *umma* is stripped of any substantive political
content in their thought. A second subcategory of secularists would include such authoritarian "state builders" as Mustafa Kemal Atatürk in Turkey and Reza Shah in
Iran, as well as the Iranian intellectual Ahmad Kasravi. These secularists quite consciously reject Islamic tradition as being antithetical to the creation of a "modern"
state and society.

Secular nationalism has made profound and irreversible inroads into the political
consciousness of Muslims, and it has dominated the actual practice of most Muslim
states in the postcolonial era. Nevertheless, secular nationalism remains peripheral
in influencing the content of Islamic political thought. The clearest example of its
marginality is the fact that not even Kemalist Turkey, the most advanced case of applied secularism in the Muslim world, has produced a single secularist ideologue of
international stature, let alone Islamic legitimacy.[8]

A second group of *modernist* intellectuals may be identified whose agenda is to reinterpret the Qur'an and *sunna* in such a way as to find an accommodation between
Islamic ideals and prevailing realities. Many figures could be cited as proponents of
this school, including Muhammad 'Abduh and Rashid Rida in Egypt, and Ziya
Gökalp in Turkey. Among the most influential and articulate is Muhammad Iqbal,
the poet-philosopher whose thought is commonly cited as providing the ideological

basis for the creation of Pakistan. Iqbal argued that "tribal or national organizations on the lines of race or territory are only temporary phases in the unfoldment and up-bringing of collective life, and as such I have no quarrel with them; but I condemn them in the strongest possible terms when they are regarded as the ultimate expression of the life of mankind."[9]

Iqbal's argument thus attempts to justify the emergence of Muslim nation-states as a transitional, perhaps necessary phenomenon, but still far short of the ideal. The ideal for him is not a pan-Islamic state but a confederation of Muslim nation-states acting in concert, a "Muslim League of Nations," as he himself terms it.[10] The league's specific powers and purposes are left blissfully unelaborated in the corpus of his work. But his idealistic vision did significantly influence Pakistani foreign policy during its first decade, much to the annoyance of secular Arab leaders who were attempting desperately to inculcate the ideology of Arab nationalism as a counter to pan-Islamism and other competing loyalties within their own states.

The third strand of Muslim thought is avowedly and unabashedly *pan-Islamic*. This group not only denies the acceptability of the nation-state according to Islamic theory but also condemns it as a vestige of European colonialism intended to perpetuate the weakness of the Muslim *umma*. Again, we could cite a number of proponents of this view, including the Egyptian leaders of the Muslim Brotherhood, Hasan al-Banna and Sayyid Qutb, and the Indian/Pakistani founder of the Jama'at-i Islami, Abu'l-A'la Mawdudi. Perhaps the most influential recent figure and certainly the best known is Ayatollah Ruhollah Khomeini. Khomeini's thought evinces the most uncompromising Islamic cosmopolitanism. The nation-state system with its emphasis on territorial integrity was described by him at one point as being the product of the "deficient human mind."[11] Iran's Islamic revolution was frequently described as the epicenter for the propagation of the universal Islamic revolution.

Much of Khomeini's revolutionary rhetoric may be dismissed as political and war-time propaganda. He, like Banna, Qutb, Mawdudi, and most other Islamic activists, proved willing to bend their Islamic cosmopolitan ideals to achieve their political ends. During the Iran–Iraq War, for example, Khomeini resorted to the language of Iranian nationalism. As a result, the Iranian claim that Khomeini be acknowledged as the leader of the universal revolution met with less than enthusiastic support in most of the Muslim world, including among religious groups. Nevertheless, the essential elements of Khomeini's call for a unified political community resonates in the programs of most Islamic groups in virtually every Muslim country today.

In short, the concept of the unified Muslim community, the *umma*, remains very much a point of discussion and debate for most Muslim theorists and very much an aspiration for most Islamic activists. This fact is inevitable given the explicit moral value that the Qur'an invests in the one community and the condemnation it reserves for those who attribute any moral worth to essentially linguistic, tribal, or ethnic ascriptions. As is evident in the thought of Iqbal, even modernist Muslim intellectuals cannot escape the conclusion that even a nation-state with liberal institutions cannot be embraced as the summum bonum of Islamic political life.

## THE QUR'ANIC ETHICS OF JUST INTERVENTION

So where does this lead us in trying to discern an Islamic approach to humanitarian intervention? Two points need to be emphasized at the outset. First, the rejection of the moral value of the nation-state does not necessarily negate the possibility of particularistic political communities short of the universal *umma*. The Qur'an states that God made humankind into "nations and tribes, so that you might come to know one another" (49:13). Thus, the Qur'an embraces the validity of group identities, but only as a means of self-reference and facility of human interaction, not as the basis for racism, chauvinism, or extreme nationalism. This verse is frequently cited by Muslim modernists today to establish an Islamic sanction for the present international system built on nation-states.

However, the reasoning behind such a claim appears strained when this verse is read in the context of all the other verses describing the Muslims as one *umma*. One may read Q. 49:13 as sanctioning the division of humanity into nation-states, with "nation" being defined according to racial or ethnic criteria, as a *functional* requirement. If the majority of the world's peoples at this time choose this form of political organization as the one best suited to their happiness and welfare, then it is not necessarily averse to Islamic principles. Indeed, most modern Muslim theorists and activists express no opposition to the structure of the modern international system *beyond the Muslim world*. The nation-state model is challenged primarily as it functions *among Muslim peoples*, when claims of state sovereignty and nationalism intrude upon the demands of the Muslim *umma*.

Second, because Muslim nation-states enjoy a limited, functional value as long as they promote the happiness and welfare of their people, the universal Islamic *umma* may not be brought about through violence. Not even most pan-Islamists would argue that a politically unified, universal Islamic state could or should be created through war. For example, Khomeini often asserted that the Islamic revolution must be propagated through nonviolent means, claiming that Islamic ideology, due to its self-evident truths, did not require enforcement upon anyone.[12] Of course, violent means are not rejected by all radical groups operating in the Muslim world today, some of which justify their tactics on the religious obligation to resist tyranny and moral corruption even through violence.

A general sanction for unlimited forceful intervention in the affairs of sovereign states may not be derived from the uncertain, qualified status of the nation-state in Islamic ethics. But a sanction for humanitarian intervention, I would argue, may be. Forceful intervention by Muslims to stop the massacre or severe abuse of human beings is not only a right of the Muslim community; it is also a moral obligation. The reason is that the Qur'an endows the collective community of Muslims—not the state in which Muslims happen to live—with moral standing, as long as the *umma* enjoins the right and forbids the wrong. The commandment to act justly and to enforce justice is a collective obligation devolving upon the community, not particular classes or divisions within the community. The justice which the Qur'an enjoins Muslims to uphold consists of universally applicable principles that emanate from a divine source and are invested in human beings by virtue of their humanity and not by their affiliation to any particularistic human grouping, whether it be racial, ethnic, or "national." It is in this context of enforcing justice that the Islamic theory of *jihad*, or "virtuous struggle," was elaborated. Thus, the ethics of humanitarian intervention in Islam must be seen as a subset of the general theory of *jihad*.

First, let us consider intervention on behalf of Muslims facing oppression by non-Muslims, either within a non-Muslim state or in Muslim areas controlled by others. The Qur'an here suggests a two-step course of action. The first is physical removal (*hijra*) of the Muslims from the territory of the oppressors (4:97). The second is a collective response of the Muslim community in support of the grievances of the oppressed community. The verse reads:

> And why should you not fight in the cause of God and of those who being weak are ill-treated and oppressed: Men, women and children whose cry is: "Our Lord! rescue us from this land whose people are oppressors. And raise for us by Your grace one who will protect; and raise for us by Your grace one who will help." (Q. 4:75)

In describing the oppressed community, in both cases the Qur'an uses the same word, *mustad'afun*. The two recommendations it gives, flight and resistance, appear to be a tactical consideration. If the oppressed are able to relocate, it is better for them to do so and seek a propitious moment to reclaim their rights, presumably with the assistance of the Muslim community. This contention is supported by the verse that first permitted Muslims to use force collectively against the polytheist Arabs, namely: "To those against whom war is made, permission is given to fight because they are wronged, and truly God is most powerful in His aid" (22:39). A subsequent verse converted the permission into an injunction: "Drive them out from where they drove you out. For persecution is worse than killing" (2:191).

This first case of intervention on behalf of Muslims being persecuted by non-Muslims is the most unequivocal example of *jihad* cited by both the classical and modern jurists. In modern cases, it has, of course, been used to legitimate anticolonial struggles and the Palestinian struggle against Israel. The latter conflict has evoked more just war rhetoric and concerted action than any other contemporary issue facing Muslims, especially since the 1967 Israeli occupation of Jerusalem.[13]

We need cite only two cases here as representative of the prevailing thought. The first is that of the Iranian scholar Ayatollah Murtaza Mutahhari, perhaps the second most influential clerical figure after Khomeini in the revolution. Mutahhari defines *jihad* as "defensive" war on behalf of oppressed Muslims. He writes:

> We may be in a situation whereby a party has not transgressed against us but has committed injustice against a group from another people, who may or may not be Muslims. If they are Muslims—as in today's plight of the Palestinians, who have been exiled from their homes, whose wealth has been seized, who have been subjected to all kinds of transgression—whereas for the moment the transgressor has no intentions against us, it is permissible for us to give assistance to

the oppressed Muslims and deliver them. This is not only permissible, but obligatory, because they are Muslims. Such action would not be a case of commencing hostilities, but rather of rushing to the defense of the oppressed in order to deliver them from the clutches of oppression.[14]

Similar arguments were advanced by leaders of the Muslim Brotherhood in Egypt when they denounced the Egyptian–Israeli peace treaty as Islamically illegitimate. In their extended legal-ethical debate with the state-supported 'ulama of al-Azhar, the Brotherhood repeatedly charged the government of Anwar Sadat with shirking a cardinal aspect of *jihad* by withdrawing from a conflict in which Muslims remained oppressed. Their arguments have found wide support in most Muslim countries.

Two other recent conflicts that also evoked widespread support as cases of *jihad* against foreign aggression were the decade-long war in Afghanistan and the conflict in Bosnia. Both wars elicited large-scale financial support by several Muslim governments, as well as relief services provided by several Muslim nongovernmental organizations. Both conflicts have also involved the participation of volunteer, self-financed *mujahidin* units consisting of fighters drawn from different Muslim countries.[15]

One question, however, troubled the classical jurists and continues to dog modern writers: What if the Islamic state has a treaty of noninterference with a non-Muslim state? Can it break its treaty obligations in order to assist Muslims in distress in the non-Muslim state? The issue arises because the final lines of Qur'an 8:72 read: "And should they seek help from you in the matter of religion, it is incumbent on you to provide help, unless it be against a people with whom you have a pact. God is aware of all you do." Qur'anic commentators have understood this verse as relating to the Treaty of Hudaybiyya, a pact between the Muslims and the polytheistic Meccans concluded in 6 A.H. Among other things, the Prophet pledged to return to the Meccans any Muslim convert remaining in Mecca who fled to Medina after the agreement was concluded. This provision of the pact proved particularly controversial in the Muslim ranks, especially when some converts sought asylum with the Muslims and were forcibly repatriated to their families or clans.[16]

The twentieth-century commentator Abu'l-A'la Mawdudi summarizes the general view among Qur'anic exegetes that this verse and Prophetic precedents make faithfulness to treaty obligations paramount over all other considerations, even assisting oppressed Muslims:

> If Muslims living in a non-Islamic state are persecuted and seek help from the Islamic state or its citizens, it is incumbent upon the latter to help the persecuted Muslims. . . . If the Islamic state happens to be bound in a treaty relationship with a nation which inflicts wrong on Muslims, the oppressed Muslims will not be helped in a manner which is inconsistent with the moral obligations incumbent on the Islamic state as a result of that treaty.[17]

According to this interpretation, the only recourse open to oppressed Muslims who have no means of defending themselves is to flee their homes and seek asylum or the means to defend themselves among people who are not bound by treaty obligations to the oppressors. This would not theoretically preclude other Muslims who are not parties to the noninterference treaty from assisting the oppressed Muslims, because even in the time of the Prophet, when there was only one Islamic state, there were scattered Muslim communities living outside that state who did not enjoy the rights and obligations of citizenship.[18]

Not all scholars, however, have shared the view that treaty relations prevent Muslims from assisting co-religionists being oppressed by a non-Muslim state. Muhammad b. al-Hasan al-Shaybani, one of the most influential classical writers on international law, sanctions Muslim residents in a non-Muslim territory rushing to the aid of fellow Muslims being victimized by their common "hosts." Even if the Muslims had entered the non-Muslim territory under a peace treaty, they could not refrain from denouncing the agreement and then providing assistance to the victims. The reason Shaybani cites is that "it would not be lawful to make a pact [to the contrary]."[19]

Shaybani's argument from the eighth century is equally compelling in the twenty-first. No peace treaty, no agreement of noninterference in the internal affairs of other states, can absolve human beings of the basic obligation to prevent murder and other extreme abuses if they have the capability to do so. No treaty between an Islamic state and non-Muslim powers can be considered legitimate if it provides a screen behind which Muslims are systematically abused. This point is in fact emphasized in the Prophet's interpretation of the Hudaybiyya pact. He returned male Muslim émigrés under the terms of the agreement, but he refused, with the Qur'an's sanction (see 60:10), to return female refugees because of their greater vulnerability to abuse.[20]

A second possible scenario for humanitarian intervention involves the persecution of non-Muslims living within a non-Muslim state. The duty for Muslims to intervene in such a case is a bit more uncertain than in the previous case. Prudential considerations, the relative costs and benefits of action versus inaction, must be weighed more carefully: Do Muslims possess the material means to intervene? How will they be received by the suffering population or by neighboring states? Are the prospects for genuine relief of the suffering population greater than the likely costs of intervening for either the victims or the Muslim forces? Given these uncertainties, classical jurists and modern scholars have generally counseled against Muslim involvement in the affairs of non-Muslims living outside the jurisdiction of Islam.[21]

Aside from these important pragmatic concerns, the *principle* in support of humanitarian intervention remains the same as in the previous case. The Qur'anic verse 4:75 cited above speaks generally of the weak and oppressed (*mustad'afun*). Although the immediate context is that of the Muslim community, there is certainly no Qur'anic limitation on the verse's import to only oppressed Muslims. Another verse explicitly declares that the *jihad* waged in the cause of God includes not only the safeguarding of Muslims, but of other religious communities as well: "Had not God checked one group of people by means of another, there would surely have been destruction of monasteries, churches, synagogues, and mosques, in all of which the name of God is abundantly extolled" (22:40).

A third scenario is as complex as the last, though for different reasons, and is perhaps more germane to our present topic: a conflict in which both parties are Muslims. Traditional Sunni discussions of this topic are ambivalent on whether to place such conflicts within the purview of *jihad*. Some classical jurists preferred to treat intra-Muslim disputes as a special category of legitimate warfare dealing with the suppression of *fitna*, or "civil discord." This problem does not arise in Shi'i thought because the first Shi'i imam, 'Ali b. Abu Talib, spent his entire tenure as caliph (656–61 C.E.) trying to suppress Muslim revolts against his rule. As a result, in Shi'i thought, there is no ambiguity as to whether *jihad* may be waged against other Muslims. All those who reject or challenge the authority of the Shi'i imam, Muslim or non-Muslim, are equally targets of *jihad*.

Both the Sunni and the Shi'i legal traditions developed elaborate rules, known as *ahkam al-bughat*, for dealing with rebellion against the authority of the state.[22] In the face of mounting internal political dissension and serious external challenges to the power of the caliphate, the formative legal literature on this subject tended toward extreme conservatism, in the end virtually outlawing all challenges to the ruler in power with the argument that tyranny is preferable to civil strife. Thus, classical Islamic political treatises are conspicuously devoid of provisions to remove despotic rulers or to counter the authoritarian bent of the political theory. However, it is important to emphasize that the jurists' desperate attempts to maintain the cohesiveness and authority of the caliphal institution were, in fact, attempts to uphold and enforce the rule of Islamic law, the *shari'a*. Widespread juristic consensus existed that no obedience was due any ruler who renounced or systematically violated the *shari'a*.[23]

Renewed interest in the nature of political authority and obligation reemerged as a central concern of Muslim scholarship in the nineteenth century. Of course, this topic figures quite prominently in the works of most contemporary revivalist thinkers. These thinkers have developed a right of rebellion against tyrannical and unjust rulers by returning to the Qur'anic and Prophetic sources that enjoin the establishment of a just political regime as a primary goal of the Muslim community on earth.[24] Yet this aspect of modern Islamic political thought remains still very inchoate, as evinced graphically by the turbulent politics of virtually every Muslim state. The operative Qur'anic verse on the subject of intra-Muslim disputes states:

> If two parties of the believers fall into quarrel, make peace between them; but if one of them transgresses beyond bounds against the other, then fight all of you together against the one that transgresses until it complies with the command of God. But if it complies, then make peace between them with justice, and be fair: For God loves those who are fair. (Q. 49:9)

The first stage prescribed in this verse is one of nonviolent intervention, seeking reconciliation between the parties. The Muslim collectivity has not only a right but also a duty to engage in preventive intervention, to resolve a dispute before hostilities begin. The second stage is the permission—rather, injunction—to launch a collective intervention on behalf of the aggrieved party. It should be noted that the verse maintains a neutral stance regarding the merits of either party's case. Collective intervention is justified and based not so much on *ad bellum* as on *in bello* criteria. The party to be collectively fought is the one that has resorted to unacceptable means to achieve its ends.

This was certainly the way the Muslim coalition partners of the United States in the Gulf War read this verse in their frequent use of it. Iraq was the *baghi*, the rebel, not because it had crossed the territorial frontiers of a sovereign state (this argument was reserved for "secular" international forums, such as the Arab League and the United Nations), but because it had employed unacceptable means in resolving its dispute with Kuwait.[25]

The same reasoning could and should have been applied with greater emphasis to justify collective Muslim intervention on behalf of Iraqi minorities. If the relative merits of the Kurdish or Shi'i positions versus the Iraqi government's position are discounted, as required by the Qur'anic verse, then the Muslim community has the obligation to intervene against the party employing unacceptable means. The killing of innocents, the use of chemical weapons, and the forced expulsion and terrorizing of entire populations all fall within the category of unacceptable means according to Islamic theories of *jus in bello*, which are applicable to Muslims and non-Muslims alike.

Finally, the verse concludes by stipulating the ends for which collective intervention is permitted, namely, the cessation of hostilities, not the elimination of one or the other party to the original dispute. Arguably, stopping the fighting short of the complete defeat and destruction of the oppressive regime is rarely possible in circumstances so grave as to justify humanitarian intervention, at least as the circumstances are defined by most Western theorists. In the face of genocide or "ethnic cleansing," is it not a moral solution to eliminate the perpetrators rather than risk a future resumption of their atrocities?

But the counterarguments also deserve careful consideration. First, it is rarely practical or prudent for outside forces to stipulate who should rightly rule a particular community. When forcible intervention moves from saving people's lives to building their state or civil society, it rapidly moves in the perception of its intended beneficiaries from humanitarianism to imperialism. The inevitable result is the weakening of the authority of whomever is designated or supported by the intervenors as the leader. Moreover, evil on such a mass scale as to justify intervention is rarely the responsibility of one person or even a small group of people. Waging war to eliminate the perpetrators may well prove futile, prolong the conflict, and in the end exacerbate the suffering of those caught up in it.

The second consideration is the moral issue itself. The moral force for intervention comes from its limited objectives: to end the murder and suffering of large numbers of human beings. When the goals are broadened to include ensuring political stability or state building, the moral case for intervention is swiftly vitiated, in spite of all the good intentions of the intervenors.

Therefore, cessation of hostilities may not definitively eliminate the evil that necessitated the intervention, but it may forestall even greater evils that lurk in the uncertainties of continued conflict. Perhaps the most prudent and moral end to be pursued in humanitarian intervention is to stop the killing, to provide the means for the oppressed party to defend itself, and then to help the parties resolve their own future relationship.

The fourth scenario is that of Muslims oppressing non-Muslims. This case does not require much elaboration beyond the arguments for intervention in the previous cases. For Islamic ethics require the protection of *all* innocent lives. There is no relevant moral distinction to be drawn between the Muslim and non-Muslim victims of a repressive Muslim state. The Qur'an reaffirms the command given to the Children of Israel: "If anyone kills a person—unless it be for murder or the spreading of mischief in the land—it would be as if he had killed all people. If anyone saves the life of one person, it would be as if he had saved the life of all people" (5:32).

In the classical theory of the Islamic state, non-Muslim residents were accorded the status of *ahl al-dhimma*. This concept resembles in many ways the notion of "limited autonomy" for minorities in modern states. Non-Muslims were guaranteed the right to order their communal affairs according to their own religious laws and customs without interference from Muslims. In return for a poll tax levied on all able-bodied, free, adult males (the *jizya*), they were exempt from military service. The obligation to protect their lives and property against harm from Muslims or non-Muslims fell upon the guaranteeing authority, namely, the Islamic state. "Protection" is in fact what the term *dhimma* means. If the non-Muslims fought alongside the Muslim forces, they were exempt from *jizya* payments.[26] If the Islamic state could no longer protect the non-Muslims, their *jizya* payments were to be returned to them.[27] There are historical examples of such returns being made.[28]

What if the Islamic state itself is abusing its non-Muslim citizens? Again, the duty to enforce justice rests with the Muslim community as a whole, not the state, which is merely its agent. If the rulers are errant, Islamic ethics repeatedly enjoins the *umma* to correct them, first by speaking out against the injustice and then by forcefully intervening to end the abuse if all other measures fail. Many of the measures relating to the mutual rights and obligations of Muslims and non-Muslims within the Islamic state date from the time of the second caliph, 'Umar b. al-Khattab (r. 634–44 C.E.). He is reported to have said: "I enjoin him [who succeeds me] as regards those under the protection of Allah and the protection of His Messenger [*dhimmis*], that the covenant made with them shall be fulfilled, and that battles shall be fought for their defense, and that they shall be burdened only with what they can bear."[29]

Today, many Muslim scholars would suggest that the classical notion of *ahl al-dhimma* ought to be replaced (as it has in practice in many countries) by modern understandings of equal citizenship of all people regardless of religion. The *jizya* tax would in particular be obsolete because all citizens are expected to defend their state. The duty of the state to protect all its inhabitants, under such an understanding of citizenship, is therefore even greater. When a state run by Muslims—secular, nominal, or religious in their ideology—systematically violates its obligations toward its citizens, the moral obligation of the Muslim community to intervene remains in force.

This last scenario of Muslims oppressing non-Muslims raises in full force a subsidiary and relatively more contentious issue, the question of who may legitimately enforce humanitarian principles in the Muslim world. Should Muslim governments collaborate with non-Muslim states in collective intervention against other Muslim regimes that are violating the rights of their own people, whether they are Muslim or non-Muslim? If Muslim powers fail to act, do non-Muslims have the right to intervene, particularly if the victims are their co-religionists or of the same ethnicity?

Western justifications for the right to intervene to protect or liberate oppressed Christians living under Muslim rule date back to the early Muslim-Byzantine wars and later to the Crusades. As the right of military intervention in international law was debated by modern Western theorists, it was frequently in the context of the Christian nations of Europe acting against the Ottoman Empire. From the late 1700s, with Russian advances in the Caucasus and the Black Sea basin, to the late 1800s, with British and French interventions in Greece, Lebanon, and other regions, Europeans consistently expanded the sphere of authority they claimed to act in the interests of the Christian subjects of the Ottoman sultan.[30] Against this history, Muslims naturally approach the question of whether outsiders should enforce humanitarian intervention inside Muslim states with a large dose of skepticism.

This issue lay at the core of the vociferous debate in the Muslim world on the ethics of the Gulf War, especially because the Iraqi invasion of Kuwait and the Iraqi regime's treatment of its own population were viewed in the Muslim world as internal Muslim matters. The deployment of an American-led military coalition in areas very close to the spiritual center of Islam, namely, Mecca and Medina, effectively shifted the Muslim ethical discourse away from the Iraqi invasion of Kuwait to the American intervention in the dispute. Those 'ulama who had earlier cited the Qur'anic verse 49:9 in justifying a collective Muslim response to the Iraqi aggression were now faced with the task of answering criticism of the Western intervention based on the very same verse.

As the critics pointed out, this verse commands *Muslims* to resolve disputes among themselves with justice. The Qur'anic injunction makes no mention of involving external parties, particularly those who had palpably demonstrated their antipathy for Muslims (the example given was invariably American support for Israel) or shown indifference and even support for Saddam Hussein when he was not seen as a threat to Western interests in the region (e.g., when he invaded Iran in 1980 or used chemical weapons against Iranian soldiers and Kurdish civilians).

Moreover, this line of argument continued, the Qur'an explicitly proscribes Muslims from taking unbelievers generally (4:144) and Christians and Jews specifically (5:51, 57) as *awliya'*, a broad term meaning "associates," "allies," or "protectors." These verses provided the basis for the widely held juristic prohibition in *ahkam al-bughat* against taking non-Muslim allies to suppress Muslim rebellions, particularly if control of military operations was in non-Muslim hands. Thus, by designating the

Iraqi regime as *bughat*, the pro-coalition *'ulama* opened the door for strong condemnation of Western involvement on both ethical and legal grounds.[31]

Echoes of the same argument against reliance upon non-Muslim powers for protection of oppressed Muslim peoples were commonplace in Muslim attitudes toward the conflict in Bosnia. The contrast between the rapid mobilization and prosecution of the war to repulse the Iraqi aggression, coupled with continuing enforcement of UN sanctions against Iraq, was indeed stark when compared with the relatively timid international response during the initial three years of Serbian aggression against Bosnia.

The varying responses to each crisis are, of course, ultimately reflections of many complex political-military factors. But the varying responses cannot but seriously undermine the emerging moral and legal consensus on the principles of humanitarian intervention, particularly in developing countries, where humanitarian intervention is still largely suspect as a guise for the pursuit of Western interests by military force. This is precisely why the international discourse on humanitarian intervention must include non-Western ethical perspectives. Such discourse would enable the peoples of the developing world, including Muslims, to understand both the rights as well as the obligations inherent in the concept of humanitarian intervention. So let us delve into the question before us: Should Muslims ally themselves with non-Muslims to fight an oppressive Muslim state?

The answer, on a superficial level, is self-evident: Of course, Muslim states should be foremost in undertaking humanitarian intervention and conflict resolution within the Muslim world. This is unambiguously demanded by Qur'anic ethical principles. Moreover, nothing in international law would prevent Muslim states organized in an international body from enforcing principles of collective security and humanitarian intervention. Indeed, Article 33 and Chapter VIII of the UN Charter emphasize the primacy of regional organizations in maintaining international peace and security.

The prosecution of the Gulf War highlights the importance of strong and timely collective Muslim action to resolve intra-Muslim disputes. The absence of an effective Islamic organization created a power vacuum that made Western intervention in the dispute all too easy and all too necessary. Initial skepticism in the Muslim world about allied intentions for the intervention was replaced by outrage once the scale of the air campaign against Iraq became apparent. Iraq may have been the precipitator of the crisis, the *baghi*, but Islamic conceptions of *jus in bello* cannot countenance the suppression of *fitna* by means of the most sophisticated and—for all their "smartness"—lethal military hardware in the world today.[32]

The lingering resentment in many parts of the Muslim world over the conduct of the Gulf War, and the general disapproval of Western military involvement in Muslim countries, may in time be translated into constructive action to create more effective Muslim collective security mechanisms and a more principled application of the Islamic ethics of political behavior. The lesson of the war is clear: Muslims should have undertaken collective action against Saddam Hussein's megalomaniacal ambitions in September 1980 when he invaded Iran and not August 1990 when he turned against his erstwhile ally Kuwait.

If we approach the issue of Muslim cooperation with non-Muslims against an oppressive Muslim regime from a more complex theoretical level, we may once again firmly assert the principle of humanitarian intervention on the basis of the general argument thus far advanced. The duty of humanitarian intervention within an Islamic ethical framework derives directly from the obligation to struggle for justice, which the Qur'an specifically asserts to be of universal applicability. In the fourth chapter, we find a clear exposition of what may be termed a deontological conception of justice: "O you who believe! Stand out firmly for justice, as witnesses to God, even as against yourselves, or your parents, or your kin, and whether it be against rich or poor" (4:135). Again, in the fifth chapter is the admonition: "O you who believe! Be ever steadfast in your devotion to God, bearing witness to the truth in all equity, and never let hatred of anyone lead you into the sin of deviating from justice. Be just: this is closest to piety. And remain conscious of God: surely God is aware of all that you do" (5:8).

These verses are addressed to the Muslim *umma*, but they do not preclude the relevance of their general moral principles to non-Muslims nor do they suggest any intrinsic moral superiority of Muslims over non-Muslims. If humanitarian intervention is a moral cause worthy of pursuit, its implementation in Muslim countries cannot be limited to Muslims. Islamic legitimacy for a truly cosmopolitan principle of humanitarian intervention is not challenged or obviated by the Qur'anic verses counseling Muslims not to ally themselves with non-Muslims against Muslims. For coupled with these warnings are verses elaborating that this caution should be exercised against only those non-Muslims who have clearly demonstrated their hostility to Muslims and to Islam. But those who are not responsible for such enmity should be treated with "kindness" and "justice" (60:7–9).

The Qur'an does not stop at mutual toleration or an uneasy coexistence of different communities, a religious cold war. Rather, it envisions a dynamic moral–political cooperation of the righteous, whereby all human beings are challenged to contribute positively and according to their own moral traditions to the building of a just and equitable human community on this planet:

> To each among you have We prescribed a law and an open way. If God had so willed, He could have made you a single community, but His aim is to test you in what He has given you. So strive as in a race in all the virtues. The goal of you all is to God. It is He who will show you the truth of the matters in which you differ. (Q. 5:48)

What more urgent struggle or what more commonly held virtue can there be than the enforcement of the most fundamental human rights? To presume that Muslims alone are empowered to realize the purposes of humanitarian intervention in the Muslim world is to presume a moral parochialism that is inherently alien to the Qur'an's catholic vision. If Muslims cannot or will not assume this responsibility, they must be prepared to accept international action, whether the victims are Muslims or non-Muslims.

Ayatollah Mutahhari may once again be cited as a representative exponent of this argument. He states: "No one should have any doubts that the most sacred form of *jihad* and war is that which is fought in defense of humanity and of human rights." Such a struggle, he continues, cannot be limited to Muslims:

> During the period in which the Algerians were at war with the French colonialists, a group of Europeans helped them in their war, either by actually fighting alongside the Algerians or otherwise. . . . The *jihad* of such people was in fact even more sacred than that of the Algerians, because the Algerians were defending the cause of their own rights, whereas the cause of the others was more ethical and sacred.[33]

## PROSPECTS FOR HUMANITARIAN INTERVENTION IN THE MUSLIM WORLD

If we move from the theory to the practice of humanitarian intervention in the contemporary Muslim world, the situation is disheartening at best. The issue faces all the problems of implementation that it encounters elsewhere in our current international system: first, the lack of any clear and commonly supported conception of humanitarian crises requiring immediate collective intervention; second, the lack of any dependable institutional machinery for implementing international resolutions on collective intervention.

Above, we encountered the Organization of the Islamic Conference (OIC), an intergovernmental organization that was created in September 1969 on the rhetoric of universal Islamic ethics yet has been mired ever since in the reality of the politics of its constituents, today fifty-six disparate and often mutually hostile states. The catalyst for the formation of the OIC was the Israeli occupation of Jerusalem in 1967. The charter specifically acknowledges the centrality of the Palestinian-Israeli dispute in its stated objectives: "To coordinate efforts for the safeguard of the Holy Places and support of the people of Palestine, and help them to regain their rights and liberate their land."

In the next clause, the charter expands the scope of the OIC's commitment to include support "of all Muslim peoples with a view to safeguarding their dignity, independence, and national rights."[34] However, beyond these rhetorical commitments, the charter is silent on the actual mechanisms whereby these goals may be realized. There is certainly no attempt to institute any collective security mechanism for the "safeguarding" of the human rights of Muslim peoples.

Not surprisingly, the OIC's record in responding to international crises has been dismal to date. In 1971, it failed to respond to the Pakistani atrocities in Bangladesh; throughout the eight-year Iran–Iraq War, its peace initiatives were repeatedly rebuffed by Khomeini, who castigated the organization's failure to condemn Iraq's aggression; throughout the course of the Soviet war in Afghanistan and the subsequent intra-Afghan fighting, it was effectively paralyzed; and finally in the Gulf War, it took no concerted action to mount a Muslim response to the Iraqi invasion of Kuwait or later to intervene inside Iraq.[35] Indeed, the August 1991 Council of Foreign Ministers' meeting in Istanbul essentially absolved OIC members of any responsibility for the miseries visited upon the Iraqi people and blamed them all on the Iraqi government. The communiqué also included a ritual condemnation of Israeli violations of Palestinian rights but was conspicuously silent on the flagrant abuses of human rights that Palestinians and others have faced in postwar Kuwait.[36]

Similarly, in the tragedy of the Balkan wars, in which large numbers of Bosnian Muslims and Albanian Kosovars were murdered or displaced, the OIC's role was primarily one of verbal declarations from the sidelines. Before and during the meeting of foreign ministers on June 17–18, 1992, in Istanbul, the OIC states had hinted at their willingness to undertake collective Muslim intervention, either unilaterally or through the United Nations, to check the Yugoslav army's military assistance to local Serbian militias. Yet in the end, the meeting yielded nothing more than calls for the strengthening of UN economic sanctions against Serbia.

Spurred by mounting domestic outrage at reports of Serbian atrocities in Bosnia, the OIC states initiated measures in early November 1992 to exempt Bosnia from the UN arms embargo against Yugoslavia in effect since September 1991. This request was formally incorporated into a resolution adopted by the foreign ministers' conference in Jidda on December 1–2, 1992. The resolution also included demands for UN enforcement of the no-fly zone over Bosnian territory and for immediate measures "against Serbia and Montenegro, including the use of force prescribed under Article 42 of Chapter VII of the United Nations Charter." There were again intimations by some OIC foreign ministers that unilateral Muslim action might be taken if the UN Security Council failed to adopt sterner measures to curb the Serbian aggression.[37] Yet, other than limited arms shipments by individual OIC states, most notably Iran, and support for the quite limited UN peacekeeping operations in Bosnia, the OIC member states did not undertake any joint intervention.

More recently, the conflict in Chechnya prompted the OIC to declare the Muslim world's concern with the disproportionate loss of civilian lives in the Russian campaign against rebels. A high-level OIC delegation met with Russian officials in Moscow on January 17–18, 2000. It affirmed that the OIC respected the sovereignty and territorial integrity of the Russian Federation, but it expressed grave concern that Russian military action only "leads to further aggravation, which hinders the political process aimed at long term stability, isolates moderation and breeds extremism."

The OIC delegation urged the Russians to resume talks with the rebels and offered "to help in the achievement of a fair, lasting and honorable political settlement in Chechnya, which will guarantee stability and peace in the region." As for the suffering of the Chechen people, the OIC representatives noted the increasing humanitarian catastrophe in Chechnya, and it offered to step up the humanitarian relief work that various OIC countries had already initiated. But beyond this limited involvement, the OIC has not sought either among its own member states or in the United Nations to undertake more forceful intervention.[38]

In short, as it is presently constituted, the OIC cannot be expected to play any decisive role in implementing the principle of humanitarian intervention in Muslim countries, even if a consensus could be developed among the ruling elites that such a right exists. However, the OIC, like the United Nations itself, cannot long remain immune to the current forces of change in the international system. The crisis in Bosnia and the many other humanitarian disasters in other parts of the Muslim world have created a popular climate that not only permits but demands consideration of principles of intervention. Indeed, in all the crises to date, the OIC member states have been moved to whatever belated action they have taken by strong internal pressure.

What then can we realistically expect from the OIC in the short term? First, the OIC could potentially play an important supportive role in humanitarian efforts of the United Nations. With strong impetus and leadership being provided by the Security Council, the OIC, in conjunction with other regional organizations, could be encouraged to develop within the UN system a series of guidelines establishing the conditions or "emergency threshold" that would trigger collective intervention. Such regional organizations are much better suited to maintain—again, under ultimate UN sanction—standing peacekeeping forces that are empowered to intervene rapidly, not only after the fact, as at present, but before the onset of hostilities. Such a proposal would also better meet the needs of most humanitarian crises, for regional organizations and not ad hoc UN peacekeeping forces are much better suited to provide the long-term presence in a crisis situation necessary for any meaningful conflict resolution.

In the long term, the OIC needs to define with much greater clarity its own place and the place of Islamic thought in the international system. One essential first step toward this goal would be the convening of the International Islamic Law Commission and for a truly open and systematic discussion of the place of Islamic theory in the contemporary international system. With greater ideological consensus on its own role and given its large constituency—approximately a third of the total UN membership and a fifth of humanity—a reconstituted OIC could potentially play a crucial role in the preservation of international peace and security generally, and not just in humanitarian intervention. As the world community evolves toward a more universalist ethics based on the reevaluation of traditional concepts of state sovereignty, the OIC and Muslim peoples generally are well positioned by virtue of the Qur'an's universalist ethics to contribute to a new international society.

## NOTES

1. Doctors Without Borders lists the continuing threat of starvation, epidemic, and violence in Chechnya, Somalia, and Sudan in its "Top 10 Most Underreported Humanitarian Stories of 2002." See www.doctorswithoutborders.org/publications/reports/2002/top10_2002.html.
2. Michael Akehurst, "Humanitarian Intervention," in *Intervention in World Politics*, ed. Hedley Bull (Oxford: Oxford University Press, 1984), 99.

3. Richard N. Gardner, *Three Views on the Issue of Humanitarian Intervention* (Washington, D.C.: United States Institute of Peace, 1992), 21–27.

4. Jarat Chopra and Thomas G. Weiss, "Sovereignty Is No Longer Sacrosanct: Codifying Humanitarian Intervention," *Ethics & International Affairs* 6 (1992): 95–117.

5. For a succinct description of the classical theory, see Majid Khadduri, "International Law," in *Law in the Middle East: Origins and Development of Islamic Law*, ed. Majid Khadduri and Herbert J. Liebesny (Washington, D.C.: Middle East Institute, 1955).

6. Abdullah al-Ahsan, *OIC: The Organization of the Islamic Conference* (Herndon, Va.: International Institute of Islamic Thought, 1988), 36.

7. See Bernard Lewis, "Politics and War," in *The Legacy of Islam*, ed. Joseph Schacht and Clifford E. Bosworth (Oxford: Oxford University Press, 1974); Hamilton A. R. Gibb, "Constitutional Organization," in *Law in the Middle East*, ed. Khadduri and Liebesny.

8. For a review and critique of the impact of secularism on Islamic political thought, see Fazlur Rahman, *Islam* (Chicago: University of Chicago Press, 1979), 212–34.

9. Cited in Parveen Feroze Hassan, *The Political Philosophy of Iqbal* (Lahore: Publishers United Ltd., 1970), 204.

10. Muhammad Iqbal, *Reconstruction of Religious Thought in Islam* (Lahore: Institute of Islamic Culture, 1989), 126.

11. Cited in Farhang Rajaee, *Islamic Values and World View: Khomeini on Man, the State, and International Politics* (Lanham, Md.: University Press of America, 1983), 77.

12. Rajaee, *Islamic Values and World View*, 82–85.

13. See Rudolph Peters, *Islam and Colonialism: The Doctrine of Jihad in Modern Times* (The Hague: Mouton Publishers, 1979).

14. Mehdi Abedi and Gary Legenhausen, eds., *Jihad and Shahadat: Struggle and Martyrdom in Islam* (Houston: Institute for Research and Islamic Studies, 1986), 96.

15. Reports of volunteer Muslim fighters in Bosnia range from 400 to 500. Many had prior combat experience in Afghanistan. See the *New York Times*, November 14, 1992, 5, and December 5, 1992, 1.

16. See Ibn Ishaq, *The Life of Muhammad*, trans. Alfred Guillaume (Karachi: Oxford University Press, 1990), 504–8.

17. Abu'l-A'la Mawdudi, *Tafhim al-Qur'an* (Toward Understanding the Qur'an), ed. and trans. Zafar Ishaq Ansari (Leicester, U.K.: Islamic Foundation, 1990), vol. 3, 172 n. 51.

18. This fact is attested by Q. 8:72 itself, which includes the following statement: "As to those who believed but came not into exile, you owe no duty of protection [or political obligations of any sort] until they come into exile [that is, migrate to the Islamic state in Medina].

19. Muhammad b. al-Hasan al-Shaybani, *The Islamic Law of Nations: Shaybani's Siyar*, trans. Majid Khadduri (Baltimore: Johns Hopkins University Press, 1966), 245.

20. See Ibn Ishaq, *Life of Muhammad*, 509–10.

21. E.g., Shaybani's treatise contains the brief comment, "I disapprove of Muslims fighting along with unbelievers against unbelievers." The reasons are not specified, but seem to be based on the fact that Muslims do not have jurisdiction in non-Muslim territory and therefore cannot control the fighting. Shaybani, *Islamic Law of Nations*, 244–45.

22. For a review of the Sunni legal literature, see Khaled Abou El Fadl, "Ahkam al-Bughat: Irregular Warfare and the Law of Rebellion in Islam," in *Cross, Crescent, and Sword*, ed. James T. Johnson and John Kelsay (New York: Greenwood Press, 1990). For a review of Shi'i approaches to the same subject, see Etan Kohlberg, "The Development of the Imami Shi'i Doctrine of Jihad," *Zeitschrift der Deutschen Morgenländischen Gesellschaft* 126 (1976): 66–78.

23. See the discussion by Gibb, "Constitutional Organization," 3–27.

24. See the review by Muhammad Salahuddin, "Political Obligation: Its Scope and Limits in Islamic Political Doctrine," *American Journal of Islamic Social Sciences* 3 (1986): 247–64.

25. See, e.g., the text of the "Declaration of Mecca," a statement of Muslim scholars and activists meeting under the auspices of the People's Islamic Conference, justifying collective Muslim action against Iraq. Foreign Broadcast Information Service (Near East and South Asia), January 14, 1991, 4–7.

26. In one such agreement, the inhabitants of Jurjan, a region bordering the southeastern shores of the Caspian Sea, were given the following terms: "You have our covenant, while it is our duty to protect [you], on condition that you pay tribute annually according to your capacity, everyone who has reached the age of puberty. Any one of you whose help we seek shall pay his tribute in the form of assistance he renders instead of his [regular] tribute." Muhammad b. Jarir al-Tabari, *Ta'rikh al-rusul wa'l-muluk* (The history of al-Tabari), vol. 14, *The Conquest of Iran*, trans. G. Rex Smith (Albany: State University of New York Press, 1994), 28–29.

27. As Khalid b. al-Walid contracted in 633 C.E. with the people of Basma and Banqiya in the region of Iraq: "I give you a covenant on condition [of payment] of the *jizyah* in return for protection. . . . Therefore, you have a guarantee of security and protection, so that, if we protect you, we are entitled to the *jizyah*, but, if not, then not until we do protect you." Jarir al-Tabari, *Ta'rikh al-rusul wa'l-muluk*, vol. 11, *The Challenge to the Empires*, trans. Khalid Yahya Blankinship (Albany: State University of New York Press, 1993), 40.

28. One of the most famous such cases is the return of *jizya* to the Christians and Jews of northern Syria when the Byzantine emperor Heraclius invaded in 639 C.E. The Muslims were forced temporarily to withdraw from the region in order to regroup further south. See Ahmad b. Jabir al-Baladhuri, *Kitab futuh al-buldan* (The origins of the Islamic state), trans. Philip Hitti (Beirut: Khayats, 1966), 210–11.

29. Narrated by Bukhari. Maulana Muhammad Ali, *A Manual of Hadith* (New York: Olive Branch Press, 1988), 408.

30. A very interesting, late-nineteenth-century study on this subject was produced by a French diplomat: Ed. Engelhardt, *Le droit d'intervention et la Turquie: Étude historique* (Paris: A. Cotillon and Co., 1880).

31. For a more detailed analysis, see Sohail H. Hashmi, "But Was It *Jihad*? Islam and the Ethics of the Persian Gulf War," in *The Eagle in the Desert: Looking Back on U.S. Involvement in the Persian Gulf War*, ed. William Head and Earl Tilford (Westport, Conn.: Praeger, 1996).

32. Many Western theorists have also argued the problematic conduct of the war according to *jus in bello* criteria. See Stanley Hoffmann, "Bush Abroad," *New York Review of Books*, November 5, 1992, 56; and the essays by Jean Bethke Elshtain, Stanley Hauerwas, and Michael Walzer in *But Was It Just? Reflections on the Morality of the Persian Gulf War*, ed. David E. Decosse (New York: Doubleday, 1992). See also Middle East Watch, *Needless Deaths in the Gulf War* (New York: Human Rights Watch, 1991).

33. Abedi and Legenhausen, *Jihad and Shahadat*, 105.

34. Al-Ahsan, *OIC*, 128.

35. For reviews of the OIC's role in the conflicts in Bangladesh, Iran–Iraq, and Afghanistan, see Al-Ahsan, *OIC*, and Haider Mehdi, *Organization of the Islamic Conference (OIC): A Review of Its Political and Educational Policies* (Lahore: Progressive Publishers, 1988).

36. "OIC Renews Its Condemnation of Iraq, Calls for Continuation of Economic Sanctions," *Saudi Arabia* 8(9) (September 1991): 2.
37. *Impact International,* December 11, 1992, 21.
38. "Senior Official Delegation Concerned over Continued Military Operations in Chechnya, Calls for Speedy Political Settlement," OIC Press Release, January 27, 2000; www.oic-un.org/pr/2000/17.html.

# FIVE

# Principles, Politics, and Humanitarian Action

## Thomas G. Weiss

The tragedies of the past decade have shaken humanitarians to the core. The mere mention of Afghanistan, Bosnia, Liberia, Rwanda, Sierra Leone, or Somalia profoundly disturbs their composure. Traumas in these countries have become synonymous with the dilemmas of humanitarian action, that is, with international attempts to help victims through the provision of relief and the protection of their human rights.

Until recently, the two most essential humanitarian principles—neutrality (not taking sides with warring parties) and impartiality (nondiscrimination and proportionality)—have been relatively uncontroversial, as has the key operating procedure of seeking consent from belligerents.[1] However, a host of developments in the 1990s altered this attitude toward humanitarian action. These include the complete disregard for international humanitarian law by war criminals and even by child soldiers, the direct targeting of civilians and relief personnel, the use of foreign aid to fuel conflicts and war economies, and the protracted nature of many so-called emergencies that in fact last for decades. The result has been a collective identity crisis among aid workers in war zones as well as among those who analyze such efforts.

The International Committee of the Red Cross (ICRC), which was founded in 1864, has shined as the beacon of humanitarianism through its apolitical practices and principles. In 1986, the International Court of Justice chose not even to define humanitarianism but rather to equate it with the work of the ICRC. The father of the organization's Fundamental Principles, Jean Pictet, defined each principle as "a rule, based upon judgment and experience, which is adopted by a community to guide its conduct."[2] In addition to providing life-saving ministrations, the ICRC has pushed governments to adopt the rules of war. Indeed, it fulfills a unique role as the custodian of the Geneva Conventions of 1949 and the Additional Protocols of

1977. The ICRC's prominence among humanitarian agencies is suggested by its having won four Nobel Peace Prizes.

Yet in many ways, international humanitarian law seems to have been formulated mainly to deal with a different world from today's—a world populated by governments and regular armies whose interests were served by adhering to the rules of warfare. Concepts once widely respected, especially domestic jurisdiction and sovereignty, have been breached even by humanitarians; for instance, nongovernmental organizations (NGOs) at times have been among the most numerous and vociferous proponents of military intervention, a position quite inconceivable a decade ago.

In today's environment, humanitarian tragedies have become "normal." Cynics even view them as growth opportunities for aid agencies, whereas others see winners as well as losers in a new international political economy of war.[3] Severe criticism of the aid establishment in general and relief agencies in particular has fueled the identity crisis experienced by humanitarians and analysts and has polarized debate.[4]

Understanding the differences between two groups of humanitarians is crucial. "Classicists," led by the ICRC, believe that humanitarian action can and should be completely insulated from politics. "Political humanitarians" believe that political and humanitarian action "could not and should not be disassociated."[5] I place myself in the latter camp.

Even classicists increasingly acknowledge the need for parallel, politically savvy action. According to ICRC president Cornelio Sommaruga, "humanitarian, political, and development actors manage crisis in a comprehensive manner."[6] Thus, in the words of the ICRC's chief medical officer, projects must be "specifically tailored to the needs [of victims] while minimizing the undesirable effects of aid."[7] This is a rhetorical step beyond earlier acknowledgments by the ICRC that its activities sometimes have political implications. The organization still maintains an apolitical veneer, however, and is unwilling publicly to admit that its principles should be adapted to political exigencies, although it has commissioned a new volume about "hard choices."[8] David Forsythe has consistently argued that the ICRC has always pursued "humanitarian politics—the struggle to implement humanitarian values as part of public policy."[9] At the same time, the organization has underestimated the impact of two other types of politics, realpolitik among states and factional politics within them.

The UN high commissioner for refugees, Sadako Ogata, notes that "political and humanitarian actors are uncomfortable bedfellows," an apt image for this awkward reality because politics and humanitarianism are intimately intertwined.[10] As a result, classical proponents of apolitical humanitarianism increasingly encounter problems in relating to those political humanitarians pursuing either "minimalist" or "maximalist" objectives. Minimalists aim to "do no harm," whereas maximalists have a more ambitious agenda of employing humanitarian action as part of a comprehensive strategy to transform conflict.

Classicists have always disagreed adamantly with a third group of political humanitarians—"solidarists," who choose sides and abandon neutrality and impartiality as well as reject consent as a prerequisite for intervention. Although solidarists first appeared during the Spanish Civil War, the most visible contemporary representatives are Médécins Sans Frontières (MSF), or Doctors Without Borders, which was established as a "counter" ICRC in the midst of the Biafran civil war by a group of ICRC field staff who could no longer abide by the organization's principles. The judgment of these renegade ICRC professionals that the application of traditional principles did more harm than good for the Ibos foreshadowed the current debate.

In many contemporary conflicts, humanitarians find neutrality and impartiality problematic at best and impossible at times. They also encounter serious difficulties in seeking the consent of numerous and undisciplined belligerents whose antics often have led to coercive economic and military sanctions. Even when they attempt to be neutral and impartial, aid agencies often are perceived to favor one side over the other. Here, though, "political humanitarianism" refers to conscious decisions to employ humanitarian action as an integral part of an international public policy to mitigate life-threatening suffering and protect fundamental human rights in active wars.

It is useful to situate humanitarians along the analytical spectrum depicted in table 5.1. The table locates classicists, minimalists, maximalists, and solidarists according to their degree of political involvement and their willingness to respect traditional principles. From left to right, the scale indicates low to high political involvement, from the extremes of no political ties at all to complete identification with victims by fervent proponents. Humanitarian action for each group from left to right in the table is, respectively, warranted as long as it is charitable and self-contained, defined only by the needs of victims and divorced from political objectives and conditionalities; worthwhile if efforts to relieve suffering do not make matters worse and can be sustained locally; defensible when coupled with steps to address the roots of violence and as part of a conscious and comprehensive political strategy; and justifiable when it sides with the main victims. A blurring of categories is inevi-

Table 5.1. The Political Spectrum of Humanitarians and Their Attitudes toward Traditional Operating Principles

| *Principle* | *Classicists* ↔ | *Minimalists* ↔ | *Maximalists* ↔ | *Solidarists* |
|---|---|---|---|---|
| Engagement with political authorities | Eschew public confrontations | ←————————————→ | | Advocate controversial public policy |
| Neutrality | Avoid taking sides | ←————————————→ | | Take the side of selected victims |
| Impartiality | Deliver aid using proportionality and nondiscrimination | ←————————————→ | | Skew the balance of resource allocation |
| Consent | Pursue as sine qua non | ←————————————→ | | Override sovereignty as necessary |

table because the four positions are not hard and fast but are tempered by realities on the ground.

Nonetheless, these ideal types are helpful for understanding the current acrimony in international discourse, the focus of the first section of this chapter. They also provide useful background for the second section, which examines why humanitarians feel such a sense of despair and defeat in the face of recent tragedies. The pros and cons of impartial versus political humanitarianism and the differing approaches by the four kinds of actors on the spectrum are the subject of the third section.

## THE CURRENT DEBATE

In their most straightforward form, contemporary criticisms of humanitarian practices range from moderate analyses about how to reform the international humanitarian system to fundamental questions about whether it is worthy of reform at all. Possible responses from aid agencies range from making the existing system more effective and thereby rekindling the trust of donors and recipients to revamping the conceptual basis of what it means to be "humanitarian" and making humanitarian action as relevant to problem solving and conflict management as it is to natural disasters. Representatives across the spectrum agree that substantial alterations in past practices are required; few foresee a return to the "good old days" when neutrality, impartiality, and consent were unquestioned tactics.

I situate myself to the right of center on the spectrum, but I do not believe that humanitarian action is anachronistic. Traditional principles may be helpful in one context, but in others, hard-headed and hard-hearted calculations—including triage and "tough love"—are more relevant than a formulaic recitation of the classical humanitarian mantra. Andrew Natsios has argued persuasively that "the advocates of neutrality are losing ground in the debate."[11]

Yet within the same theater of conflict, classicist principles and the call to intervene can clash. Leading the charge is usually MSF, the most visible and vocal of the solidarists, arguing that agencies should employ humanitarian action within a political strategy on behalf of victims. The ICRC position is giving way to the notion that the two types of action—political and humanitarian—cannot and should not be dissociated. This shift was remarkably stated in a background document for the second ICRC Wolfsberg Humanitarian Forum: "It is difficult to imagine how humanitarian assistance could remain fully neutral in complex emergencies."[12]

Recent complex emergencies have given rise to a clarion call for improved collaboration and perhaps integration among the "intervention trio" of the military, the political and diplomatic elements, and the humanitarian agencies. As a guide to action, the "do no harm" position of minimalists seems hard to dismiss on logical grounds alone. Furthermore, it is plausible that humanitarian help as part of an ambitious political package, as recommended by maximalists, could ultimately relieve more life-threatening suffering than similar help in a political vacuum, however effectively it is delivered.[13] Many situations require calculations with which few are comfortable and by which many will be appalled.[14]

Cornelio Sommaruga and Adam Roberts caution that "we should not be too hasty in announcing that barbarism is back."[15] I am tempted to ask when it disappeared. David Rieff has asserted that ignoring the resurgence in grisly violence is a "humanitarian illusion" and that "disillusionment is the beginning of wisdom in the analysis of this terrible reality, this time of piety and iron."[16] A striking fact of contemporary international society is that the number of individuals and organizations fostering humanitarian norms and action has risen dramatically, along with media attention to the plight of victims. The paradox is that barbarism has kept pace. In the words of the late historian Eric Hobsbawm, there has been a "return to what our nineteenth-century ancestors would have called the standards of barbarism."[17]

Traditional humanitarian principles are now under siege. The extent to which they can be applied depends on the context. Classicists are becoming aware of the unacceptable results of applying neutrality, impartiality, and consent when dealing with unprincipled actors in a variety of armed conflicts. Humanitarian action has never been easy, but abiding strictly by traditional principles used to be a better tactical guide to sustaining the vast majority of impulses to rescue war victims than it is today. Although this approach led to dissension in ICRC ranks and the creation of MSF, in the late 1960s it was possible for classicists to view the Biafran civil war as anomalous and to dismiss the claims of dissenters. But in the post–cold war period, Biafras have become routine, and classicists are obliged to engage in a conversation with representatives from most of the spectrum of political humanitarians.

In many war zones, context is as important as principles because the latter often clash. Thoughtful reflection thus has come to assume a growing role relative to visceral reaction. At the beginning of this decade and in the face of new challenges in Kurdistan and Bosnia, Larry Minear and I spelled out an alternative to the ICRC's practices, the Providence Principles, which are more flexible than the classical ones.[18] This approach was a step toward modifying established rules to guide the conduct of humanitarians in a new and troubled period. The ICRC's own Fundamental Principles are not immutable, although this is frequently overlooked. Last modified in 1965 during "an orgy of rule-making," these principles may be adapted when necessary to reflect the changing nature of war, humanitarian agencies, and donor policies.[19]

Operational principles thus are not moral absolutes. Whether from the ICRC or other agencies, they are norms toward which to strive, but without the illusion that their application is possible in every situation or that their success is guaranteed. They are means to achieve ends but not ends in themselves. Differences exist in the interpretation given to principles by various individuals and agencies, in the importance of some relative to others, and in the extent to which a given principle or set of principles will prevail in particular circumstances. The need for case-by-case judgments has been reinforced by recent experience. From sustaining vulnerable groups in the African Great Lakes region while feeding thugs and fueling the war to moving threatened populations in Bosnia while facilitating ethnic cleansing, operational situations in the 1990s were tortuous—for victims as well as their humanitarian benefactors.

Because morally wrenching contexts are now the rule rather than the exception, it is increasingly difficult for humanitarians to occupy unequivocally the moral high ground. For those few on pedestals, it is a precarious perch. Michael Ignatieff anguishes that "almost everyone who tries . . . has a bad conscience; no one is quite sure whether our engagement makes things better or worse."[20] Bill Maynes recommends "ethical realpolitik" as an alternative for American foreign policy.[21] Mark Duffield calls for a "new ethics of working in political crises . . . [where] 'good guys' no longer exist."[22] Joanna Macrae states, "The idea that it is easy to distinguish the bad guy from the good woman and child is no longer sustainable."[23] Evoking Dante's Inferno, where the hottest room was reserved for those who vacillated, a Norwegian research group confronts the distinct possibility that "neutrality is a form of moral bankruptcy."[24]

To date, responses to these critics have often been semantic gymnastics, stretching concepts to such a degree that they become meaningless. For example, the UN secretary general and others utilize the oxymoron "induced consent,"[25] while Hugo Slim calls for a "robust form of impartiality which allows them [NGOs and UN forces] not just to dish out relief in proportion to needs, but also to dish out criticism (advocacy) or military bombardment in proportion to human rights wrong doing."[26]

What is the value of principles if problems are not uniform across war zones, and if neutrality, impartiality, and consent may be more or less pertinent depending on the type and phase of an armed conflict? The clear articulation of principles provides an emergency brake on the slippery slope of shameless opportunism. When principles bump into one another, compromise and tough trade-offs are inevitable; but those who deviate from principles should be aware of the costs. Humanitarians who are clear about the costs of departing from principles undoubtedly will be more successful in helping and protecting victims than those who have none or who are inflexible. The only absolute principle is the respect for human life. Other principles are standard operating procedures reflecting empirical judgments about experience. They amount to finding ways to make things happen in individual situations.

Scholars and practitioners frequently employ the term "dilemma" to describe painful decision making; but "quandary" would be more apt.[27] A dilemma involves two or more alternative courses of action with unintended but unavoidable and equally undesirable consequences. If consequences are equally unpalatable, then remaining inactive on the sidelines is an option rather than entering the scrum on the field. A quandary, conversely, entails tough choices among unattractive options with better or worse possible outcomes. Though humanitarians are perplexed, they are not and should not be immobilized. The solution is not indifference or withdrawal but rather appropriate engagement. The key lies in making a good faith effort to analyze the advantages and disadvantages of different alloys of politics and humanitarianism, and then to choose what often amounts to the lesser of evils.

Thoughtful humanitarianism is more appropriate than rigid ideological responses, for four reasons: goals of humanitarian action often conflict; good intentions can have catastrophic consequences; there are alternative ways to achieve ends;

and even if none of the choices is ideal, victims still require decisions about outside help. What Myron Wiener has called "instrumental humanitarianism" would resemble just war doctrine because contextual analyses and not formulas are required.[28] Rather than resorting to knee-jerk reactions to help, it is necessary to weigh options and make decisions about choices that are far from optimal.

Many humanitarian decisions in northern Iraq, Somalia, Bosnia, and Rwanda—and especially those involving economic or military sanctions—required selecting least-bad options. Thomas Nagle advises that "given the limitations on human action, it is naive to suppose that there is a solution to every moral problem."[29] Action-oriented institutions and staff are required in order to contextualize their work rather than apply preconceived notions of what is right or wrong. Nonetheless, classicists continue to insist on Pictet's "indivisible whole" because humanitarian principles "are interlocking, overlapping and mutually supportive. . . . It is hard to accept the logic of one without also accepting the others."[30]

The process of making decisions in war zones could be compared with that pursued by "clinical ethical review teams," whose members are on call to make painful decisions about life-and-death matters in hospitals.[31] The sanctity of life is complicated by new technologies, but urgent decisions cannot be finessed. It is impermissible to long for another era or to pretend that the bases for decisions are unchanged. However emotionally wrenching, finding solutions is an operational imperative that is challenging but intellectually doable. Humanitarians who cannot stand the heat generated by situational ethics should stay out of the post–cold war humanitarian kitchen.

## PRINCIPLES IN AN UNPRINCIPLED WORLD

Why are humanitarians in such a state of moral and operational disrepair? In many ways, Western liberal values during the past few centuries have been moving toward interpreting moral obligations as going beyond a family and intimate networks, beyond a tribe, and beyond a nation. The impalpable moral ideal is concern about the fate of other people, no matter how far away.[32] The evaporation of distance with advances in technology and media coverage, along with a willingness to intervene in a variety of post–cold war crises, however, has produced situations in which humanitarians are damned if they do and if they don't. Engagement by outsiders does not necessarily make things better, and it may even create a "moral hazard by altering the payoffs to combatants in such a way as to encourage more intensive fighting."[33]

This new terrain requires analysts and practitioners to admit ignorance and question orthodoxies. There is no comfortable theoretical framework or world vision to function as a compass to steer between integration and fragmentation, globalization and insularity. Michael Ignatieff observes, "The world is not becoming more chaotic or violent, although our failure to understand and act makes it seem so."[34] Gwyn Prins has pointed to the "scary humility of admitting one's ignorance" because "the new vogue for 'complex emergencies' is too often a means of concealing from oneself that one does not know what is going on."[35] To make matters more frustrating, never before has there been such a bombardment of data and instant analysis; the challenge of distilling such jumbled and seemingly contradictory information adds to the frustration of trying to do something appropriate fast.

International discourse is not condemned to follow North American fashions and adapt sound bites and slogans. It is essential to struggle with and even embrace the ambiguities that permeate international responses to wars, but without the illusion of a one-size-fits-all solution. The trick is to grapple with complexities, to tease out the general without ignoring the particular, and still to be inspired enough to engage actively in trying to make a difference.

Because more and more staff of aid agencies, their governing boards, and their financial backers have come to value reflection, an earlier policy prescription by Larry Minear and me no longer appears bizarre: "Don't just do something, stand there!"[36] This advice represented our conviction about the payoffs from thoughtful analyses and our growing distaste for the stereotypical, yet often accurate, image of a bevy of humanitarian actors flitting from one emergency to the next.

Searing experiences have led to such a voluminous literature that analysts are now categorizing the types of criticism.[37] Countless conferences and internal agency debates indicate a cultural change under way in institutional behavior as practitioners grapple to comprehend the ugly terrains where they operate, to put what they are doing into a political context rather than react viscerally with the hope that good intentions alone will suffice. Even the most critical of critics, Alex de Waal, observes that "as critiques of humanitarianism become more common and more accepted, some thoughtful agency staff are becoming more questioning."[38]

"Humanitarianism" means helping and protecting victims, irrespective of who and where they are and why they are in need. The three main types of "politics" are the competition among states for survival and supremacy and for maximizing national interests in an anarchical world (realpolitik); the struggle for power and influence within donor and crisis states (partisan or factional politics depending on the existence of democratic rules or the law of the jungle); and efforts to agree upon desirable international public policies within governmental, intergovernmental, and nongovernmental arenas. Humanitarians have a stake in political outcomes at every level, and their actions influence and are influenced by such outcomes.

The intersection of politics and humanitarianism—obvious to elected officials, pundits, and political scientists but not to classicists—alters considerably the usual procedure of seeking consent from belligerents and respecting neutrality and impartiality.[39] Much contemporary humanitarian action occurs in countries torn by civil war (i.e., in countries of origin and not of asylum) where civilians are targets and outside military forces are sometimes deployed despite objections from sovereign authorities. Outside resources—usually favoring one side (or so perceived)—are actively fought over by local factions, and have unintended and unanticipated negative consequences. Because civilians are now prime targets instead of accidental victims, humanitarians often are obliged to confront those responsible for massive abuses of fundamental rights. In 1992, Jarat Chopra and I wrote "Sovereignty is no longer sacrosanct."[40] A fitting corollary in 1999 is "Humanitarian principles are no longer sacrosanct."

The sanctity of human life is the first principle of all humanitarians and overrides other considerations; but neutrality, impartiality, and consent are second-order principles that may or may not be accurate tactical guides. Traditional principles were developed as means to safeguard life, but they no longer provide unequivocal guidance and should be modified when necessary. Classicists disagree with this conclusion, but not with the painful reality suggested by such conference titles as "Principled Aid in an Unprincipled World," which was sponsored in April 1998 in London by the European Community Humanitarian Office and the Overseas Development Institute.

In a 1997 speech, ICRC president Sommaruga pointed to the need for dialogue among humanitarian and political players because they have "different roles but complementary responsibilities."[41] The argument here is different. Whether these players are dealing with the disproportionate burdens on vulnerable groups of economic sanctions, the complications from military enforcement, or the need to balance tensions between protection of human rights and access, they face not only intense interactions and complementary responsibilities but also clashes between political and humanitarian imperatives.

It is crucial to flush out differences and not airbrush them away. The assumption that politics and humanitarianism can be entirely separated, as if they were parts of two different and self-contained worlds, is a fiction. The "dark side" of humanitarian action would include: food and other aid usurped by belligerents to sustain a war economy (e.g., in Liberia); assistance that has given legitimacy to illegitimate political authorities, particularly those with a guns economy (e.g., in Somalia); aid distribution patterns that have influenced the movement of refugees (e.g., in eastern Zaire); resource allocations that have promoted the proliferation of aid agencies and created a wasteful aid market that encourages parties to play organizations against one another (e.g., in Afghanistan); elites that have benefited from the relief economy (e.g., in Bosnia); and resources that have affected strategic equilibriums (e.g., in Sierra Leone).

There is also a subtle and often-ignored "bright side" of humanitarian action in that humanitarians can exert a modest positive influence on peace building and conflict resolution. Humanitarians can play diplomatic roles by taking advantage of their local connections and knowledge to build bridges among warring parties. Rehabilitation and development undoubtedly can take place concurrently with relief, particularly in parts of a country where relative peace is present. Finally—and although it has been minimized in both analyses and budgetary allocations—enhanced protection of human rights also can result from the mere presence of outside humanitarians and military forces.

In brief, reflection is becoming a priority for the staffs of most aid agencies, wherever they are on the spectrum of humanitarianism. The laudable action-oriented humanitarian ethos is being tempered with more consideration of missions, mandates, performance, operating styles, and results. Complexity is not an excuse for complacency or a pretext to abandon large numbers of people to their Hobbesian fate in civil wars, but it does introduce elements of confusion and frustration in the formerly more certain and straightforward worldview of humanitarians. Contemporary complex emergencies can and must be understood better, just as humanitarian agencies can and must train and equip their personnel to be more effective.

## APPROACHES TO HUMANITARIAN ACTION

What are the pros and cons of impartial versus political humanitarianism, and what form do differences in approach take in designing assistance and protection activities? Although agencies frequently have performed well under arduous circumstances, the disastrous consequences of much contemporary humanitarian action constitute a serious enough indictment of past procedures to force a thorough reexamination of how all humanitarian agencies approach their work in war zones. Classicists, whose impulses and mores have compelled them to respond automatically to the plight of victims in the past, now face a painful quandary. If the objective of relieving suffering suffices, there is no reason to scrutinize the short- or long-term effects of assistance— responding with one's heart and guts is adequate.

However, if the effects beyond the immediate intervention are as, or more, important than the immediate relief of suffering, then a painful process of questioning should begin. Classicists are obliged to take adequately into account the results of the realpolitik calculations by states, factional politics within war zones and partisan politics in donor countries, and outcomes of international public policy debates. Honest questions should be asked about engagement and disengagement. Rushing immediately to the scene of a disaster is not preordained. Doing nothing is an option.

Reflections and not reflexes are required because, in Rieff's words, "despite the best intentions of aid workers, and at times because of them, they become logisticians in the war efforts of warlords, fundamentalists, gangsters, and ethnic cleansers."[42] The 1998 background document for the second off-the-record Wolfsberg Humanitarian Forum organized by the ICRC was less poignant but similar in its conclusion: "Aid in complex emergencies is always determined by a highly politicized context and has political implications itself, whether as a direct consequence of its provision or by way of intentional or unintentional side-effects."[43]

The "good Samaritan" figures prominently in ICRC documentation, and many humanitarians agree implicitly or explicitly with Sommaruga's biblical interpretation and his perennial praise for apolitical humanitarianism as an "act of charity."[44] Paul's First Letter to the Corinthians praises charity as the greatest of virtues, but John Hutchinson has criticized the "champions of charity" on the grounds that they helped make war more palatable.[45]

In light of substantial evidence of the counterproductive effects of well-intentioned humanitarian action, there are still other reasons to question visceral charity. Altruism should infuse debate but not constitute policy. It is impermissible to cede to virtue if it hinders rather than helps a political solution, leads to more violence and conflict, unduly supports the growth of a war economy, or undermines local coping capacities. Classical humanitarianism may seem unequivocally noble, but counterproductive efforts are uncharitable. Benign motivations are insufficient if the results are dreadful—just as selfish motivations are sufficient if the results are beneficial. Alain Destexhe, former secretary general of the international office of MSF and now president of the International Crisis Group and a member of the Belgian Senate, argues: "Humanitarian action is noble when coupled with political action and justice. Without them, it is doomed to failure and . . . a conscience-salving gimmick."[46]

Although politics and humanitarianism are inextricably linked, senior ICRC officials continue publicly to defend the apolitical fiction.[47] Anything added to or subtracted from the traditional mandate of saving lives allegedly diminishes the humanitarian mission. There is no need to denigrate unselfish acts or compassion and courage. Analysts should be clear, however, that classicists do not engage in the task of—indeed they remain agnostic about—linking emergency help to the longer-term requirements of bringing a society back to some type of equilibrium. Their claims are limited to saving lives and reducing suffering today, to a discrete incrementalism that can be praised or lambasted as the "one more blanket" theory.[48] This reality creates serious problems for classicists in coming to grips with minimalist and maximalist objectives of a more conscious political humanitarianism, and it continues to compel classicists to reject out of hand the approach of solidarists.

The minimalist approach, associated especially with the work of Mary Anderson,[49] allows the ICRC and other classicists to engage in a conversation to determine the conditions under which it is possible, in two recent formulations, "to do good without doing harm" or "to do the least harm."[50] Both classicists and minimalists acknowledge that poorly designed humanitarian action can promote or nourish violence. Thus, project design and implementation should take into account, for instance, such matters as the location and lighting of women's latrines, which can reduce dramatically instances of rape. Moreover, they should ensure, to the extent possible, that projects take advantage of development possibilities that could be sustainable once expatriates and external resources evaporate. Public relations and speeches emanating from Geneva notwithstanding, the most savvy field staff of the ICRC already act on such insights. In many ways, this is common sense for reflective humanitarians, although it may not be for reflexive ones.

This is not the place to examine criticisms of this modified Hippocratic oath, which include the lack of empirical evidence to warrant an emphasis on humanitarian institutions instead of states; the difficulties in disaggregating the effects of humanitarian shortcomings from the effects of local war economies; the inappropriateness of applying concepts from natural disasters to manmade ones; the anecdotal nature of successful cases of peace building; and the questionable sustainability of most projects once outsiders and their funds disappear. There is no pejorative connotation to the term "minimalist," which is intended to indicate a location left of center on the spectrum. Indeed, given the nature of contemporary tragedies, accomplishing the minimalist agenda is ambitious.

If humanitarian agencies are persuaded by the evidence that they are not exacerbating conflict or causing more harm than good, they are pursuing a defensible strategy. Whether or not they maintain the fiction of separating humanitarianism from politics, they can choose to respect the humanitarian imperative and alleviate life-threatening suffering as a stopgap until political actors catch up. They can take advantage of opportunities, however limited, to pursue "developmentalist relief" that helps build sustainable local capacities for peace.[51]

Humanitarian angst results because doing nothing or withdrawing under some circumstances may be necessary, and such eventualities go against the impulse to help. Thus, even the commonsensical notion that relief should do more good than harm is not without controversy. In the United Kingdom, some observers are so determined to counteract pessimism and halt any erosion in public funds devoted to relief and development that they have attacked the do-no-harm notion with a vehemence ordinarily reserved for the political opposition.[52] This short-sighted stance, which verges on humanitarian know-nothingness, is hard to fathom because counterproductive efforts are more of a threat to public support over the long haul than is the minimalist position.

The partial entente between classicists and minimalists does not extend much farther along the spectrum of political humanitarianism. The long-standing feud by classicists with solidarists, especially MSF, is well known. But maximalists also pursue a brand of political humanitarianism that is anathema to apolitical classicists. A serious conversation between maximalists and classicists is virtually unthinkable, because overt and self-conscious political considerations supposedly corrode the pure humanitarian imperative. Maximalists go beyond compassion and charity to argue that the relief of life-threatening suffering can no longer be the sole justification for outside assistance. They are determined to tackle the underlying causes of violence and to reform humanitarianism to prevent, mitigate, and resolve conflicts. Sommaruga described the maximalist agenda as "dangerous" because it amounts to "subordinating humanitarian action to political considerations, for instance, or bringing humanitarian issues into broader negotiations where diplomatic or military bargains can sometimes be struck at the expense of humanitarian concerns."[53]

At this juncture, maximalists are arguing on behalf of a largely untested proposition—indeed, their harshest critics would argue that results thus far have demonstrated that politicized aid has made matters worse, not better. Careful empirical research is required to verify the hypothesis, but it is plausible that placing humanitarian activities within a conflict resolution framework could ultimately work in favor of humanitarian interests, to bring substantially more benefits to victims than myopic or misplaced humanitarian action.

Properly conceived politically motivated assistance would use carrots and sticks, with conditionalities to reward or punish behavior. The notion is that such maximalist projects can reduce violence—effectively turning on its head the argument that aid can be manipulated by belligerents and exacerbate armed conflict. The calculation would be that the greatest good for the greatest number over the longer term would be better served by successful conflict management than by successful relief. In spite of billions of dollars in aid, the "well-fed dead" in Bosnia and the African Great Lakes suggest why emergency aid may not maximize the relief of suffering, even in the medium term.

The British, Canadian, Dutch, and Swedish governments have reorganized to foster better programmatic connections between humanitarian assistance and conflict resolution, and the World Bank has become a major actor in postconflict peace building in such places as Bosnia, thereby reviving the "R" in its original IBRD acronym (International Bank for Reconstruction and Development). A recent report financed by the government of Norway, with guidance from former UN undersecretary-general Marrack Goulding, recommends "close cooperation between the political and humanitarian parts of the United Nations, which implies that in certain circumstances the purely humanitarian mandate may have to be adjusted temporarily to take account of political requirements."[54] Recent donor practice in Afghanistan and Sierra Leone suggests that political humanitarianism has gained ground and that relief appeals must increasingly aim to do more than save lives to sustain financing. Mark Duffield has characterized these institutional changes as a "shift in aid policy away from humanitarian assistance towards attempting to support development in conflict situations."[55] There are clear implications of this shift in mainstream policy toward developmental relief for both UN agencies and NGOs that have, in the market-driven aid economy, come to depend on government funding or intergovernmental subcontracts.[56]

Instead of the neutral and impartial provision of aid, humanitarian action as a tool of conflict management implies choice, and choices involve political decisions. In describing aid conditionality for peace processes, two observers note: "In an inversion of the children's fable, the unmentionable truth is that the emperor does indeed wear clothes, tailored to the political fashion of the day. . . . The real issue is not whether political effects will result, but what these will be."[57]

The difficulty of outsiders' making decisions about the legitimacy and desirability of different national institutions should not be underestimated. An in-depth familiarity with local values and institutions is required to begin to act effectively. Even in Western societies themselves, social engineering experiments have hardly been unalloyed successes. Moreover, well-intentioned and well-informed outsiders without a long-term stake in the local economy and political outcomes have no right to influence decisions. At the same time, it is inevitable that the leverage from resources necessarily entails judgments by outsiders about what is just and right, about whose capacities are built, and about which local groups are favored. Power imbalances provide at least a cautionary note for political humanitarians.

Moreover, there are risks for political humanitarians. Aid can be held hostage to politics or withheld without commensurate payoffs. Politicians can seize upon the expanded objectives in order to justify isolationism and a reduction in resources devoted to emergency succor. The primacy of humanitarian values can be further eroded. And the overselling of humanitarian action could lead to additional disenchantment by politicians and the public if the more ambitious efforts to link emergency aid and conflict resolution fail. Thus, the maximalist experiment could lead to the worst of many worlds just as the minimalist one can be tritely inadequate.

Nonetheless, growing programmatic emphasis on doing no harm and linking relief with conflict resolution means that major donors increasingly are asking humanitarians to save lives in acute emergencies while simultaneously finding better ways to address underlying vulnerabilities. It is worth considering dispassionately that political humanitarianism may not necessarily be a threat to classicists. Under the right circumstances, the maximalist approach could be viewed as an opportunity to address the roots of violence rather than place emergency Band-Aids, however well funded and effective, on wounds. Nonetheless, some of the more grandiose claims of maximalists should lead to extreme skepticism: There literally is no space for conflict resolution or development activities when deep insecurity prevails. In the darkest moments of civil war, only emergency relief efforts are plausible, and even these often are under siege.

## CONCLUSION

Minimalists, maximalists, and solidarists contribute to today's international toolkit in spite of protests by classicists. Keeping politics and humanitarian action separate appears increasingly problematic. Oxfam, for example, is calling upon humanitarian agencies to conduct "conflict impact assessments" before undertaking what previously would have been apolitical and knee-jerk reactions to come to the rescue.[58]

Conceptions of both "humanitarianism" and "politics" are changing, but stereotypes persist. The ideal is a humanitarianism that is unaffected by political factors in the countries that receive or provide assistance or by the bureaucratic politics of aid agencies themselves. Humanitarianism, after all, means helping and protecting innocent victims. Such undertakings, being rooted in morality and principle, are unequivocally noble.

There is a mirror image of this stereotype: If humanitarianism claims the moral high ground, politics occupies the nether terrain because it refers to jockeying for power, prestige, and a piece of the pie. Whether one cites Niccolò Machiavelli or Henry Kissinger, international politics is the self-interested struggle among states over raisons d'état. Within borders, partisan or factional politics occur where deals or threats are cut and where integrity is in short supply. At the level of international public policy, politics refers to the competition and struggle to pursue one's own definition of a desirable outcome, and this can also seem ignoble.

The experience of the post–cold war era suggests that the reality in Bosnias, Rwandas, and Somalias is more complicated than these stereotypes. Humanitarian organizations have attenuated human suffering and saved lives; but they have not been apolitical. Although humanitarian agencies go to great lengths to present themselves as nonpartisan and their motives as pure, they are deeply enmeshed in politics. Budget allocations and turf protection require vigilance. Humanitarians also negotiate with local authorities for visas, transport, and access, which all require compromises. They feel the pain of helping ethnic cleansers, feeding war criminals, and rewarding military strategies that herd civilians into camps. They decide whether or not to publicize human rights abuses. They look aside when bribes occur and food aid is diverted for military purposes. They provide foreign exchange and contribute to the growth of war economies that redistribute assets from the weak to the strong.

Humanitarians not only need to understand the prevailing political environment to secure resources and protect organizational mandates. They also need to deal with and accommodate host governments and a variety of opposition or insurgent political authorities. Local economic, political, and power dynamics are altered whenever outsiders enter a resource-scarce environment. To pretend that pragmatic political calculations are not taken into account as part of legitimate compromises in choosing among several unpalatable options obfuscates the actual nature of humanitarian decision making in complex emergencies. At a minimum, the vast majority of humanitarians now acknowledge the need to minimize their impact on the relative power of warring parties or to affect them as equally as possible. And they certainly influence and are influenced by the outcomes of realpolitik and partisan politics in donor countries as well as by debates on international public policy.

At the same time, political and military responses have demonstrated on occasion the centrality of humanitarian values to governments and policy debates. In the post–cold war era, governmental interpretations of vital national interests and of international conventions have been present along with notions of human solidarity. There is no exit strategy for humanitarians if states do not take their humanitarian responsibilities seriously and use coercion to halt genocide and other massive abuses of civilians. Involvement in politics by humanitarians is necessary in war zones and elsewhere. In the words of Jeffrey Herbst: "It is naive, at best, to believe that peace will break out in some countries without a change in the balance of power given that political influence often flows from the barrel of the gun. Such a reversal of political fortunes can only be achieved through the use of force."[59] A more subdued version of this idea comes from UN secretary-general Kofi Annan in a 1997 Economic and Social Council document: "Humanitarian activities take place in a political environment and thus are affected by and affect that environment."[60]

It is hard to square this view with the ICRC's official stance, shared by other classicists, that "humanitarian work must be disassociated from military operations aimed at ensuring security and restoring law and order in regions affected by conflict."[61] In more and more wars, efficacious remedial efforts have little to do with consent and traditional peacekeeping. Rather, effective action often requires such robust coercion as seizing airports in the midst of a Rwandan genocide, creating truly safe areas in a Bosnia, disarming thugs in Somalia, and eliminating war criminals from the management of camps in eastern Congo or Tanzania. These actions are, by definition, coercive and partial. They are political and humanitarian; they certainly are not neutral, impartial, or consensual.

Humanitarians cannot deny political realities. Or if they do, which has been the practice for decades, they do so increasingly at their own peril and to the detriment of victims. They cannot set themselves above the political fray, because they are part of it, in both the countries where they work and the countries where they are incorporated. They should realize that humane values are best served by understanding and minimizing the manipulation inherent in civil wars. They should make use of political momentum and advocate political involvement to halt violence and ensure respect for human rights. They should determine the ultimate impact of emergency assistance on the conflict arena and adapt or even withhold aid if it increases violence, fuels conflict dynamics, legitimizes armed factions, or supports the growth of a war economy. And they should employ their leverage, whenever and wherever possible, to foster conflict transformation.

The fact that humanitarian space cannot be opened or maintained by humanitarians themselves suggests clear benefits from thinking politically and collaborating with diplomatic and military institutions. This political vision transforms humanitarianism. At the same time, the political sphere needs to be widened to ensure that the international arena is as hospitable as possible for both emergency aid and the protection of rights. Politics at its best embraces a vision of human solidarity and works to operationalize a strategy for making that solidarity real rather than rhetorical.

Political actors have a newfound interest in principles, while humanitarians of all stripes are increasingly aware of the importance of politics. Yet there remain two distinct approaches—politics and humanitarianism as self-contained and antithetical realities or alternatively as overlapping spheres.

Nostalgia for aspects of the cold war or other bygone eras is perhaps understandable, but there never was a "golden age" when humanitarianism was insulated from politics. Much aid was an extension of the foreign policies of major donors, especially the superpowers. Nonetheless, it was easier, conceptually and practically, to compartmentalize humanitarianism and politics before the present decade. Then, a better guide to action was provided by an unflinching respect for traditional principles, although they never were absolute ends but only intermediate means.

In today's world, humanitarians must ask themselves how to weigh the political consequences of their action or inaction, and politicians must ask themselves how to gauge the humanitarian costs of their action or inaction. The calculations are tortuous, and the mathematics far from exact. However, there is no longer any need to ask whether politics and humanitarian action intersect. The real question is how this intersection can be managed to ensure more humanized politics and more effective humanitarian action. To this end, humanitarians should be neither blindly principled nor blindly pragmatic.

## NOTES

For their thoughtful suggestions and comments on earlier versions of this chapter, the author thanks David P. Forsythe, Ian McAllister, S. Neil MacFarlane, Larry Minear, and Peter Uvin, as well as the International Committee of the Red Cross, for having challenged him to develop these ideas for the Second Wolfsberg Humanitarian Forum, June 5–7, 1998. Responsibility for the views expressed and any remaining errors in fact or interpretation are the author's.

1. Neutrality and impartiality are important because they are central to the humanitarian ethos and give rise to much controversy. Consent is emphasized here, because nonintervention in domestic affairs is the glue of international relations, and consent guides virtually all UN actions with the exception of Chapter VII coercion. See Marion Harroff-Tavel, "Neutrality and Impartiality: The Importance of These Principles for the International Red Cross and Red Crescent Movement and the Difficulties Involved in Applying Them," *International Review of the Red Cross* 273 (November–December 1989): 536–52. See also Yves Sandoz, "The International Committee of the Red Cross and the Law of Armed Conflict Today," *International Peacekeeping* 4 (winter 1997): 86–99.

2. Jean Pictet, "The Fundamental Principles of the Red Cross," *International Review of the Red Cross* 210 (May–June 1979): 130–40, at 135; and Jean Pictet, *Development and Principles of International Humanitarian Law* (Dordrecht: Martinus Nijhoff, 1985). Humanity, impartiality, neutrality, independence, universality, voluntary service, and unity are principles of "humanitarian action" (guiding relief and protection of rights), as distinct from principles of "international humanitarian law" (e.g., the distinctions between combatant and noncombatant), which are not the subject of this inquiry.

3. Mark Duffield, "The Political Economy of Internal War: Asset Transfer and the Internationalisation of Public Welfare in the Horn of Africa," in *War and Hunger: Rethinking International Responses to Complex Emergencies*, ed. Joanna Macrae and Anthony Zwi (London: Zed Books, 1994). For a discussion of humanitarian tragedies as growth opportunities see, e.g., Michael Maren, *The Road to Hell: The Ravaging Effects of Foreign Aid and International Charity* (New York: Free Press, 1997). See also David Keen, *The Economic Functions of Violence in Civil Wars*, Adelphi Paper 320 (Oxford: Oxford University Press, 1998); and François Jean and Christophe Rufin, eds., *Economies des Guerres Civiles* (Paris: Hachette, 1996).

4. The debate was initiated by Alex de Waal and Rakiya Omaar, *Humanitarianism Unbound? Current Dilemmas Facing Multi-Mandate Relief Operations in Political Emergencies*, Discussion Paper 5 (London: African Rights, 1994).

5. Steering Committee, "Background Paper: Humanitarian and Political Action: Key Issues and Priorities for a Concerted Strategy," in *Report on the Second Wolfsberg Humanitarian Forum, 5–7 June 1998* (Geneva: International Committee of the Red Cross, 1998), 1; hereafter, *Report Second Wolfsberg.*

6. Cornelio Sommaruga, "Concluding Remarks," in *Report Second Wolfsberg*, 3.

7. Pierre Perrin, "The Impact of Humanitarian Aid on Conflict Development," *International Review of the Red Cross* 323 (June 1998): 332.

8. Jonathan Moore, ed., *Hard Choices: Moral Dilemmas in Humanitarian Intervention* (Lanham, Md.: Rowman & Littlefield, 1998).

9. David P. Forsythe, *Humanitarian Politics: The International Committee of the Red Cross* (Baltimore: Johns Hopkins University Press, 1977), 3.

10. Sadako Ogata, "Keynote Address," in *Report Second Wolfsberg*, 1.

11. Andrew Natsios, "Commentary," *Ethics & International Affairs* 11 (1997): 133.

12. Steering Committee, "Background Paper," 4.

13. See Jarat Chopra, *Peace-Maintenance: The Evolution of International Political Authority* (London: Routledge, 1999); and Jarat Chopra, ed., *The Politics of Peace-Maintenance* (Boulder, Colo.: Lynne Rienner, 1998).

14. See Michael J. Smith, "Humanitarian Intervention: An Overview of the Ethical Issues," *Ethics & International Affairs* 12 (1998): 63–80.

15. Adam Roberts, "Threats to Humanitarian Action: Remedies," in *Report on the Wolfsberg Humanitarian Forum, 8–10 June 1997* (Geneva: International Committee of the Red Cross, 1997), 1; hereafter, *Report First Wolfsberg.*

16. David Rieff, "The Humanitarian Illusion," *New Republic,* March 16, 1998, 29.

17. Eric Hobsbawm, *The Age of Extremes: A History of the World, 1914–1991* (New York: Vintage, 1996), 13.

18. These are: relieving life-threatening suffering, proportionality to need, nonpartisanship, independence, accountability, appropriateness, subsidiarity of suffering, and contextualization. See Larry Minear and Thomas G. Weiss, *Humanitarian Action in Times of War: A Handbook for Practitioners* (Boulder, Colo.: Lynne Rienner, 1993), 7–41.

19. Forsythe, *Humanitarian Politics,* 28. See also Jean-Luc Blondel, "The Fundamental Principles of the Red Cross and the Red Crescent: Their Origin and Development," *International Review of the Red Cross* 283 (July–August 1991): 349–57.

20. Michael Ignatieff, *The Warrior's Honor: Ethnic War and the Modern Conscience* (New York: Henry Holt, 1997), 5.

21. Charles William Maynes, "'Principled Hegemony,'" *World Policy Journal* 14 (fall 1997): 36.

22. Mark Duffield, "The Symphony of the Damned: Racial Discourse, Complex Political Emergencies and Humanitarian Aid," *Disasters* 20 (September 1996): 191.

23. Joanna Macrae, "The Death of Humanitarianism? An Anatomy of the Attack," *Disasters* 22 (December 1998): 316. This is part of a special issue titled "The Emperor's New Clothes: Charting the Erosion of Humanitarian Principles."

24. Chr. Michelsen Institute, *Humanitarian Assistance and Conflict* (Bergen, Norway: Chr. Michelsen Institute, 1997), 3; this publication contains a good review of the literature of the 1990s.

25. See Donald C. F. Daniel and Bradd C. Hayes, "Securing Observance of UN Mandates through the Employment of Military Force," *International Peacekeeping* 3 (winter 1996): 105–25; and Kofi Annan, "Challenges of the New Peacekeeping," in *Peacemaking and Peacekeeping for the New Century,* ed. Olara A. Otunnu and Michael W. Doyle (Lanham, Md.: Rowman & Littlefield, 1998).

26. Hugo Slim, "International Humanitarianism's Engagement with Civil War in the 1990s: A Glance at Evolving Practice and Theory," briefing paper for ActionAid UK, document dated December 19, 1997, 16.

27. See Thomas G. Weiss and Cindy Collins, *Humanitarian Challenges and Intervention: World Politics and the Dilemmas of Help* (Boulder, Colo.: Westview, 1996), 97–134.

28. Myron Wiener, "The Clash of Norms: Dilemmas in Refugee Policies," *Journal of Refugee Studies* 11 (1998): 1–21. See also Dan Smith, "Interventionist Dilemmas and Justice," in *Humanitarian Force,* ed. Anthony McDermott (Oslo: International Peace Research Institute, 1997), 29–31.

29. Thomas Nagle, *Moral Questions* (New York: Cambridge University Press, 1991), 74.

30. Pictet, "Fundamental Principles," 136; and Nicholas Leader, "Proliferating Principles or How to Sup with the Devil without Getting Eaten," *Disasters* 22 (December 1998): 305.

31. The author is grateful to Charles Keely for this point.

32. International Committee of the Red Cross founder Henry Dunant's efforts could be contrasted with the more circumscribed assessment of his Swiss compatriot Jean-Jacques

Rousseau, who earlier had emphasized the importance of kin, kith, and ken: "It appears that the feeling of humanity evaporates and grows feeble in embracing all mankind, and that we cannot be affected by the calamities of Tartary or Japan, in the same manner as we are by those of European nations." Jean-Jacques Rousseau, "A Discourse on Political Economy," *The Social Contract and Discourses* (New York: Dutton, 1950), 301. See also Nancy Sherman, "Empathy, Respect, and Humanitarian Intervention," *Ethics & International Affairs* 12 (1998): 103–19.

33. Dave Rowlands and David Carment, "Moral Hazard and Conflict Intervention," in *The Political Economy of War and Peace*, ed. Murray Wolfson (The Hague: Kluwer, forthcoming), 2; emphasis in original.

34. Ignatieff, *Warrior's Honor*, 8.

35. Gwyn Prins, "Modern Warfare and Humanitarian Action," keynote lecture to a European Community Humanitarian Office–International Committee of the Red Cross conference titled "Humanitarian Action: Perception and Security," Lisbon, March 27–28, 1998, 6.

36. Minear and Weiss, *Humanitarian Action in Times of War*, 37.

37. See, e.g., Macrae, "Death of Humanitarianism?"; and Cindy Collins, "Critiques of Humanitarianism and Humanitarian Action," in *Humanitarian Coordination: Lessons Learned* (New York: Office for the Coordination of Humanitarian Affairs, 1998).

38. Alex de Waal, *Famine Crimes: Politics and the Disaster Relief Industry in Africa* (Oxford: James Currey, 1997), 145.

39. See, e.g., Taylor B. Seybolt, "The Myth of Neutrality," *Peace Review* 8 (1996): 521–27; and Richard Betts, "The Delusion of Impartial Intervention," *Foreign Affairs* 73 (1994): 20–33.

40. Jarat Chopra and Thomas G. Weiss, "Sovereignty Is No Longer Sacrosanct: Codifying Humanitarian Intervention," *Ethics & International Affairs* 6 (1992): 95–118.

41. "Objectives and Agenda of the Forum," in *Report First Wolfsberg*, 1.

42. Rieff, "Humanitarian Illusion," 30.

43. Steering Committee, "Background Paper," 4.

44. "Introductory Address by Dr. Cornelio Sommaruga," in *Report First Wolfsberg*, 3.

45. John F. Hutchinson, *Champions of Charity: War and the Rise of the Red Cross* (Boulder, Colo.: Westview, 1996).

46. Alain Destexhe, "Foreword," in *Populations in Danger 1995*, ed. François Jean (London: Médécins Sans Frontières, 1995).

47. Eric Roethlisberger, "Faced with Today's and Tomorrow's Challenges, Should the International Red Cross and Red Crescent Movement Rethink Its Code of Ethics?" speech given March 20, 1998, 2; and "Guiding Principles on the Right to Humanitarian Assistance," *International Review of the Red Cross* 297 (November–December 1993): 519–25.

48. Forsythe, *Humanitarian Politics*, 234.

49. Mary B. Anderson, *Do No Harm: Supporting Local Capacities for Peace through Aid* (Cambridge, Mass.: Collaborative for Development Action, 1996).

50. Astri Surhke and Kathleen Newland, "Humanitarian Assistance in the Midst of Armed Conflict," paper presented at a conference titled "The Evolution of International Humanitarian Response in the 1990s," sponsored by the Carnegie Endowment for International Peace and the Gilman Foundation, Yulee, Fla., April 23–26, 1998, 2; and Michael Bryans, Bruce D. Jones, and Janice Gross Stein, *Mean Times: Humanitarian Action in Complex Political Emergencies—Stark Choices, Cruel Dilemmas* (Toronto: Program on Conflict Management and Negotiation, 1999), vi.

51. See Mary B. Anderson and Peter J. Woodrow, *Rising from the Ashes: Development Strategies in Times of Disaster* (Boulder, Colo.: Westview, 1989); and Ian McAllister, *Sustaining Relief with Development* (Dordrecht: Martinus Nijhoff, 1993).

52. See Dylan Hendrickson, *Humanitarian Action in Protracted Crises: The New Relief "Agenda" and Its Limits*, RRN Network Paper 25 (London: Overseas Development Institute, 1998).

53. "Concluding Remarks by Dr. Cornelio Sommaruga," in *Report First Wolfsberg*, 2.

54. Norwegian Institute of International Affairs, *Development Assistance as a Means of Conflict Prevention* (Oslo: Norwegian Institute of International Affairs, February 1998), 14.

55. Mark Duffield, *Aid Policy and Post-Modern Conflict: A Critical Review*, Occasional Paper 19 (Birmingham, U.K.: School of Public Policy, 1998), 3.

56. See Development Assistance Committee, *Policy Statement on Conflict, Peace and Development Co-operation on the Threshold of the 21st Century* (Paris: Organization for Economic Cooperation and Development, 1997).

57. James K. Boyce and Manuel Pastor Jr., "Aid for Peace: Can International Financial Institutions Help Prevent Conflict?" *World Policy Journal* 15 (summer 1998): 42.

58. Edmund Cairns, *A Safer Future: Reducing the Human Cost of War* (Oxford: Oxfam Publications, 1997), 94.

59. Jeffrey Herbst, *Securing Peace in Africa*, WPF Report 17 (Cambridge, Mass.: World Peace Foundation, 1998), 10.

60. "Review of the Capacity of the United Nations System for Humanitarian Assistance: Report of the Secretary-General," UN Document E/1997/98, July 10, 1997, para. 6.

61. Jean de Courten, "ICRC Statement on Security Environment," Geneva, draft presented at the Humanitarian Liaison Working Group, April 24, 1997, 2. For a discussion opposing the use of force from the classicist perspective, see Umesh Palwankar, ed., *Symposium on Humanitarian Action and Peace-keeping Operations* (Geneva: International Committee of the Red Cross, 1994).

# PART II
# CHALLENGES

# SIX

# The Politics of Rescue: Yugoslavia's Wars and the Humanitarian Impulse

Amir Pasic and Thomas G. Weiss

The humanitarian impulse is remarkably prevalent in the post–cold war world. Whether or not we have actually entered "the age of humanitarian emergencies" is open to debate,[1] but the dramatic increase in the number of humanitarian interventions since 1991 has been widely noted, as has sobriety after debacles or disappointments in Somalia and elsewhere.[2] Humanitarianism as an expression of concern for the victims of armed conflict and political disorder has traditionally been spearheaded by nonstate actors. That states themselves have begun to include humanitarianism in their policy architectures is evidence of the extent to which this orientation has become a prominent feature of both contemporary transnational civil society and interstate relations.[3] The notion of rescue is also emerging in the philosophical and policy literature.[4]

There is, however, a dramatic downside to what might otherwise be considered a positive moral development at the international level. Rushing to rescue victims on the basis of a visceral reaction to their suffering may, depending on the circumstances, be a palliative or, even worse, counterproductive. A poor basis for policy, it builds erroneously on the metaphor of saving a drowning stranger and distorts the context surrounding humanitarian efforts. It seems to initiate a new relationship with distant peoples who are suddenly of concern to us because they are subject to unacceptable suffering. At the same time, this link is exceptional and limited only to the duration of a particular rescue effort. It does not alter significantly the relationship between the rescuers and the rescued.

The multiple ties that bind rescuers and victims long before the onset of a complex emergency, and throughout its evolution, are ignored. In particular, rescue does not capture sufficiently the absence of secure ground in war zones to which to bring imperiled victims. Furthermore, those in danger are not as foreign, unknown, and unconnected to us as often is implied by the rescue metaphor. Before, during, and after complex emergencies, rescuers and victims are related through many relationships that their representatives conduct in economic, diplomatic, and cultural domains.

States have always intervened in one another's affairs. Justifications and rationalizations for incursions across sovereign boundaries have included past grievances and the protection of co-religionists or nationals.[5] Remarkably, interventions along with other less invasive but more routine human rights intrusions into domestic affairs are now being justified in terms of humanitarian concerns.[6] National interests and other justifications have not disappeared, nor will they, but they have acquired a definite humanitarian flavor.

Moreover, the humanitarian impulse is not limited to the most obvious agents: protectors, aid deliverers, peacekeepers, and journalists.[7] It has also seeped into foreign ministries and security agendas as heads of states proclaim the virtues of "doing the right thing," despite the usual warnings that moral sentiments should not guide the ship of state.[8]

Indeed, pundits and professors use that nebulous term, "the international community," as a stock concept to analyze contemporary world politics, increasingly with the implication that there is a moral obligation to act even if there is no consensus about the requirement to do so.[9] Furthermore, a focus on multilateral military endeavors with humanitarian justifications is becoming a standard feature of strategic, operational, and doctrinal discourse in the United States military and NATO.[10] In the process, humanitarians from both the United Nations and nongovernmental organizations (NGOs) are being recognized as natural partners in what the British military first labeled "operations other than war," now the preferred term in most militaries.[11]

Given the surge in humanitarian intervention and its impact on foreign policy, it is imperative to examine its limitations. This chapter explores the ethical challenges presented by the emergency mode of humanitarianism in war zones. One example is the former Yugoslavia, where the Office of the UN High Commissioner for Refugees (UNHCR) was designated the lead agency by the UN secretary-general and orchestrated rescue operations in Europe's largest involuntary displacements since World War II.[12] The UNHCR's relative success in bringing assistance to 4 million victims in the Balkans reflected a principled extension of the organization's charge to take care of refugees—that is, people who have no state to protect them.

At the same time, the experience of the refugee agency in this instance demonstrates the limits of rescue. The Balkans benefited from a substantial resource abundance vis-à-vis the rest of the world, and the international community is unlikely to devote such ample material resources and political attention to other complex emergencies. In 1995, the former Yugoslavia received more than 100 percent of estimated aid requirements—as it had in previous years—which contrasted with less than 50 percent received by Angola, Sudan, Somalia, Afghanistan, Iraq, Sierra Leone, and others.[13]

However, rescue served also as a substitute for robust diplomatic and military engagement and prolonged the need for assistance. Moreover, as former U.S. assistant secretary of state Richard Holbrooke has pointed out, "the damage that Bosnia did to the UN was incalculable."[14] As long as something was being done to assuage the suffering, international leadership could declare that it had a policy for dealing with the former Yugoslavia. The means available amounted to what the former UN senior political adviser characterized as "trying to hold back the tide with a spoon."[15] The outpouring of help was manipulated by those political authorities who did not share humanitarian goals, thus damaging the long-term interests of endangered populations and the quest for peace and stability. Aid was diverted, access to civilians was denied in order to extort resources and recognition of territorial claims, and the multilateral humanitarian presence became a pawn in the capricious maneuvers of irresponsible demagogues whose policies would ultimately exacerbate the difficulties that the region would have in rehabilitating itself when peace finally came.[16] The delivery of relief settled into a bizarre pattern, sustaining civilians who were being manipulated by leaders whose primary political resource was their capacity to threaten civilians and even humanitarians. Simultaneously, scores of opinion leaders in the West and in the Islamic world agonized over the rescue effort and its meaning for the moral identities of all of us who were witnessing the tragedy.[17]

Although it seeks to moderate the ugly realities of international politics, rescue—even with the exceptional level of commitment it received in the former Yugoslavia—in actuality adds new ethical dilemmas to international politics. Perhaps the foremost of these dilemmas regards the proportionality of needs and the affirmation that life is as precious in one part of the globe as another. Thus, the "privileged position" of Yugoslavia's victims should trouble us as much as the failure of a policy based on such an extensive expenditure of resources.

Rescue affects the political lives and identities not simply of victims but of the rescuers as well. It reveals a troubled and unsettled link to sovereignty, which separates humanity into integral units, each pursuing a distinctive way of life. Does rescue seek to establish a new kind of "revolutionary" humanitarian relationship among peoples or is it "restorative," seeking to rebuild the capacity of endangered populations to continue their distinctive way of life under state authority as before the crisis? The former option would establish a transcendent moral link among human beings as such, thus overriding or at least going beyond sovereignty; the latter would seek to restore the autonomy of suffering populations within a self-contained polity, thus sustaining traditional sovereignty.

On the one hand, revolutionary humanitarianism makes rescuers self-conscious participants in a "foreign" political community, thus rearranging the boundaries of the political space occupied by victims. Restorative humanitarianism, on the other hand, accepts the necessity of tolerating blatant abuses of rights because relief efforts are fundamentally directed toward reestablishing the endangered population's autonomy with as little outside political involvement as possible. Rescue is thus a radically ambiguous principle, persisting incoherently between revolutionary and restorative humanitarianism. Although these two points are at either end of a continuum, with many gradations between them, they are not merely heuristic devices to amuse analysts. They are principled choices that circumscribe policy options. The fundamental purpose of this chapter is to explore the normative tension between them, hoping to better explain why rescue founders.

We begin with an overview of apolitical attempts to rescue the "wretched of the earth," during which both outside aid personnel and victims are implicated in the politics of rescue. Then, by focusing on the UNHCR and its attempt to deal with the people displaced by Yugoslavia's wars, we discern the shortcomings of any episode of rescue and the implicit principles that could guide future rescue missions. This serves as background for a discussion of the ambiguity of humanitarianism—a principle that can be used either to buttress sovereignty or to challenge it. Whether one opts for the more conservative (restorative) or, alternatively, the more radical (revolutionary) vision, the Yugoslav case suggests the limits of humanitarianism.

## THE POLITICS OF RESCUE

Distinctions between humanitarian and political concerns are instructive, reflecting the difference between the goals of rescue and of stability. In spite of the initial lofty rhetoric of the post–cold war world, the various members of the international community are becoming aware of the necessity for more reflection and fewer automatic responses to humanitarian tragedies. Removing superpower rivalry clearly has been insufficient for the international humanitarian system to move from the pursuit of rescue to the institution of political order.[18]

There are inevitable trade-offs between the two goals. To pursue rescue is to seek the immediate and unconditional alleviation of human suffering. To institute political order is to seek to create and sustain viable social institutions that will prevent the need for subsequent rescue efforts. Political strategies to create an enduring sociopolitical order will sometimes require reining in the impulse to save lives and alleviate the suffering of noncombatants with all available means.[19] In the prescient prose of Alain Destexhe, the former secretary general of Médécins Sans Frontières (Doctors Without Borders):

> All over the world, there is unprecedented enthusiasm for humanitarian work. It is far from certain that this is always in the victims' best interests. . . . In dealing with countries in ongoing wars of a local nature, humanitarian aid has acquired a near-monopoly of morality and international action. It is this monopoly that we seek to denounce. Humanitarian action is noble when coupled with political action and justice. Without them, it is doomed to failure and especially in the emergencies covered by the media, becomes little more than a play thing of international politics, a conscience-solving gimmick.[20]

To complicate matters, the use of the term "peace" as a synonym for "stability" is philosophically loaded. Decolonization, for example, showed that everything cannot be sacrificed at the altar of peace, and that not all political orders are worth preserving no matter how apparently stable. We confront the age-old tensions between order and justice. There are situations in which it would be justifiable to increase suffering and create disorder for the purpose of fashioning a more equitable and sustainable political order in the long run. It is, of course, by no means obvious when we may justifiably calculate the costs and benefits of such endeavors.

In fact, conflicts between order and justice have been temporarily obscured by a superficial consensus about the values of democratization and liberalization. Orderly, just, and peaceful liberal democracies and their mutual relations do not necessarily provide guidance for states going through the potentially destabilizing transition to democracy, where violence may become a favored option.[21] Also, the normative guidelines are even less clear for a conflict that has become about whom to include or exclude from membership in a state. When the bounds of a state and its identity are contested, it is also not clear for whom there should be order and justice.

What makes the problems of rescue, order, and justice stand out so vividly is the conventional wisdom regarding the impulse—some, for example, the International Committee of the Red Cross (ICRC), would say "imperative"—of rescue even in cases where de jure sovereignty presents a prima facie legal prohibition.[22] Most humanitarian endeavors without the consent of a state take place in areas of turmoil supposedly governed by failed or collapsed states.[23] That sovereignty should be subordinated to the demand for rescue from calamity is less problematic than the moral and operational implications of actually assuming responsibility for those rescued. The subordination of sovereignty, even if it is only in situations where effective political authority is absent, still implies an obligation to assume a longer-term perspective, a commitment to the sustainability and health of a society rather than merely to one episode of rescue. Without such a commitment, rescue can become self-defeating.

No matter how intense and heroic an intervention to deliver food, resettle people, or even eliminate an irresponsible tyrant or an armed threat, such an intervention is only a start. A simple declaration that sovereignty presents no bar to our intervention against intolerable suffering only begins to expose obligations across borders.[24] We do not know how the decentralized international humanitarian system might work to maintain order after an intervention. Nor do we possess normative criteria to trigger interventions and guide them so that there is more consistency, or perhaps less selectivity, in unleashing the humanitarian impulse.[25] The dilemmas of humanitarian challenges—in particular the reality of unanticipated negative consequences resulting from well-meaning but counterproductive humanitarianism—are thus truly unsettling.[26]

Ideas move people figuratively and can also serve to displace them literally, especially as manipulated by Serbian and Croatian politicians to justify ethnic cleansing. And in situations where people are not threatened at gun point, fear can move them whether or not it is ultimately warranted. In the Yugoslav context, ethnic identity became a potent guiding principle, even for those national and international actors who most wanted to stop hostilities and were appalled by the disappearance of a multiethnic society. As Susan Woodward writes of the September 1992 peace conference in the Hague, convened under the auspices of the European Community: "No pro-Yugoslav parties were represented in the formulation, nor were the representatives of non-ethnic parties, the civilian population, or the many civic groups mobilizing against nationally exclusive states and war consulted."[27] Genocidal extermination, forced migration to achieve ethnic purity, and national animosity did not fester in a vacuum. They were clearly and faithfully reported and legitimated by the actions of humanitarians, governments, and the media even before violent hostilities commenced.

The overarching lesson to be extracted from the lot of war victims in the former Yugoslavia is the extent to which humanitarianism and politics are inextricably intertwined. The policy response thus should not be to try to keep the two as separate as possible, but rather to understand how they should be addressed simultaneously. Those who support the apolitical approach of separating the two advocate keeping the issue of who makes decisions about the distribution of aid to those at risk their own affair. As such, humanitarians can only provide relief to those in need, making whatever compromises are required. Aid providers typically respond viscerally to massive human suffering. As such, immediate and direct access to civilian victims becomes an absolute priority. Issues of sustainable order, much less its quality, appear so distant that even thinking about them detracts from the immediacy of the life-saving tasks at hand. Thus, humanitarianism becomes the emergency-response mechanism of the sovereign state system, seeking to restore the viability of sovereign compartments that have temporarily become irresponsible and dysfunctional, as revealed by the gross suffering that they contain. Mitigating the suffering begins to restore the viability of the sovereign container.

That outside intervention can save lives and reduce suffering without advancing anyone's political agenda is at best an outmoded notion. This notion—long championed by the ICRC and many other humanitarians—is increasingly viewed by critics as naive and wrong. Humanitarian efforts have never really been neutral; there is no such thing as "pure" humanitarianism because the distribution of aid always has political ramifications. As former U.S. secretary of state for African affairs Chester A. Crocker reminded us in commenting upon the November 1996 crisis in Zaire, "intervention (just like nonintervention) is an inherently political action with inescapable political consequences."[28]

Even without military forces, humanitarian efforts are profoundly political; and unless they are carefully designed, they can actually exacerbate conflicts.[29] If done properly, civilian humanitarian efforts, and certainly ones supported by the use of military forces, should alter the balance of power in favor of victims. Decisions to remain on the sidelines can be considered a form of intervention in that by failing to help the oppressed, humanitarians comply with the oppressors. This latter view, championed especially by Médécins Sans Frontières, has been gaining ground in the debate with the more traditional view espoused by the ICRC.

Those of us who support the more calculating and political approach recognize that virtually all humanitarian agencies, even the 125-year-old ICRC, are necessarily involved in political calculations and have had to compromise in many post–cold war efforts.[30] For example, the ICRC, in spite of its principles, relied upon armed escorts, including the infamous "technicals" in Somalia, because sometimes only such private mini-armies or gangs can secure access and protect humanitarians in areas of turmoil. By actually diverting a portion of aid as bribes to those who control infrastructure, or giving in to extortion, humanitarian efforts are already deeply involved in political affairs.[31] As UN high commissioner for refugees Sadako Ogata has stated, ignoring the political consequences of humanitarianism is not an option: "Mass displacement of the most cruel kind imaginable has become a conscious objective of the combatants in many armed conflicts. Humanitarian assistance is used as a weapon of war."[32]

An incident in Bosnia can serve as a particularly poignant illustration of how politicized humanitarian efforts have become despite their purveyors' fervent desire to remain neutral and impartial. At the beginning of 1993, the United Nations was unable to convince the Bosnian Serbs to let humanitarian convoys through to besieged towns in eastern Bosnia where people faced imminent starvation. Radovan Karadzic, the Bosnian Serb president who was subsequently indicted for war crimes, offered to guarantee "humanitarian corridors" of safe passage to the Muslims of Gorazde, Srebrenica, and Zepa, provided that they removed themselves from their besieged towns and thus from their islands in territory occupied by Bosnian Serbs.

The Bosnian government—responding with indignation to what it saw as a proposal for an abandonment of political commitment to eastern Bosnia and ethnic cleansing under humanitarian auspices—banned all aid deliveries to Sarajevo with the intention of goading the United Nations into a more aggressive stance vis-à-vis the Bosnian Serbs. Viewing this as blackmail and a clear indication that the warring parties were unwilling to respect internationally sanctioned procedures, Ogata suspended all relief in Serb-held Bosnia and ordered staff to withdraw from Sarajevo. On the next day, February 19, then–UN secretary-general Boutros Boutros-Ghali reversed Ogata's decision.

This incident illustrates the degree to which humanitarian endeavors can become part of the local political landscape, especially when they help to change the demographic composition of an area in an ethnically charged war over territory. Even though Karadzic's plan for eliciting humanitarian endorsement for ethnic cleansing was not accepted, on many occasions well-meaning humanitarians have greased the wheels of ethnic resettlement. This has been especially the case, understandably, when the apparent alternative was the death of civilians.

Ethnic cleansing is an utter abomination. At the same time, accepting Karadzic's offer had a strong allure. It might have been sensible, especially because the alternative would have been unmentionably worse for the endangered people as a result of the West's unwillingness to use adequate military force. We now know that Srebrenica and Zepa were overrun by Bosnian Serbs in the summer of 1995, and that the flight of tens of thousands from the area led to mayhem and murder, including a massacre in Srebrenica under the watch of Dutch UN soldiers.[33] Our humanitarian impulse would have us turn back the clock and accept Karadzic's "humanitarian corridor."

Yet, this perspective and calculation are incomplete because Srebrenica's citizens would not have been the only victims of Karadzic's proposal. The movement out of the enclaves in eastern Bosnia would also have changed the strategic situation dramatically by creating what the Serbs had long sought—an ethnically homogenous swath of territory bordering on Serbia itself. The delicate balance on the ground, however fragile, maintained by the various actors would have been altered.

The moral justification for order is conservative, reflecting fears that tampering with established procedures could bring about an even worse state of affairs. Although the rejection of Karadzic's proposal seems to have included embracing the argument on the need to preserve the strategic order, it also went beyond that to considerations of justice and morality, in that the welfare of other potential victims, especially in Sarajevo and other so-called safe areas, was part of the policy calculation.

Sometimes the need to preserve order does not dominate. We are often confident that improvements can be made without risking chaos, and we even judge that dramatic changes are imperative. In such situations, the long-term collective good may require a sacrifice of the short-term interests of a group. Although the Bosnian government and the United Nations did not have to sacrifice themselves, they did face the almost certain prospect of institutional failure if all of eastern Bosnia turned into killing fields. They could not bow to Karadzic even though he seemed to have the capacity to realize his implied threats. In the case of Karadzic's corridors, governmental and intergovernmental officials went beyond the knee-jerk reaction characteristic of restorative humanitarianism. They ignored the injunction against political involvement to become thoroughly enmeshed in the political fate of threatened populations.

There are many moral facets in judging appropriate responses to Karadzic, but ultimately the justifiable rejection of his proposal involved a political judgment by both the United Nations and the Bosnian government that overrode the normal and visceral impulse to do anything in order to rescue the Muslims of eastern Bosnia. There was a greater value to be gained by not rushing to succor victims. There was also the outright rejection of the manner in which Karadzic's proposal was framed. His implied threat that aid would not be allowed was met with a momentary stiffening of NATO resolve. His proposal made him even more of a pariah because its consequences were beyond what was considered imaginable abuse even by the deteriorating standards of behavior in the Balkans.

It took some time for the United Nations and the West to realize that negotiating with Karadzic was not fruitful, even if the failure to negotiate was at loggerheads with the humanitarian impulse. Can we generalize about the unspoken, yet pragmatic, political judgments that rejected Karadzic as a partner? Can we find a systematic way to consider relevant factors? Are there ways to analyze conflicts and leaders more quickly and directly so that we do not waste so many lives and resources in the process of blundering our way into situations where help is counterproductive?

A logical starting place would be to spell out political and ethical principles that might guide, and occasionally constrain, the humanitarian impulse. An unusual case of principled adaptation can be seen from the UNHCR's experience in the former Yugoslavia.

## RESCUING THE DISPLACED FROM YUGOSLAVIA'S WARS

Humanitarian action requires effective management of inevitable political pressures rather than maintenance of the myth that humanitarianism and politics occupy separate spheres. In the former Yugoslavia, the UNHCR's performance illustrated the most that can be expected even from the most successful rescue effort.

What was especially vital to the UNHCR's leadership was the expansion of its guiding mission to include not just the right of asylum and the protection of refugees but also assistance for all those with a well-founded fear of persecution. From its inception, the refugee agency has operated in the interstices of sovereignty, catering to the one right in the pantheon of human rights that is both national and international.[34] In the process of expanding its mandate to cover internally displaced persons (IDPs) and even those who were not displaced but whose lives were endangered, the UNHCR extended the legitimate purview of international organizations, although the debate will continue as to whether states have consented to this extension or been unable to mount an effective protest.[35]

Whom should humanitarians rescue? Here it is instructive to adopt and extend the definition of displacement. "Refugees" in the sense discussed here are no longer only those persons who have crossed the border of a sovereign state with a legitimate fear of persecution, as they were defined by the 1951 Convention on the Status of Refugees. They also include those who have not crossed state boundaries and thus are not entitled to special treatment by host states.[36] Most are confined to the states of which they are citizens or nationals. Furthermore, in war zones such as Bosnia and Croatia, many of the neediest victims are not physically removed from their homes at all. Rather, the economic and social conditions necessary for survival are removed from them, just as they are for involuntary migrants. Displacement broadly defined to include all the victims of war is the most appropriate focus of rescue. It encompasses all those who do not have a polity or a state to which they can appeal and through which they might alter their condition without outside assistance.

In the former Yugoslavia, involuntary migration was not a side effect of armed conflict; it was an explicit war aim. The theme of forceful displacement was mixed with vituperative rhetoric, and this volatile combination preceded the actual uprooting of groups and individuals. Being a Muslim or a Serb in the "wrong" suburb of Sarajevo or a Muslim or a Croat in Mostar or a Serb or a Croat in Vukovar meant being "in the wrong place." The idea spread that each ethnic group had exclusive rights to certain geographic areas, and that these physical spaces could not be shared. This sentiment then accompanied political developments that situated ethnic or national groups within legal jurisdictions that they or their leaders found unacceptable.[37]

People were aware that they found themselves in the wrong political space before they were physically displaced from it. The political process—which reconstructed relations between people and their places of residence as well as made an issue of "who" would govern, rather than "how"—eliminated the basic trust that allows politics to proceed without violence. For too many people, even those who did not suffer physical displacement, fear and hatred dominated as they were excluded from a common social and political space because of their ethnic backgrounds.

The former Yugoslavia's proximity to Western Europe and the relative socioeconomic privilege of its populations distinguish this case from most other complex emergencies. Geopolitical position had consequences for a variety of issues, ranging from military logistics and journalistic coverage to emigrant destinations and humanitarian access. Distances, logistics, the literacy of the populations, and available infrastructure were obstacles only because they were affected by the political conflict. Unlike other complex emergencies, there was no shortage of material resources; like others, however, political will was certainly absent.

Another atypical characteristic of Yugoslavia's wars was the prevalence and salience of international security organizations as actors, including the European Community (now Union), NATO, the Conference (now Organization) on Security and Cooperation in Europe, and the Western European Union. Although their impact was limited—and some observers would argue counterproductive—such a formidable array of politically powerful and resource-rich actors is unusual in current war zones. A comparable range and depth of involvement by the West or other powerful military actors in other future cases of displacement would be hard to imagine.

The substantial military presence meant that the UNHCR, as lead agency for the first time in the midst of armed conflict, was obliged to innovate with military liaison and personnel. Officers borrowed from Western armed forces were temporarily based at UNHCR headquarters to help plan the airlift and manage large numbers of new recruits in the field who had no previous military experience. Subsequently, a recently retired military officer was engaged as an adviser to the high commissioner, and the UNHCR published a manual for staff who were working side by side with outside military forces.[38] Nonetheless, these organizational innovations and formidable military capabilities proved largely beside the point until there was political will to use them to stop the carnage in tandem with a Croatian-Bosnian military offensive in August through September 1995.

Most important, with the urging and financial backing of a host of donors, the UNHCR succored all casualties of Yugoslavia's wars, whatever their juridical status or physical location—a sharp departure from its traditional mandate and previous reluctance to pursue this task with the energy and enthusiasm required. As is demonstrated by the data presented in table 6.1, "populations of concern" to the refugee agency included all the casualties of Yugoslavia's wars, 85 percent of whom fell outside the mandate of the refugee agency. The UNHCR helped everyone who needed help.

From the beginning, the UNHCR has expanded its protection and assistance activities. After its inception as a temporary institution with a restricted scope for refu-

TABLE 6.1. Populations of Concern to the Office of the UN High Commissioner for Refugees (UNHCR), 1991–95 (year-end statistics)

| Country | Population | 1991 | 1992 | 1993 | 1994 | 1995 |
|---------|-----------|------|------|------|------|------|
| UNHCR | Refugees | .. | .. | 0 | 0 | 0 |
| Assistance | IDPs | .. | .. | 1,290,000 | 1,282,600 | 1,097,800 |
| | War victims | .. | .. | 1,450,000 | 1,456,700 | 1,442,800 |
| | Total | 0 | 810,000 | 2,740,000 | 2,739,300 | 2,540,600 |
| Croatia | Refugees | .. | .. | 280,000 | 183,600 | 188,600 |
| | IDPs | .. | .. | 344,000 | 307,000 | 198,700 |
| | War victims | .. | .. | 176,000 | 0 | 60,000 |
| | Total | 0 | 648,000 | 800,000 | 490,600 | 447,300 |
| FYROM | Refugees | .. | .. | 15,000 | 14,900 | 9,000 |
| | IDPs | .. | .. | 0 | 0 | 0 |
| | War victims | .. | .. | 12,000 | 0 | 0 |
| | Total | 0 | 32,000 | 27,000 | 14,900 | 9,000 |
| Yugoslav FR | Refugees | .. | .. | 479,100 | 195,500 | 650,000 |
| | IDPs | .. | .. | 0 | 0 | 700 |
| | War victims | .. | .. | 150,000 | 0 | 0 |
| | Total | 500 | 516,500 | 629,100 | 195,500 | 650,700 |
| Slovenia | Refugees | .. | .. | 45,000 | 29,200 | 22,300 |
| | IDPs | .. | .. | 0 | 0 | 0 |
| | War victims | .. | .. | 0 | 0 | 0 |
| | Total | 0 | 47,000 | 45,000 | 29,200 | 22,300 |
| Total | Refugees | .. | .. | 819,100 | 423,200 | 869,900 |
| | IDPs | .. | .. | 1,634,000 | 1,589,600 | 1,297,200 |
| | Warvictims | .. | .. | 1,788,000 | 1,456,700 | 1,502,800 |
| | Total | 500 | 2,053,500 | 4,241,100 | 3,469,500 | 3,669,900 |

*Note:* IDPs = internally displaced persons; FYROM = Former Yugoslav Republic of Macedonia; Yugoslav FR = Yugoslav Federal Republic.
*Source:* Compiled from various data issued by the Office of the UN High Commissioner for Refugees.

gees following World War II, it became permanent under the 1951 Convention on the Status of Refugees, and global under the 1967 protocol. A concern for IDPs emerged in the 1990s, though it has not been codified. The organizing principle is protecting and assisting people who require refuge in the broadest sense—those who do not have access to a state's protection and are vulnerable to persecution.

The UNHCR has been struggling to square its mandate, which is confined to refugees, with the stark reality that other persons involuntarily displaced by wars are "refugees in all but name," while still others live in "refugee-like conditions." With civil wars on the increase in the 1990s, IDPs began to outnumber refugees in many crises and eventually worldwide. The UN secretary-general and donors increasingly asked the UNHCR to assume responsibility for assisting and protecting both refugees and IDPs. UN high commissioner for refugees Ogata commissioned a study to spell out a "comprehensive approach to coerced human displacement."[39]

The UNHCR truly acted as the "lead agency" in the former Yugoslavia; in UN jargon, it was in the humanitarian driver's seat. It played a role that a growing number of observers see as vital: a "UN Humanitarian Organization for Casualties of War." With the blessing of donors, the UNHCR moved away from its usual statistical preoccupation with categorizing refugees—as distinct from other civilians in need—and ceased to restrict assistance and protection efforts to those victims who had crossed an international boundary. The UNHCR seized responsibility where the leaders of the former Yugoslavia had failed dismally. This is not to say that the UNHCR's activities were without problems. It is rather the enterprising interpretation of its mission along with competent implementation in difficult circumstances that needs to be emphasized.[40] Accompanied by the lack of international political will, however, helping victims was clearly insufficient.

## HUMANITARIANISM AND SOVEREIGNTY

Observers of and participants in humanitarian endeavors in the former Yugoslavia see these efforts as reweaving a tattered social fabric. They work to reconstitute a society in disrepair whose rescue was as successful as any such effort is ever likely to be. But this approach avoids confronting sovereignty—the principle that upholds the autonomy of populations and their polities. Humanitarian practice points us toward the ambiguity of the principles that regulate the crossing of lines demarcating autonomous societies, cultures, and nations as well as the states that represent and protect them.

In normal times, these sovereign boundary lines are indispensable. In the words of Article 2(7) of the UN Charter, "nothing contained in the present Charter shall authorize the United Nations to intervene in matters which are essentially within the domestic jurisdiction of any state." When the fabric of a community has been shredded, seeking that community's consent for aid is problematic; its weakened condition does not allow it to respond as it might in less trying times.[41]

In discussions about when humanitarian intervention is justified, the fact is often overlooked that even forceful intrusions do not necessarily challenge the principle of autonomy, but rather may seek to bolster what outside soldiers are violating temporarily, for the sake of restoring it. This is because there are temporarily no viable institutions to exercise or express the autonomy that is presumed to be present. Humanitarianism is not exclusively a cosmopolitan effort to unite all humanity at the expense of the autonomy of political communities encapsulated by sovereign states. The humanitarian impulse is triggered precisely in circumstances in which the autonomous continuation of a population under minimal standards of human dignity is jeopardized. The UNHCR's efforts in pre-Dayton Yugoslavia can be usefully viewed as a response to the condition of displacement broadly understood, whereby people had no ground on which to stand, no place in which to exercise their autonomy.

The essential question then becomes not one of respecting it but rather one of understanding the nature of the processes through which outside humanitarians participate in reweaving an unraveled autonomy. Are humanitarians restoring the autonomy of the people whom they rush to rescue or are they participating in a more revolutionary process through which they are establishing a lasting link with the endangered population, contravening the habit of moral separation reflected by sovereignty? A direct examination of this question should help clarify the difficulties in defining the exact role of the humanitarian impulse in contemporary world politics.

The activation of the humanitarian impulse shines a new light on the boundaries that once preserved the integrity of a polity and its dignity as an independent culture. We suddenly recognize the salience of boundaries that in normal times are taken for granted. Populations "over there" are no longer primarily an autonomous strand of the global fabric; they become humans in inhuman distress. Is the goal to restore autonomy along pre-emergency lines or to reweave a cloth so that it will be better able to withstand future crises, something that implies a deeper intrusion into the political lives of the distressed population?

Before considering the justification for each alternative, it would be useful to delineate the relationship between humanitarianism and sovereignty. The original overriding concern of the former—best exemplified by the venerable ICRC and international humanitarian law—was to limit the most destructive and indiscriminate consequences of armed conflicts among sovereign states and a few aspects of civil war.[42] If there were questions regarding the status of the belligerents and their links to populations for whom they claimed to be fighting, their control over such populations and a fixed territory provided a reliable guideline to the domain of their responsibilities.[43] Outsiders would adjust their relations to a particular conflict or complex emergency by recognizing a specific government or authority as reflective of legitimate sovereignty. Today, the humanitarian impulse often responds to situations in which there are no integral polities—no viable unities of government, people, and territory to serve as candidates for sovereignty.

With the agents of outside assistance as the saintly executors of a universal moral sense, the humanitarian impulse collapses the barriers that normally separate Americans and Swedes from Bosnians and Rwandans. The moral barriers between "us" and "them" dissolve as we encounter naked humanity and are exposed to misery that is no longer mediated by social differences and distance. No culture, custom, religion, or ethnicity ever justifies the suffering that befalls individuals in a complex emergency. Individuals just like us, possibly huddling together in families or family-like groups, await assistance from those to whom they have established a direct link of common humanity by virtue of having fallen out of the social and cultural web that had made them closer to one another than they were to us. Now, as humanitarian subjects, they are equally close to all of us.

The recent unleashing of the humanitarian impulse reveals the extent to which sovereignty is no longer sacrosanct.[44] When the suffering of entire populations overwhelms their capacity to fend for themselves, we sometimes bound over the barriers of sovereignty because the victims are no longer strangers. Their threatened existence connects them intimately to us through their ineffable humanity. Differences of culture, nation, ethnicity, and religion are no longer a concern because they will persist only in diminished form, if at all, should their carriers perish. In such times, distressed humanity is "over here," unadorned by social artifice and shorn of its differences and exoticism.

Nonetheless, the shibboleth of sovereignty remains key when decision makers contemplate humanitarian intervention. Sovereignty should be examined dispassionately; we should not delude ourselves into thinking that it is anatural fact.[45] It is not an insurmountable mountain. As a conceptual shorthand, sovereignty summarizes a series of other moral considerations.[46]

Sovereignty promises and protects much that is valuable.[47] It is meant to preserve autonomy, in the same way that we mean to preserve the independence of our communities, workplaces, and family life in domestic politics. In particular, we expect and insist that others, especially the state, respect our separateness and autonomy. In international affairs, sovereignty delineates the units of survival and the boundaries of identity. But it is not only for the protection of people who want to preserve their distinctiveness. Humanity benefits from knowledge—no matter how limited—about the variety of potential modes of human existence and association. But sovereignty also remains frustrating for humanitarians because it divides peoples by protecting their diversity. Sovereignty establishes a moral distance and provides no guide when the autonomy that it so absolutely enshrines collapses or is used to justify intolerable abuse.

Humanitarianism can thus be viewed as a principle that indirectly links human beings, recognizing the fallen barrier of sovereignty to resurrect it. In its reformist, restorative guise, humanitarianism is not an end in itself but a means for reestablishing the sovereign separateness of target populations. Humanitarian responses to the failures of sovereign divisions can be compared with the emergence of social work in domestic polities. The progress of capitalism and modernization inevitably generates victims whose suffering demands mitigation, and social workers help people regain their autonomy.[48]

The comparison of humanitarian efforts to social work is apt because of the contrast with conventional notions of foreign policy practice.[49] Mortally endangered populations lose their diplomatic voice because no one in particular is authorized to speak or act on their behalf.[50] In spite of their broad mandates, various intergovernmental and nongovernmental humanitarian organizations inevitably seek to negotiate with authoritative representatives, but there is no indigenous sovereign to assume responsibility. And the relationship of other sovereigns to the endangered population is not clear. Conventional recognition does little to alleviate the suffering that indigenous aspirants to sovereignty are usually unprepared or unwilling to address. Humanitarianism, then, helps reconstitute a moral community so that it may once again function as an autonomous member of international society, permitting us to return to and reinforce the habits of moral separation that undergird the international society of sovereigns.

Diplomacy rests on a process of competition, be it cooperative or conflictive, through which agents of sovereign populations occasionally gather to conduct business and reaffirm the distinctiveness of the peoples for whom they speak. In the humanitarian context, there is no sovereign to speak for the destitute. Those mortally endangered have lost the capacity to assert their separate identities, and they require outside humanitarian attention because the vessel that carried them has run aground. Foreign ministers and heads of state have seen their role in the emergence of humanitarianism as an effort to simultaneously save the drowning wretches and rebuild their vessel—to relocate them in the ship of state that carried them before the onset of disaster. That the person at the helm may be a war criminal who has offended humanity itself is frequently attributed to the unavoidable realities of world politics. Certainly the more privileged sovereigns may come to the conclusion that social work is not their business, and that there is virtually no national interest to be pursued or protected in complex emergencies.

If that is to be the case, we should recognize and acknowledge the nature of such decisions, being careful not to delude ourselves into thinking that to resist the humanitarian impulse is simply to realize that there are limits to what can be done in the uncertain and insecure international realm. Such decisions also question the limits of our identities and what we think of ourselves.[51]

When humanitarians rush to rescue, sovereignty fades. Moral barriers crumble as the suffering of now-intimate others authorizes assistance and insists upon access to victims. The invocation of boundaries that preserve diversity and pluralism becomes a weak excuse for not acting according to our moral sense, which says that we cannot stand apart from naked humanity. We may choose to reinforce our side of the fence of sovereignty once we get tired and discouraged or when the demand on limited resources for multiple rescues exceeds the supply. But that is a peculiar choice that requires justification. The appeal to sovereignty diminishes in moral weight during complex emergencies because endangered populations cannot assure their own survival, which obviously is the precondition for their continued dignity. This line of argument is further complicated because the benefits of rescue are often difficult to ascertain. One dilemma is a heightened dependence that distorts and displaces indigenous survival mechanisms,[52] which has led one analyst to a new bottom line: "Do no harm."[53]

The humanitarian impulse is a reflection of a universal moral sense that sovereignty does not bar our concern for strangers in distress. The expansion of humanitarian efforts in the post–cold war era indicates that sovereignty is waning, though not necessarily irreversibly. At the same time, those whose powers, prerogatives, and privileges may be threatened by humanitarian action routinely invoke sovereignty as a barrier and point to the supposed weakness of the obligation flowing from the direct connection to distressed humanity.

Humanity, however, is not a category for which we have prepared our political concepts, despite the seeming internationalization of human rights and humanitarian discourse.[54] Hannah Arendt, who drew on her own experience of displacement, discussed "the terror of the idea of humanity" and the existential burden that it placed on fellow humans.[55] Indeed, the history of the stateless and of refugees was a prominent theme in the twentieth century as states jockeyed to adjust the precise distributions of populations for whom they would assume responsibility. Through

Arendt, we can appreciate the challenge displaced populations represent to the decision makers of sovereign states.

One of the great tribulations in the twentieth century was statelessness, which Arendt equated with rightlessness. For her, the exercise of rights that was fundamental to the human condition was not a question of moral philosophy or legal doctrine but a matter of political action. The horror of displacement was the condition of not being engaged in the political construction of one's life. She looked to a politics across state domains as an alternative to the arbitrary decisions of states to include or exclude portions of humanity. And this mode of politics was to be built by and around precisely those people who had no state to call their own.

Rescue in complex emergencies is problematic because it is triggered precisely when the autonomy of a society is in jeopardy. To return to our original metaphor, we seek to bring the drowning person back to a beach whose sands shift continually and which is occupied by deadly armed combatants who hamper relief efforts and often menace victims and aid personnel as well. Such rescue efforts attempt to return the endangered populations to a status quo ante. The central paradox of rescue thus is that it seeks to restore a social order that has failed to protect its members from natural or manmade deprivations. Triggering the humanitarian impulse, social collapse leads to justifications for the rush of aid, relief, and crisis diplomacy. It is then, at best, short-sighted to restore any social order that will be autonomous only to the extent that outsiders will have politically disengaged themselves.

The case of the former Yugoslavia illustrates that while we may want to do the right thing, the right thing to do is not always obvious, although we have often deceived ourselves into embracing a simplistic idea of rescue as an absolute good. This concept implies that one is going to pull drowning strangers from a turbulent sea and restore them to firm ground, whereupon they will be able to continue a dignified life as the same strangers they were before the peril. In spite of the reluctance to utter the "N-word"—nation building—after Vietnam and Somalia, we hope to restore populations to conditions in which they will be able to sustain themselves and remain a self-contained entity "foreign" to us and separated by the legal and moral boundaries of state sovereignty.

What happens when the need for rescue becomes episodic and almost routinized? Interventions closely modeled after Good Samaritan rescue often seem to require repetition—for example, Liberia, the Sudan, and Rwanda. In the past few years, the term "exit strategy," which provides a deadline for disengagement and not a criterion of success, has entered the humanitarian lexicon. However, future rescue efforts almost become assured in such cases, as experiences in Somalia and Haiti suggest. The exit of outsiders is simply not an adequate test for the autonomy of the target, if that is to be our concern. As UN high commissioner for refugees Ogata has stated, time and patience are required because "there is certainly no such thing as a humanitarian surgical strike."[56]

We have not yet thought through what it will mean to move beyond the ineffective and sporadic conscience-salving variety of rescue whose main motivation is the removal of horrific images from our television screens and newspapers.[57] Populations in danger require sustained commitments that are different from the current approach of rescue.

Institutionalizing such a sustained humanitarianism is problematic because it would establish a direct moral link to "foreigners" and a lasting responsibility toward them. Moreover, we could not easily extricate ourselves, contrary to George Kennan's argument with respect to the U.S. role in today's humanitarian interventions. He has proposed that the United States return to the kind of policy promoted by John Quincy Adams, whereby we would help not by actually getting involved but by concentrating on perfecting our own polity and allowing it to serve as an example for others:

> The interventions in which we are now engaged or committed represent serious responsibilities. Any abrupt withdrawal from them would be a violation of these responsibilities. . . . Only when we have succeeded in extracting ourselves from the existing ones with dignity and honor will the question of further interventions present itself to us in the way it did to Mr. Adams.[58]

Kennan implies a responsibility to ourselves and to those whom we seek to help, but the nature of this responsibility is unclear. Removing the official agents of states from the territory of a failed sovereign makes matters appear simpler for those who have the capacity to help. But it does nothing to clarify the inevitable continuation of relations among different populations and their representatives, which relations are neither terminated nor simplified by outside military and diplomatic engagement or disengagement.

To see sovereignty as an unquestioned idea that aims to preserve the good of a plurality of nations, societies, and cultures seeking to survive on their own is to evade responsibilities that attach to already existing relations among societies. At present, we are trapped between two principles: one that asks us to restore sovereignty and one that tells us to embrace the long-term transnational responsibilities that emerge from the pursuit of humanitarianism as an end in itself.

## CONCLUSION

Bridging the normative gap between restorative and revolutionary humanitarianism—between actions that seek to rebuild state sovereignty and those that seek to transcend it—is a central foreign policy challenge. Groping to go beyond rescue—having learned, often painfully, about its limitations—is the priority agenda item for humanitarians, be they scholars or practitioners. We cannot rely on sovereignty to take care of itself, nor are we certain how to control the humanitarian impulse that causes us to rush in to rescue those who can no longer look to a sovereign to assure their survival. Rescue is misleading in that it fails to acknowledge the possibly irreparable disorder that preceded the crisis that motivated the rescue. Moreover, rescue fails to recognize the moral implications of humanitarian connections across borders.

The UNHCR's experience in the former Yugoslavia exemplified its role as an institution located at the interstices of sovereignty. It was designed to help the community of states manage the people who fled beyond the borders of certain members, relocating them in appropriate sovereign jurisdictions. With the emergence of internal displacement as a global problem and its direct, violent politicization in the case of the former Yugoslavia, the UNHCR extended the principle of caring for refugees to encompass all victims. Its legitimacy rested on its charge to assist all those without refuge, whatever their physical location or juridical status. However limited its discretion as an agent of member states, the UNHCR and the humanitarian community that it led sought to rescue endangered populations where neither indigenous nor outside political authorities took their responsibilities to these populations seriously.

Although the UNHCR extended itself admirably as rescue coordinator in the former Yugoslavia, it was not in a position to challenge the political problems that caused the suffering in the first place and, in fact, allowed it to continue.[59] The management of the conflict almost exclusively through the politics of rescue also served to delay and perhaps eclipse consideration of the mutual obligations of the rescuers and the rescued beyond the immediacy of the emergency phase. The final outcome of the Dayton process is far from clear as of this writing, but the international community, with the United States at the helm, seems intent on restoring minimally sustainable sovereign boundaries as a prelude to an eventual disengagement of outside military forces.[60]

The peoples of the former Yugoslavia were rescued under the restorative principle of humanitarianism. We should realize the limits of humanitarianism inherent in the politics of rescue; otherwise, we can do additional injustice by not considering the political relationships that accompany the humanitarian impulse. Thus, it is not so much the separation of humanitarianism and politics that presents a challenge for the future as it is the conscious analysis and management of the tensions between them. From a global perspective, dilemmas attending the scarcity of resources and the burgeoning demands for rescue can be compared with triage in medical emergencies.[61] Decisions regarding who gets first attention and scarce medical resources are based on a stock of medical knowledge and a corpus of medical ethics supported by well-worn practice. In the rapidly changing field of politically conscious humanitarian engagement, however, we have only begun to digest the profound implications of "humanitarian war"[62] and the inherent limits of multilateral military efforts.[63] There is no return to the apparent clarity and simplicity of the decades when cold war politics persuaded us too easily that who was worth rescuing and who was not depended upon ideological or geopolitical affiliations.

We can continue to assume the appropriateness and applicability of an apolitical and automatic response to earthquakes or other natural disasters. Although these also will have political implications, they will be relatively minor in comparison with the straightforward charge to alleviate suffering. Complex humanitarian emergencies, however, are different. They often overwhelm in not just short-term but also long-term local coping capacities, as well as the coping capacities of the international humanitarian system. It is necessary to contemplate the need, rationale, and consequences of lending helping hands in such circumstances. Developments that bring about deterioration in the human condition, cause international outrage, and catalyze responses are also part of the social fabric that outside assistance is supposed to mend. Humanitarians must proceed into this maelstrom with care, reflecting before responding rather than acting impulsively. They must recognize that they are not simply mending a rent fabric but also participating in the process through which it is being repaired.

The rescue model of intervention implies discrete acts of assistance that seek to restore a person or a group of persons to a position of autonomy. The person in need is a stranger, a fellow human with whom we share little besides our common humanity. When we help, we also enlarge and dignify ourselves. Our humanity becomes more expansive and encompassing. The relationship between the rescuer and the rescued is based on a simple occurrence. Nothing significant changes in the relations between the strangers—except perhaps a warm afterglow of common affection—because isolated acts of kindness are not integrated into an ongoing relationship.

But this image misrepresents the mutual involvement of the agents of the international humanitarian system and the peoples of the former Yugoslavia. Thus, rescue provides no guidance or justification for the politics that it is supposed to guide. This was clear from 1991 to 1995, and it also was evident from the implementation of the Dayton agreements. Bosnia's displaced people—those who were rescued and promised the choice of returning to their homes—continue to complicate what might otherwise have been a symbolically multiethnic state divided along orderly ethnic lines.[64] It is in our vacillating commitment to the promise made that we again see the inadequacy of rescue as a guiding principle. If we are unable or unwilling to provide a clear justification for the political action that we undertake in response to the humanitarian impulse, we should at least be honest and skeptical about our own kindness.

# NOTES

This chapter draws on the authors' study of human displacement in the former Yugoslavia. See Weiss and Pasic, "Dealing with Displacement and Suffering from Yugoslavia's Wars: Conceptual and Operational Issues," in *Masses in Flight*, ed. Roberta Cohen and Francis M. Deng, (Washington, D.C.: Brookings Institution Press, 1998). The authors thank Jarat Chopra for his comments and Béla Hovy for his help in generating statistics.

1.  Raimo Vayrenen, "The Age of Humanitarian Emergencies," draft working paper, World Institute for Development Economics Research, Helsinki, June 1996.

2. See Samuel M. Makinda, "Sovereignty and International Security," *Global Governance* 2 (May–August 1996): 149–68; and Thomas G. Weiss, "Military–Civilian Humanitarianism: The 'Age of Innocence' Is Over," *International Peacekeeping* 2 (summer 1995): 157–74.

3. Paul Wapner, "Politics beyond the State: Environmental Activism and World Civic Politics," *World Politics* 47 (April 1995): 311–40; and Kelly Kate Pease and David P. Forsythe, "Human Rights, Humanitarian Intervention, and World Politics," *Human Rights Quarterly* 15 (1993): 290–314.

4. See a special issue, "Rescue—The Paradoxes of Virtue," *Social Research* 62 (spring 1995), especially Michael Walzer, "The Politics of Rescue," 53–66. See also David Rieff, "The Humanitarian Trap," *World Policy Journal* 12 (winter 1994–95): 1–11.

5. See Stephen Krasner, "Sovereignty and Intervention" in *Beyond Westphalia? State Sovereignty and International Intervention*, ed. Gene Lyons and Michael Mastanduno (Baltimore: Johns Hopkins University Press, 1995); and Hedley Bull, ed., *Intervention in World Politics* (New York: Oxford University Press, 1984).

6. Complete bibliographic information and its interpretation are found in Oliver Famsbotham and Tom Woodhouse, *Humanitarian Intervention in Contemporary Conflict* (Cambridge: Polity Press, 1996). See also John Harriss, ed., *The Politics of Humanitarian Intervention* (London: Pinter, 1995); James Mayall, ed., *The New Interventionism: United Nations Experience in Cambodia, Former Yugoslavia, and Somalia* (New York: Cambridge University Press, 1996); and Jan Nederveen Pieterse, ed., *World Orders in the Making: Humanitarian Intervention and Beyond* (London: Macmillan, 1998).

7. See Larry Minear and Thomas G. Weiss, *Mercy under Fire: War and the Global Humanitarian Community* (Boulder, Colo.: Westview Press, 1995); and Minear and Weiss, *Humanitarian Politics* (New York: Foreign Policy Association, 1995).

8. Bill Clinton, "Why Bosnia Matters to America," *Newsweek*, November 13, 1995, 55.

9. Here it is interesting to note the alteration in the French literature from *devoir* (or duty) to *droit* (right). See Bernard Kouchner and Mario Bettati, *Le devoir d'ingérence: Peut-on les laisser mourir?* (Paris: Denoël, 1987), and Mario Bettati, *Le droit d'ingérence: Mutation de l'ordre international* (Paris: Odile Jacob, 1996).

10. U.S. Department of State, *Clinton Administration's Policy on Reforming Multilateral Peace Operations*, Pub. 1061, Bureau of IO Affairs (Washington, D.C.: U.S. Department of State, 1994), which explicates a presidential directive known as PDD-25. See also Chris Seiple, *The U.S. Military/NGO Relationships in Humanitarian Interventions* (Washington, D.C.: U.S. Army War College Peacekeeping Institute, Center for Strategic Leadership, 1996); Com. Richard R. Beardsworth, Com. Richard V. Kikla, Lt. Col. Philip F. Shutler, and Col. Guy C. Swan, "Strengthening Coordination Mechanisms between NGOs and the U.S. Military at the Theater/Country Level During Complex Humanitarian Emergencies," draft, Harvard University National Security Program, Cambridge, Mass., March 1996; and Kenneth Allard, *Somalia Operations: Lessons Learned* (Washington, D.C.: National Defense University Press, 1995). For a critical perspective proposing that preparation for and engagement in peace operations diminish the military's preparedness, see Col. Charles J. Dunlap, "The Last American Warrior: Non-traditional Missions and the Decline of the U.S. Armed Forces," *Fletcher Forum for World Affairs* 18 (winter–spring 1994): 65–82.

11. See R. M. Connaughton, *Military Support and Protection for Humanitarian Assistance: Rwanda, April–December 1994* (Camberly, U.K.: Strategic and Combat Studies Insti-

tute, 1996), 71. See also Hugo Slim, "The Stretcher and the Drum: Civil–Military Relations in Peace Support Operations," paper presented at a conference in Pretoria, South Africa, March 13–14, 1996.

12. See Thomas G. Weiss and Amir Pasic, "Reinventing UNHCR: Enterprising Humanitarians in the Former Yugoslavia, 1991–1995," *Global Governance* 3 (January–March 1997): 41–57.

13. U.S. Mission to the United Nations, "Global Humanitarian Emergencies," New York, February 1996, 24. The periods vary slightly, and there may be some needs and some disbursements not reflected in the data. The accuracy of the broad comparative data and the privileged position of the former Yugoslavia, however, are clear.

14. Quoted by Alison Mitchell, "Clinton's About-Face," *New York Times*, September 24, 1996, A8.

15. Cedric Thornberry, "Saving the War Crimes Tribunal," *Foreign Policy* 104 (fall 1996): 72–85; quote at 75.

16. For an elaboration of the foundational role played by neutrality and impartiality at the core of the identity and mission of the International Committee of the Red Cross and the Red Cross and Red Crescent Movement, see Denise Plattner, "ICRC Neutrality and Neutrality in Humanitarian Assistance," *International Review of the Red Cross* 36 (March–April 1996): 161–79. Clearly, our discussion assumes that humanitarianism cannot be apolitical and that the dilemma at hand revolves around the principled relation between humanitarianism and sovereignty.

17. E.g., see Rabia Ali and Lawrence Lifschultz, eds., *Why Bosnia? Writings on the Balkan War* (Stony Creek, Conn.: Pamphleteer's Press, 1993).

18. For a review of the limits of the post–cold war ambitions of humanitarian intervention, see Stephen John Stedman, "The New Interventionists," *Foreign Affairs* 72 (winter 1993): 1–16. For a normative argument in the opposite direction, see Nigel Rodley, ed., *To Loose the Bonds of Wickedness: International Intervention in Defence of Human Rights* (London: Brassey's, 1992).

19. The most controversial analysis is Rakiya Omaar and Alex de Waal, *Humanitarianism Unbound? Current Dilemmas Facing Multi-Mandate Relief Operations in Political Emergencies*, Discussion Paper 5 (London: African Rights, 1994). There is also a rapidly growing literature on the political dimensions of humanitarian action and peacekeeping; e.g., see Jarat Chopra, "The Space of Peace-Maintenance," *Political Geography* 15 (March–April 1996): 335–57, and Antonio Donini, *The Policies of Mercy: UN Coordination in Afghanistan, Mozambique, and Rwanda*, Occasional Paper 22 (Providence: Thomas J. Watson Jr. Institute for International Studies, 1996).

20. Alain Destexhe, "Foreword," in *Populations in Danger*, ed. François Jean (London: Médécins Sans Frontières, 1995), 13–14.

21. For a recent infusion of sobriety, see Ed Mansfield and Jack Snyder, "Democratization and the Danger of War," *International Security* 20 (summer 1995): 5–38. A less technical version can be found in *Foreign Affairs* 74 (May–June 1995): 79–97. For a general argument regarding the priority of order over justice, see Hedley Bull, *The Anarchical Society* (New York: Columbia University Press, 1977).

22. For collections of essays, see Marianne Heiberg, ed., *Subduing Sovereignty: Sovereignty and the Right to Intervene* (New York: Saint Martin's Press, 1994); Lyons and Mastanduno, *Beyond Westphalia?* and Paul A. Winters, ed., *Interventionism: Current Controversies* (San Diego: Greenhaven Press, 1995).

23. See Gerald B. Helman and Steven R. Ratner, "Saving Failed States," *Foreign Policy* 89 (winter 1992–93): 3–20, and I. William Zartman, ed., *Collapsed States: The Disintegration and Restoration of Legitimate Authority* (Boulder, Colo.: Lynne Rienner, 1995).

24. See Stanley Hoffmann, *Duties beyond Borders: On the Limits and Possibilities of Ethical International Politics* (Syracuse: Syracuse University Press, 1981).

25. For a brief overview of the political obstacles that marred the humanitarian mission in Bosnia, see Mark Prutsalis, "Humanitarian Aid: Too Little, Too Late," in *With No Peace to Keep: United Nations Peacekeeping and the War in the Former Yugoslavia*, ed. Ben Cohen and George Stamkoski (London: Grainpress Ltd., 1995).

26. One analytical effort to understand this phenomenon is Thomas G. Weiss and Cindy Collins, *Humanitarian Challenges and Intervention: World Politics and the Dilemmas of Help* (Boulder, Colo.: Westview, 1996).

27. Susan Woodward, "Redrawing Borders in a Period of Systemic Transition," in *International Organizations and Ethnic Conflict*, ed. Milton Esman and Shibley Telhami (Ithaca, N.Y.: Cornell University Press, 1995), 213.

28. Chester A. Crocker, "All Aid Is Political," *New York Times*, November 21, 1996, A29.

29. See John Prendergast, *Frontline Diplomacy: Humanitarian Aid and Conflict in Africa* (Boulder, Colo.: Lynne Rienner, 1996); and Michael Maren, *The Road to Hell: The Ravaging Effects of Foreign Aid and International Charity* (New York: Free Press, 1997).

30. For discussions of the ICRC's principles and approaches, see David P. Forsythe, *Humanitarian Politics* (Baltimore: Johns Hopkins University Press, 1977), and James A. Joyce, *Red Cross International and the Strategy for Peace* (New York: Oceana, 1959).

31. See the discussion of the use of relief resources to feed soldiers and as bribes for safe passage in Åge Eknes, "The United Nations' Predicament in the Former Yugoslavia," in *The United Nations and Civil Wars*, ed. Thomas G. Weiss (Boulder, Colo.: Lynne Rienner, 1995); in mid-1994, Eknes wrote in this chapter: "The accusation that the United Nations has indirectly legitimized ethnic cleansing and territorial aggression does not bite as much today—not because it is less true but because it has become a fact of life" (p. 124). For a discussion of the possible manipulation of aid agencies by belligerents, see Gayle E. Smith, "Relief Operations and Military Strategy," in *Humanitarianism across Borders: Sustaining Civilians in Times of War*, ed. Thomas G. Weiss and Larry Minear (Boulder, Colo.: Lynne Rienner, 1993).

32. Quoted by Christopher S. Wren, "Resettling Refugees: UN Facing New Burden," *New York Times*, November 24, 1995, A15.

33. See O. van der Wind, *Report Based on the Debriefing on Srebrenica* (Assen: Netherlands Ministry of Defense, 1995).

34. Ernst Tugendhat, "The Moral Dilemma in the Rescue of Refugees," *Social Research* 62 (spring 1995): 127–41.

35. For a discussion of migration as a multifaceted security issue, see Michael S. Teitelbaum and Myron Weiner, eds., *Threatened Peoples, Threatened Borders: World Migration and U.S. Foreign Policy* (New York: Norton, 1995), and Myron Weiner, ed., *International Migration and Security* (Boulder, Colo.: Westview, 1993).

36. For an overview of the issues raised by the secretary-general on internally displaced persons, see Francis M. Deng, *Protecting the Dispossessed: A Challenge for the International Community* (Washington, D.C.: Brookings Institution Press, 1993). See also Roberta Cohen and Jacques Cuénod, *Improving Institutional Arrangements for the Internally Displaced* (Washington, D.C.: Brookings Institution Press, 1995), and Deng, "Dealing with

the Displaced: A Challenge to the International Community," *Global Governance* 1 (winter 1995): 45–58.

37. See Bogdan Denitch, *Ethnic Nationalism: The Tragic Death of Yugoslavia* (Minneapolis: University of Minnesota Press, 1994), 173–85; Norman Cigar, *Genocide in Bosnia: The Policy of "Ethnic Cleansing"* (College Station: Texas A&M University Press, 1995), 22–37; V. P. Gagnon, "Ethnic Nationalism and International Conflict: The Case of Serbia," *International Security* 19 (winter 1994–95): 130–66; Branka Magas, *The Destruction of Yugoslavia: Tracking the Breakup 1980–92* (London: Verso, 1993); Slavko Curuvija and Ivan Torov, "The March to War (1980–1990)," in *Yugoslavia's Ethnic Nightmare: The Inside Story of Europe's Unfolding Ordeal,* ed. Jasminka Udovicki and James Ridgeway (Chicago: Lawrence Hill Books, 1995); Misha Glenny, *The Fall of Yugoslavia: The Third Balkan War* (New York: Penguin, 1992); Susan Woodward, *Balkan Tragedy: Chaos and Dissolution after the Cold War* (Washington, D.C.: Brookings Institution Press, 1995); and Richard H. Ullman, ed., *The World and Yugoslavia's Wars* (New York: Council on Foreign Relations, 1996).

38. See Office of the UN High Commissioner for Refugees, *Handbook for the Military on Humanitarian Operations* (Geneva: Office of the UN High Commissioner for Refugees, 1995).

39. Office of the UN High Commissioner for Refugees, Division of International Protection, *UNHCR's Operational Experience with Internally Displaced Persons* (Geneva: Office of the UN High Commissioner for Refugees, 1994).

40. See Alex Cunliffe and Michael Pugh, "The UNHCR as Lead Agency in the Former Yugoslavia," *Journal of Humanitarian Assistance* (April 1, 1996); http://131.111.106.147/articles/A011.htm.

41. For an explication of the need to have consent and preserve "the autonomy of the 'target'," see Michael Joseph Smith, "Ethics and Intervention," *Ethics & International Affairs* 3 (1989): 1–26.

42. See Geoffrey Best, *Humanity in Warfare* (New York: Columbia University Press, 1980); Sheldon M. Cohen, *Arms and Judgment: Law, Morality, and the Conduct of Warfare in the Twentieth Century* (Boulder, Colo.: Westview, 1989); and Hilaire McCoubrey and Nigel D. White, *International Law and Armed Conflict* (Aldershot, U.K.: Dartmouth, 1992).

43. The classic text is Hersch Lauterpacht, *Recognition in International Law* (Cambridge: Cambridge University Press, 1947). See also James Crawford, *The Creation of States in International Law* (New York: Oxford University Press, 1979).

44. See Jarat Chopra and Thomas G. Weiss, "Sovereignty Is No Longer Sacrosanct," *Ethics & International Affairs* 6 (1992): 95–117.

45. See Thomas Biersteker and Cynthia Weber, eds., *State Sovereignty as Social Construct* (New York: Cambridge University Press, 1996).

46. Indeed, when scholars defend the principle of nonintervention, they elucidate the positive aspect of sovereignty. See, e.g., Michael Walzer, "The Moral Standing of States: A Response to Four Critics," in *International Ethics: A Philosophy and Public Affairs Reader,* ed. Charles Beitz et al. (Princeton, N.J.: Princeton University Press, 1985).

47. See Terry Nardin, *Law, Morality, and the Relations of States* (Princeton, N.J.: Princeton University Press, 1983).

48. See, e.g., June Axinn and Herman Levin, *Social Welfare: A History of the American Response to Need* (New York: Longman, 1992).

49. See Michael Mandelbaum, "Foreign Policy as Social Work," *Foreign Affairs* 75 (January–February 1996): 1–16.

50. For a discussion about living up to the responsibilities of sovereignty with particular reference to IDPs, see Francis M. Deng, "Frontiers of Sovereignty," *Leiden Journal of International Law* 8 (1995): 249–86.

51. For a psychological description of the processes that lead to international human rights advocacy and the concern for those outside one's own domestic polity, see Todd E. Jennings, "The Developmental Dialectic of International Human Rights Advocacy," *Political Psychology* 17 (March 1996): 77–95.

52. See John Prendergast and Colin Scott, "Aid with Integrity: Avoiding the Potential of Humanitarian Aid to Sustain Conflict; A Strategy for USAID/BHR/OFDA in Complex Emergencies," draft manuscript, Center of Concern, Washington, D.C., March 1996.

53. Mary B. Anderson, *Do No Harm: Supporting Local Capacities for Peace through Aid* (Cambridge, Mass.: Collaborative for Development Action, 1996).

54. See David P. Forsythe, *The Internationalization of Human Rights* (Lexington, Mass.: Lexington Books, 1991); Jack Donnelly, *Universal Human Rights* (Ithaca, N.Y.: Cornell University Press, 1989); and Jonathan I. Charney, "Universal International Law," *American Journal of International Law* 87 (October 1993): 529–51.

55. See Hannah Arendt, "Peace or Armistice in the Near East," in *The Jew as Pariah*, ed. Ron Feldman (New York: Grove Press, 1978). See also Jeffrey C. Isaac, "A New Guarantee on Earth," *American Political Science Review* 90 (March 1996): 61–73.

56. Sadako Ogata, "Opening Address," in *Healing the Wounds: Refugees, Reconstruction and Reconciliation* (New York: International Peace Academy, 1996), 5.

57. For discussions of this phenomenon, see Robert I. Rotberg and Thomas G. Weiss, eds., *From Massacres to Genocide: The Media, Public Policy, and Humanitarian Crises* (Washington, D.C.: Brookings Institution Press, 1996); Larry Minear, Colin Scott, and Thomas G. Weiss, *The News Media, Civil War, and Humanitarian Action* (Boulder, Colo.: Lynne Rienner, 1996); Edward Girardet, ed., *Somalia, Rwanda, and Beyond: The Role of the International Media in Wars and Humanitarian Crises*, Crosslines Special Report 1 (Dublin: Crosslines Communications, 1995); Johanna Newman, *Lights, Camera, War* (New York: Saint Martin's Press, 1996); and Nik Gowing, *Real-Time Television Coverage of Armed Conflicts and Diplomatic Crises* (Cambridge, Mass.: Harvard Shorenstein Center, 1994).

58. George Kennan, "On American Principles," *Foreign Affairs* 74 (March–April 1995): 116–26, at 124.

59. See Thomas G. Weiss, "Collective Spinelessness: U.N. Actions in the Former Yugoslavia," in *World and Yugoslavia's Wars*, ed. Ullman, 59–96.

60. The role of the International Criminal Tribunal for the former Yugoslavia as an agent of the international community in the reconciliation process may imply a more lasting commitment to the peoples who were rescued. See Madeleine K. Albright, "Bosnia in Light of the Holocaust: War Crimes Tribunals," *U.S. Department of State Dispatch* 5 (April 18, 1994): 209–12. For a more skeptical view, see Thornberry, "Saving the War Crimes Tribunal."

61. Thomas G. Weiss, "Triage: Humanitarian Interventions in a New Era," *World Policy Journal* 11 (spring 1994): 1–10.

62. See Adam Roberts, "Humanitarian War: Military Intervention and Human Rights," *International Affairs* 69 (1993): 429–49.

63. For a straightforward realist perspective, see John J. Mearsheimer, "The False Promise of International Institutions," *International Security*, winter 1994–95: 5–49.

64. See Open Media Research Institute (OMRI), "*Pursuing Balkan Peace*," OMRI Special Report 1 (Chlumova, Czech Republic: OMRI, 1996).

SEVEN

# Humanitarian Intervention: Which Way Forward?

## Richard Caplan

One of the fundamental weaknesses of the international order highlighted by the crisis in Kosovo is the gap between entitlements to human rights and the availability of mechanisms to ensure respect for these rights. By virtue of customary law and numerous international covenants, individuals enjoy formal protection from genocide, crimes against humanity, and violations of the laws of war, among other guarantees. Yet states may choose to ignore their humanitarian obligations, as several have done in recent years, and though there are a number of enforcement mechanisms at the disposal of the international community, many of these rely for their effectiveness on the consent of the parties involved or, if resort is made to the use of force, on the support of the UN Security Council.

NATO's bombing campaign against the Federal Republic of Yugoslavia in the spring of 1999 represented a bold attempt to overcome this weakness of the international order. When the UN Security Council proved unwilling to take stronger measures in defense of humanitarian principles in Kosovo, the nineteen-member NATO chose to arrogate the responsibility to itself. The absence of a Security Council mandate raised serious questions about the legality of the NATO operation, but NATO's member states saw their actions as possessing in legitimacy what they may have lacked in lawfulness. As French President Jacques Chirac explained when NATO first threatened to use force against Yugoslavia in October 1998, France "considers that any military action must be requested and decided by the Security Council [but] the humanitarian situation constitutes a ground that can justify an exception to a rule, however strong and firm it is."[1]

This approach, though perhaps effective, was and remains a risky proposition. In principle, any state would have been within its rights to come to the defense of Yugoslavia in what was construed by some, including China and Russia, to be an act of NATO aggression against a sovereign state. Of course, the political and military realities were such that countermeasures of this kind were highly unlikely. Indeed, when offered the opportunity to demand an immediate end to the air strikes, on March 26, 1999, twelve out of fifteen Security Council members voted against the Russian-sponsored resolution—an indication, arguably, of some recognition of the necessity of the NATO campaign.[2] But not all unauthorized interventions can be expected to meet with comparably weak international resistance, and the fact that chaos and violence could ensue is one reason why the principle of nonintervention has been so fundamental to international order.

The possibility that the Kosovo action may in fact augur a general attenuation of constraints on intervention has been of great concern to many states. UN secretary-general Kofi Annan expressed this concern in his address before the UN General Assembly in September 1999: "Is there not a danger of such interventions undermining the imperfect, yet resilient, security system created after the Second World War and of setting dangerous precedents for future interventions without a clear criterion to decide who might invoke these precedents, and in what circumstances?"

At the same time, Annan was mindful of the potentially tragic consequences of inaction in the absence of international consensus:

> To those for whom the greatest threat to the future of the international order is the use of force in the absence of a Security Council mandate, one might ask— not in the context of Kosovo but in the context of Rwanda: If, in those dark days and hours leading up to the genocide, a coalition of States had been prepared to act in defense of the Tutsi population, but did not receive prompt Council authorization, should such a coalition have stood aside and allowed the horror to unfold?[3]

The conundrum Annan identified is a very real one, and it is arguably one of the more urgent challenges confronting the United Nations as it enters the twenty-first century. Humanitarian intervention, it is true, is likely to remain the exception rather than the rule. Sovereignty may no longer be sacrosanct, but it still carries enormous currency, and states will always hesitate to intervene when the risks seem too great or, to a lesser degree, the crisis seems too remote. However, in an age when sovereignty is seen increasingly to be not an absolute right but a contract between a state and its people, the pressures on states to intervene in response to the violent repression of minorities are unlikely to abate.

This chapter explores the ways in which states—particularly European ones—are rethinking historic prohibitions against humanitarian intervention in the wake of NATO's actions in Kosovo. It argues that though efforts to weaken these prohibitions may succeed, thereby facilitating future interventions, the tension between legitimacy and effectiveness in the defense of humanitarian principles will remain unresolved unless a broad consensus can be achieved regarding when—and how— states may use force for such purposes.

## HISTORIC PROHIBITIONS AND RECENT TRENDS

For both principled and pragmatic reasons, states have long taken exception to the notion of humanitarian intervention. In the absence of severe constraints on intervention, states would have few formal guarantees of their political independence, with consequences not only for individual states but also for orderly international relations in general. Although in earlier centuries there existed an acknowledged right of humanitarian intervention as part of the just war tradition, abuses of that right in part explain why in the twentieth century the doctrine largely disappeared from state practice and gradually lost ground in treaty law.[4]

Although the UN Charter does not expressly proscribe humanitarian intervention, most jurists would agree that its general prohibitions on the use of force are incompatible with any notion of humanitarian intervention.[5] Article 2(4) states that "all Members shall refrain in their international relations from the threat or use of force against the territorial integrity or political independence of any State, or in any other manner inconsistent with the Purposes of the United Nations."

This position was reaffirmed twenty-five years later with the General Assembly's Declaration on Principles of International Law Concerning Friendly Relations and Cooperation among States. The declaration, a consensual interpretation of the principles of the UN Charter, asserts that "no State or group of States has the right to intervene, directly or indirectly, for any reason whatsoever, in the internal or external affairs of any other State. Consequently, armed intervention and all other forms of interference or attempted threats against the personality of the State or against its political, economic and cultural elements, are in violation of international law."[6]

The UN Charter permits the use of force in only two circumstances: in self-defense (individual or collective) in the event of armed attack against a member state; and as authorized by the Security Council in response to a threat to the peace, a breach of the peace, or an act of aggression.[7] Neither of these circumstances can be said to have existed during the Kosovo crisis. Kosovo is not an independent state entitled to exercise the right of self-defense; nor were any of the neighboring states or NATO member states subject to armed attack by Yugoslavia as part of the latter's operations against the Kosovar Albanians. And though the Security Council had judged the humanitarian crisis in Kosovo to be a threat to peace and security in the region and had found Yugoslavia to be largely responsible for the deterioration of the humanitarian situation, it did not authorize the use of force in response. The council only agreed to consider further action and additional measures as might be necessary to restore peace in the region.[8]

However, international law is not confined to treaties, and some jurists maintain that the right of humanitarian intervention has a basis in customary law.[9] Yet there have actually been very few cases since the UN Charter was signed in 1945 in which states have invoked humanitarian considerations in defense of an intervention. Although the respective interventions of India, Vietnam, and Tanzania in East Pakistan (1971), Cambodia (1978), and Uganda (1979) had the effect of putting an end to massive human rights violations in each case, the intervening states ultimately relied on arguments of self-defense to justify their actions, even if reference was also made to the humanitarian situation. These states were understandably reluctant to advance a doctrine of humanitarian intervention for which they knew there would be little international support. As it was, India's and Vietnam's actions were widely criticized.

In contrast, the Economic Community of West African States (ECOWAS) attracted broad support for its intervention in Liberia in 1990, the stated aim of which was in part to bring a halt to the massive violations of human rights occurring in the context of the civil war there. However, the intervention was endorsed by the Security Council only ex post facto; Resolution 788, which welcomed the efforts of ECOWAS to restore peace in Liberia, was adopted in November 1992. Similarly, France, the United Kingdom, and the United States enjoyed considerable support for their establishment of a "safe haven" in northern Iraq in 1991—also without a Security Council mandate—in an effort to protect the indigenous Kurdish population from violent attacks by Saddam Hussein.

These more recent examples suggest that we may well be witnessing the emergence of a right of humanitarian intervention, but it seems too soon to say that such a norm has been established. States may choose to support a practice for all manner of reasons—including convenience and political considerations. But unless that support is accompanied by an expression of belief on the part of states that the practice reflects a new rule of law—in this case, a right of humanitarian intervention—it cannot be said that a customary legal basis for such a right exists. In any event, the objections of China, India, and Russia, among others, to NATO's actions in Kosovo can hardly be said to offer evidence of the general recognition of such a norm.

What is important, however, is to see these more recent operations not just in relation to other instances of intervention but also in relation to broader developments since the end of the cold war. These three interventions—in Liberia, Iraq, and Kosovo—are part of a larger trend that has seen states give increased weight to human rights and humanitarian norms as matters of international concern—to the extent that the Security Council may now choose to characterize these concerns as threats to international peace liable to enforcement measures under Chapter VII of the UN Charter. Indeed, in the space of fewer than five years from 1992, the Security Council authorized interventions of a humanitarian nature in Somalia, Bosnia, Rwanda, Haiti, and Albania. Because many of these interventions were launched only after a crisis had assumed catastrophic proportions and were therefore judged by critics to be "too little, too late," states have come under considerable pressure to take more effective measures in advance of humanitarian disasters—as NATO arguably did in the case of Kosovo.[10]

Not only by virtue of enforcement action have humanitarian norms achieved increased prominence in the post–cold war period. The international community has also taken steps to give greater substance to humanitarian law. The establishment of two ad hoc war crimes tribunals (for Yugoslavia and Rwanda) and the initialing of a treaty in 1998 to set up a permanent international criminal court with jurisdiction over war crimes, genocide, and crimes against humanity (the Rome Statute) represent significant progress in this regard. Indeed, the day the NATO campaign began, March 24, 1999, was the same day the Appellate Committee of the United Kingdom's House of Lords ruled that the principle of sovereign immunity offered former Chilean head of state Augusto Pinochet no protection against prosecution for human rights crimes. Alongside these developments and the broad shift in international concerns they represent, NATO's enforcement actions in Kosovo, although unauthorized, begin to look somewhat less irregular. Still, the challenge remains no less urgent for states to find a way to reconcile effectiveness in defense of human rights and humanitarian law with legitimacy of process.

## A NEW FRAMEWORK FOR INTERVENTION

States have responded to the challenge in two related ways. The first has been to reinterpret existing law so as to demonstrate that their actions, as participants in the NATO campaign, were in fact consistent with international law governing the use of force. These same states have been divided, however, as to whether Kosovo represents an exceptional case or a template for future interventions. The second response has been to seek to build a political consensus in the international community in support of general principles of humanitarian intervention that can facilitate such interventions in the future. I examine each in turn.

### Rethinking the Law

Efforts to reinterpret international law in relation to NATO's intervention began even before NATO commenced its operations against Yugoslavia. In an October 1998 memorandum circulated to all its NATO allies, the British Foreign and Commonwealth Office spelled out the United Kingdom's view on the international legal basis for the possible use of force by NATO in Kosovo. UN Security Council authorization, the memo stated, would give a "clear legal base" but force could also be justified on the grounds of "overwhelming humanitarian necessity without a UNSCR [Security Council Resolution]," provided that the following three conditions were satisfied:

(a) that there is convincing evidence, generally accepted by the international community as a whole, of extreme humanitarian distress on a large scale, requiring immediate and urgent relief; (b) that it is objectively clear that there is no practicable alternative to the use of force if lives are to be saved; and (c) that the proposed use of force is necessary and proportionate to the aim (the relief of humanitarian need) and is strictly limited in time and scope to this aim—i.e., it is the minimum necessary to achieve that end. It would also be necessary at the appropriate stage to assess the targets against this criterion.[11]

Elsewhere, British and other state officials have suggested that such actions would be justified only insofar as they also supported purposes laid down by the UN Security Council, in this case Resolutions 1160, 1199, and 1203.[12]

It was not the first time that the United Kingdom had invoked humanitarian urgency in support of armed intervention. In December 1992, A. I. Aust, the British Foreign and Commonwealth Office's legal counselor, cited the "severe human rights and humanitarian situation" with respect to the Kurds in northern Iraq to justify the allied intervention there without a UN mandate. Aust referred to the "customary international law principle of humanitarian intervention" and went on to explain that "there is no agreement in the sense of rules which have been laid down by any international body, but the practice of states does show over a long period that it is generally accepted that in extreme circumstances a state can intervene in another state for humanitarian reasons."[13]

Only four years earlier, however, a Foreign and Commonwealth Office position paper had concluded that "the best case that can be made in support of humanitarian intervention is that it cannot be said to be unambiguously illegal." This document acknowledged that "the overwhelming majority of contemporary legal opinion comes down against the existence of a right of humanitarian intervention."[14] Indeed, the government's own parliamentary undersecretary of state for foreign and Commonwealth affairs, Baroness Symons of Vernham Dean, responding to questions in the House of Lords in November 1998, stated that "there is no general doctrine of humanitarian necessity in international law."[15]

The United Kingdom was not alone in arguing from humanitarian necessity in relation to Kosovo. France, Germany, the Netherlands, Spain, and the United States justified the NATO campaign on similar grounds. Belgium offered an additional legal argument in support of NATO's actions. In response to charges brought against it (and nine other NATO member states) by Yugoslavia in the International Court of Justice, Belgium asserted that the armed intervention was in fact compatible with Article 2(4) of the UN Charter proscribing the use of force in international relations. Belgium claimed that NATO's actions were not directed against the "territorial integrity or political independence" of Yugoslavia but in support of Security Council resolutions that explicitly affirmed the sovereignty and territorial integrity of Yugoslavia.[16] Hence NATO did not employ force "in [a] manner inconsistent with the Purposes of the United Nations," as Article 2(4) proscribes.[17] However, this restrictive interpretation of Article 2(4) is not supported by the *travaux préparatoires* associated with the drafting of the UN Charter; nor does it reflect the views of the vast majority of legal scholars on the subject.

Where states differed more significantly was in their view of the general as opposed to the specific legality of NATO's actions. What made it possible for Germany, among others, to justify the campaign was its view that no conclusion with respect to a general rule of humanitarian intervention could be drawn from these actions. As German foreign minister Klaus Kinkel announced in the Bundestag in October 1998: "The decision of NATO must not become a precedent. As far as the Security Council monopoly on force is concerned, we must avoid getting on a slippery slope."[18] Germany could accept the need to depart from existing norms of international law because a compelling and urgent humanitarian crisis demanded such action. But it did not want the exception to result in the establishment of a new norm.

There were several risks: that such a policy would undermine the authority of the Security Council; that it would lend itself to abuse; that it would be applied unevenly—by the powerful against the weak—which, in turn, would encourage the weak to become powerful; and that, quite simply, it would compromise a central pillar of the international order.

These concerns found concrete expression in the deliberations surrounding NATO's adoption of a new "strategic concept," which took place at NATO's fiftieth anniversary summit in Washington one month after the war over Kosovo had begun. At the summit, France is reported to have resisted U.S. efforts to assert that NATO was entitled to circumvent the Security Council when a veto threatened to inhibit the scope for NATO maneuvering.[19] A proposal of this kind had already been put forward by U.S. senator William Roth, in his capacity as president of the NATO Parliamentary Assembly (then the North Atlantic Assembly), and was adopted by the assembly in November 1998:

> NATO must preserve its freedom to act: The Allies must always seek to act in unison, preferably with a mandate from the United Nations (UN) or the Organization for Security and Cooperation in Europe (OSCE), the framework for collective security in Europe. Even though all NATO member states undoubtedly would prefer to act with such a mandate, they must not limit themselves to acting only when such a mandate can be agreed.[20]

France now insisted on the insertion of language in the strategic concept that would make clear that NATO's actions remained rooted in the alliance's original treaty, which enshrines the authority of the Security Council. The strategic concept thus reaffirms the primary responsibility of the Security Council for the maintenance of international peace and security and makes no attempt to institutionalize breaches of the UN Charter—but neither does it place any strictures on the exercise of that option.[21]

## Building a New Consensus

The choice, however, is not necessarily between accepting the need to sidestep the UN Security Council on an ad hoc basis and institutionalizing the option in a formal way. A complementary approach would be to establish a political consensus among states regarding when they may use force—and how—in support of humanitarian objectives. As part of such a consensus, states might agree to the nature of crimes that could trigger international action, perhaps using the Rome Statute of the International Criminal Court as a basis. Other aspects of a consensus would bear on the procedural requirements for an intervention, including pacific remedies that would first have to be exhausted, the role the United Nations should play, and the limitations that would apply to any use of force.[22]

To the proponents of such an approach, a consensus on intervention would contribute to the maintenance of orderly international relations in one important respect. If states are likely to find it necessary to intervene on humanitarian grounds in the future, even if only rarely, broad agreement on the relevant criteria would help to ensure that such interventions are governed by shared or at least predictable norms. A consensus along these lines, it is argued, would not eliminate the possibility that states would exploit an option to intervene, but it might help to limit the scope for abuse. Critics of such an approach maintain, to the contrary, that general criteria for intervention would serve less to restrain abuse than to provide a pretext for it, as has been the case before with the right of self-defense.[23]

Over the years, there have been numerous attempts by legal scholars and political scientists to devise various factual and procedural criteria for legitimate humanitarian intervention.[24] In the absence of major-power support, however, these efforts have had no palpable impact on international policy. It was therefore significant that British prime minister Tony Blair, in a speech before the Economic Club of Chicago one month after the Kosovo campaign began, called for the adoption of "new rules" governing decisions about when and whether to intervene in other nations' conflicts. "Non-interference has long been considered an important principle of international order," Blair acknowledged. "But the principle of non-interference must be qualified in important respects."[25] He went on to identify five general considerations that states need to bear in mind before embarking on an intervention:

> First, are we sure of our case? War is an imperfect instrument for righting humanitarian distress, but armed force is sometimes the only means of dealing with dictators. Second, have we exhausted all diplomatic options? We should always give peace every chance, as we have in the case of Kosovo. Third, on the basis of a practical assessment of the situation, are there military operations we can sensibly and prudently undertake? Fourth, are we prepared for the long term? In the past we talked too much of exit strategies. But having made a commitment we cannot simply walk away once the fight is over; better to stay with moderate numbers of troops than return for repeat performances with large numbers. And finally, do we have national interests involved? The mass expulsion of ethnic Albanians from Kosovo demanded the notice of the rest of the world. But it does make a difference that this is taking place in such a combustible part of Europe.[26]

Although Blair seemed as much, if not more, concerned with limiting demands for future interventions and with the practicality of such actions, it is clear, especially from subsequent remarks, that he also had in mind to establish an agreed-on framework for intervention that would help to ensure its legitimacy. In a speech at Guildhall, London, in November 1999, he announced his government's intention to put forward detailed proposals for "agreed principles on when we should use force, limited in scope, and proportionate in scale to the humanitarian objective of preventing major loss of civilian life."[27] The United Kingdom has since begun exploratory discussions with its partner states in the hope of gaining agreement among the five permanent members of the Security Council as well as the Group of Seventy-Seven in the General Assembly for some statement of policy guidelines.

A new rule of law would arguably be preferable to a political consensus, but even a highly circumscribed right of humanitarian intervention would be unlikely to gain widespread support among states.[28] Agreement on international legislation is always more difficult to achieve than the adoption of political principles. Moreover, in view of its prohibitions on the use of force, the UN Charter would almost certainly need to be amended to accommodate such legislation. Article 103 of the charter requires that "in the event of a conflict between the obligations of Members of the United Nations under the present Charter and their obligations under any other international agreement, their obligations under the present Charter shall prevail." In any case, a political consensus does not preclude the possibility of legal reform at a later stage and may in fact make such reform easier to achieve.

Blair admits that any "new rules will only work if we have reformed international institutions with which to apply them," yet there is little evidence that the British government, or any other major power, is contemplating fundamental UN reform in response to the need to strengthen the organization's capacity to cope more effectively with humanitarian catastrophes.[29] Greater UN control over military operations, for instance, might help to ensure that the prosecution of an intervention is consistent with agreed-on aims and with the laws of war (e.g., as regards the selection of targets—a contentious issue in the Kosovo campaign). Moreover, it would perhaps mitigate concerns, especially among developing countries, that the intervening states will exercise power in their own interests. But the United States in particular is unwilling to place its forces under foreign command,[30] and the problems arising from the NATO–United Nations "dual-key" arrangements in Bosnia have soured many states on the idea of UN control.[31] A UN voluntary force would circumvent these problems, but it would never have the firepower at its disposal to be able to carry out an intervention of the magnitude of NATO's in Yugoslavia.[32]

The area in most urgent need of reform from the standpoint of UN effectiveness is the veto power wielded by the five permanent members of the Security Council. Here, too, various proposals have been advanced over the years for diluting or eliminating the veto, and in 1993 the UN General Assembly even established an open-ended working group to consider Security Council reform.[33] But many of the same states claiming to be interested in finding a way around Security Council deadlock—including France, the United Kingdom, and the United States—are opposed to changes that would restrict their use of the veto. Although there is always scope for enhanced cooperation among the five permanent council members, barring major institutional reform, we are likely to see further deadlock in the council over the use of force in response to humanitarian emergencies.

## COLLATERAL EFFECTS

It is too early to judge what effect the trends discussed above are likely to have on state practice in the long run. In the short term, however, there can be no doubt that NATO's actions in Kosovo, together with other recent developments, are already having broad ramifications, especially in the area of national strategic policy.

The Russian assault on Chechnya has perhaps been one of the first instances of NATO's wider impact. It may seem paradoxical to suggest that Russia's brutal attacks against the renegade province were inspired by the NATO example; it was, after all, Belgrade's own campaign of violence against a civilian population that prompted NATO to unleash its arsenal on Yugoslavia. But Russia, a nuclear power, has been less worried in this case about NATO's humanitarian instincts than it has been interested in NATO's military tactics. Moscow's reliance on air power, echoing NATO's, has enabled it to minimize Russian losses—which three years earlier, when Moscow last tried to subdue Chechnya, were so heavy as to force Russia to abandon its campaign.[34]

Chinese strategists also are drawing lessons from the Kosovo experience. Hardliners in the military have invoked the United States–led "aggression"—along with NATO's eastward expansion, closer defense ties between the United States and some of China's neighbors, and Washington's accusations of Chinese espionage—as evidence of a renewed push by the United States for "hegemonic domination." Partly as a consequence, China and Russia have forged closer ties with one another than at any time since the Sino-Soviet split in the early 1960s.[35] There are also concerns that Kosovo has only confirmed the importance of nuclear weapons to India and Pakistan—newly declared nuclear powers that may now see their nuclear status as insurance against international intervention in their dispute over Kashmir.[36]

NATO's intervention has perhaps had an even greater strategic impact on Western Europe. NATO's actions in Kosovo drew attention to the enormous disparity that exists between American and combined European military capabilities. Comparative technological weaknesses—70 percent of the war planes and nearly 90 percent of the ordnance used against Yugoslav targets were American—illustrate Europe's "excessive" reliance on U.S. leadership, as some European leaders view the matter.[37] As a result, the European Union, at its December 1999 Helsinki summit, took decisive steps toward the establishment of an autonomous European defense force—numbering up to 60,000 soldiers—that could be deployed quickly to carry out humanitarian roles, such as peacekeeping in Bosnia and Kosovo.[38] Not only is it hoped that a force of this kind will allow the Europeans to act independently of the United States in limited areas, but it is also expected that it will spur reform that will eventually lead to greater European defense cooperation, especially with respect to procurement policies. It remains to be seen, however, whether there is actually sufficient political will to accept the increased military spending, force restructuring, and industrial reorganization required to realize European ambitions.

Finally, NATO's actions in Kosovo have also provided a major impetus for the regeneration of NATO itself. The Kosovo campaign—NATO's second "out of area" operation (after Bosnia)—paved the way for the enlargement of NATO's geographic scope and for the formal expansion of its mandate as reflected in the new strategic concept adopted at the fiftieth-anniversary summit. NATO—no longer committed solely to the defense of its members—now stands ready "to contribute to effective conflict prevention and to engage actively in crisis management, including crisis response operations," in the Euro-Atlantic area.[39]

Although this broader mandate arguably enhances the prospect of more NATO interventions in the future, in fact it is difficult to imagine NATO's nineteen-plus members agreeing easily to such actions. NATO's campaign against Yugoslavia was, and is likely to remain, a singular event. To the extent that states may feel compelled to use force in defense of human rights and humanitarian norms, these are likely to be interventions by ad hoc coalitions of states—that is, coalitions of the willing.

## CONCLUSION

As early as 1991, before the debacles of Bosnia and Rwanda, then–UN secretary-general Javier Pérez de Cuéllar identified the challenge that the international community faced as a result of the increased weight being given to human rights and humanitarian norms as matters of international concern:

> It is now increasingly felt that the principle of non-interference within the essential domestic jurisdiction of states cannot be regarded as a protective barrier behind which human rights can be massively or systematically violated with impunity. The fact that in diverse situations the United Nations has not been able to prevent atrocities cannot be accepted as an argument, legal or moral, against the necessary corrective action, especially when peace is also threatened.[40]

NATO's actions in Kosovo represented one form of "corrective action" in response to this challenge—but is it the way forward? Should states—singly or collectively—intervene to prevent or put an end to a humanitarian crisis when the UN Security Council is unable to do so? The genie, it seems fair to say, is already out of the bottle. We are witnessing the emergence of a customary law of humanitarian intervention. And we should welcome this evolution of norms to the extent that it bespeaks genuine humanitarian concern.

Of course, such concern may not always or entirely motivate intervening states, despite their claims, which is why it is worth persevering in current efforts to build a consensus in support of a pragmatic set of principles and conditions—narrowly defined—that would govern such actions. For in the absence of agreed-upon criteria, the risk is even greater that other states and regional organizations, or even NATO for that matter, will invoke a right to use force for similar purposes in a manner that does not elicit the relatively broad support that Operation Allied Force enjoyed. Sensitive to this problem, the NATO Parliamentary Assembly, in its plenary resolution of November 15, 1999, concluded that "humanitarian intervention cannot be left to the discretion of the intervening state or group of states and must be regulated by clear and universally accepted rules." It thus urged its member states "to work together and with Partner countries to develop a clear set of international rules to allow for humanitarian intervention in case of massive human rights violations or an impending humanitarian catastrophe and to commend them for approval by the United Nations."[41]

At present, resolution of the tension between legitimacy and effectiveness in defense of human rights continues to elude the international community. It can be hoped that in time common standards may be established on which basis the necessity, or not, of international enforcement of humanitarian norms can be agreed on. Without such a consensus, order and justice will endure an uneasy coexistence.

## NOTES

1. Press conference at Palazzo Vechio, Florence, October 6, 1998, cited in Catherine Guicherd, "International Law and the War in Kosovo," *Survival* 41 (summer 1999): 28.
2. Some states seem also to have been concerned that adoption of the resolution would have encouraged Yugoslavia in its repressive action, especially because the resolution made no mention of Yugoslavia's failure to comply with earlier UN Security Council demands. See Niko Krisch, "Unilateral Enforcement of the Collective Will: Kosovo, Iraq and the Security Council," *Max Planck Yearbook of United Nations Law 3* (The Hague: Kluwer Law International, 1999), 84–85.
3. Text of the address of UN secretary-general Kofi Annan to the 54th General Assembly, UN Press Release SG/SM/7136, September 20, 1999.
4. *Humanitarian Intervention: Legal and Political Aspects* (Copenhagen: Danish Institute of International Affairs, 1999), 11–12. Many of the minority rights "regimes" established in Europe from the eighteenth to the early twentieth century contained provisions for great-power intervention that were prone to abuse. See C. A. Macartney, *National States and National Minorities* (London: Oxford University Press, 1934).
5. See the discussion of Article 2(4) in Bruno Simma, ed., *The Charter of the United Nations: A Commentary* (Oxford: Oxford University Press, 1994), 106–28.
6. UN General Assembly Resolution 2625 (XXV), October 24, 1970.
7. Article 51 and Chapter VII of the UN Charter, respectively.
8. UN Security Council Resolutions 1160 (March 31, 1998), 1199 (September 23, 1998), and 1203 (October 24, 1998).
9. Christopher Greenwood, professor of international law at the London School of Economics and Political Science, is one of the principal exponents of this view. See his "Yes, But Is the War Legal?" *Observer*, March 26, 1999.
10. In his testimony before Parliament on April 14, 1999, British foreign secretary Robin Cook explained: "The [Yugoslav] spring offensive was planned; we knew it was coming; we knew it would be accompanied by ethnic cleansing and I am quite sure, if I were here in front of this Committee and we were doing nothing, [you] would be the first to criticize us." See House of Commons, Foreign Affairs Committee, Session 1998–99, *Kosovo: Interim Report*, HC 188, para. 111.
11. The memorandum is reproduced in Adam Roberts, "NATO's 'Humanitarian War' over Kosovo," *Survival* 41 (autumn 1999): 106. See also the Foreign and Commonwealth Office memorandum "Kosovo: Legal Authority for Military Action" (January 22, 1999), reproduced in *Kosovo: Interim Report*, 1.
12. See, e.g., the statement of George Robertson, the British defense secretary, in the House of Commons on March 25, 1999 (*Parliamentary Debates*, House of Commons, March 25, 1999, cols. 616–17).

13. See the testimony of Aust to the Foreign Affairs Committee on December 2, 1992 (*Parliamentary Papers*, 1992–93, House of Commons, HC Paper 235–iii, p. 85).

14. Foreign and Commonwealth Office, "Is Intervention Ever Justified?" (Foreign Policy Document 148), para. II.22, reproduced in *British Year Book of International Law* 57 (1986), 619.

15. *Parliamentary Debates*, House of Lords, November 16, 1998 (written answers), col. 140.

16. Legality of Use of Force (*Yugoslavia v. Belgium*), ICJ Doc. CR/99/15, p. 16.

17. A similar approach is reflected in the NATO Parliamentary Assembly's plenary resolution of November 15, 1999, which urges member governments to strive "to legitimize a new interpretation of article 2 para. 4 of the UN Charter according to which humanitarian intervention no longer be considered as 'inconsistent with the purposes of the United Nations,' but rather as a contribution to the realization of these purposes." *Plenary Resolution: NATO and Humanitarian Intervention*, adopted by the NATO Parliamentary Assembly, November 15, 1999, para. 16(f); www.naa.be/publications/resolutions/99as-res319-e.html.

18. Cited by Bruno Simma in "NATO, the UN and the Use of Force: Legal Aspects," *European Journal of International Law* 10 (1999): 13.

19. "La bataille de Jacques Chirac," *Le Figaro*, April 26, 1999.

20. North Atlantic Assembly, "NATO in the 21st Century," October 2, 1998, summary recommendations; www.naa.be/publications/special/ar5gen-e.html.

21. "The Alliance's Strategic Concept Approved by the Heads of State and Government Participating in the Meeting of the North Atlantic Council in Washington, D.C., on 23rd and 24th April 1999," Press Release NAC-S(99)65, April 24, 1999, para. 15.

22. For a discussion of procedural and factual requirements that might serve as the basis for a humanitarian intervention regime in the light of NATO's actions over Kosovo, see Jonathan I. Charney, "Anticipatory Humanitarian Intervention in Kosovo," *American Journal of International Law* 93 (October 1999): 834–41.

23. Sean D. Murphy, *Humanitarian Intervention: The United Nations in an Evolving World Order* (Philadelphia: University of Pennsylvania Press, 1996), 382–87. Noteworthy in this regard are proposals that have been made recently within the NATO Parliamentary Assembly to extend the right of self-defense to embrace the "defense of common interests and values, including when the latter are threatened by humanitarian catastrophes, crimes against humanity, and war crimes." See North Atlantic Assembly, Resolution 283, *Recasting Euro-Atlantic Security: Towards the Washington Summit*, November 1998, para. 15(e).

24. Most notable among these efforts were those of the International Law Association, which between 1970 and 1976 explored the possibility of drafting a protocol of procedure for humanitarian intervention that included criteria for legitimate intervention. The initiative was abandoned when it became apparent that there was little chance of achieving consensus among the members. See International Law Association, *Report of the Fifty-fifth Conference* 1972 (London: International Law Association, 1974), 608–24; *Report of the Fifty-sixth Conference* 1974 (London: International Law Association, 1976), 217–22; and *Report of the Fifty-seventh Conference* 1976 (London: International Law Association, 1978), 519–23.

25. Transcript of speech by Tony Blair to the Economic Club of Chicago, Hilton Hotel, Chicago, April 22, 1999; available at the British Foreign and Commonwealth Office's website, www.fco.gov.uk/news/speechtext.asp?2316.

26. Blair, speech to the Economic Club of Chicago, April 22, 1999.

27. Transcript of speech by Tony Blair at the Lord Mayor's Banquet, Guildhall, London, November 22, 1999; available at the British Foreign and Commonwealth Office's website, www.fco.gov.uk/news/speechtext.asp?3026.

28. For the view that it is better to accommodate the occasional infraction than to change the law with respect to humanitarian intervention, see Thomas M. Franck, "Break It, Don't Fake It," *Foreign Affairs* 78 (July–August 1999): 116–18.

29. Blair, speech to the Economic Club of Chicago, April 22, 1999.

30. "U.S. Presidential Decision Directive 25" (PDD-25), signed on May 3, 1994, allows for the operational control of U.S. forces by a non-American only under exceptional circumstances.

31. For a critique of the dual-key arrangements, see Rosemary Righter, "The UN & NATO: A Marriage Made in Hell," in *With No Peace to Keep: United Nations Peacekeeping and the War in the Former Yugoslavia*, ed. Ben Cohen and George Stamkoski (London: Grainpress, 1994), 21–28.

32. Brian Urquhart, "For a UN Volunteer Military Force," *New York Review of Books*, June 10, 1993, 3–4.

33. Sam Daws, "Seeking Seats, Votes and Vetoes," *World Today* 53 (October 1997): 256–59.

34. "Imitating NATO: A Script Is Adapted for Chechnya," *New York Times*, September 28, 1999, 3.

35. "China Maps Changes in Defense Strategy," *International Herald Tribune*, June 12–13, 1999. One must be careful, however, not to overstate the importance of closer ties between these two neighbors, which still harbor considerable mutual distrust.

36. Former Indian foreign secretary J. N. Dixit, claiming in July 1999 that Pakistan was hoping to create a Kosovo-like situation in Kashmir which might lead to U.S. intervention, argued that Pakistan had failed to realize that (nuclear) India was no Bosnia or Kosovo and the United States would think several times before interfering. See "Kargil Conflict Occurred Because the Country Has a Caretaker Government: J. N. Dixit," *India Today*, July 8, 1999; www.india-today.com/ntoday/newsarchives/99.7/08/n24.sthml.

37. See, e.g., the French government report on lessons learned from Kosovo, *Les enseignements du Kosovo* (Paris: Ministry of Defense, 1999), 7–12.

38. "EU Completes Plan for Own Forces," *International Herald Tribune*, December 10, 1999.

39. "Alliance's Strategic Concept," para. 10.

40. "Report of the Secretary-General on the Work of the Organization," UN Doc. A/46/1, September 13, 1991, 5.

41. "Plenary Resolution," para. 16(e).

## EIGHT

# "Immaculate War": Constraints on Humanitarian Intervention

## Martin L. Cook

In the Kosovo crisis, pundits at home and abroad charged the White House overlearned the lessons of Vietnam and Somalia and underestimated the willingness of the public for a fight when it perceives important issues at stake. The result, they argue, was a military campaign devoid of daring, so fearful of its own losses that it could not save the Kosovar refugees or effectively punish Serb atrocities:

> Contemporary American policy on the appropriate use of military force reflects deep tensions. The prevailing analysis is that the use of military force will only be politically acceptable if American casualties are kept to a minimum. Partly in negative reaction to the prolonged agony of Vietnam and the debacles of Lebanon and Somalia, and partly in positive reaction to the seemingly bloodless and very quick Persian Gulf War, so the analysis goes, American political leaders have accepted a new standard for acceptable military conflict: "immaculate war."[1]

I believe this analysis contains a large degree of truth. But I argue in this chapter that there are deeper issues of ethical principle underlying the desire to have only immaculate interventions. I will contend that the impulse to intervene comes from one particular view of international order, and of the role of the U.S. military in that order. The impulse to keep such interventions immaculate, conversely, arises from the systemic misfit between the interventionist impulse and the moral contract between political leaders and the men and women of the armed services who bear the burden of executing such interventions.

## THE INTERVENTIONIST IMPERATIVE

American political rhetoric about military intervention has always been moralistic. To the constant frustration of political realists, American political culture has been notoriously resistant to reducing intervention decisions to clear-eyed and coldhearted assessments of narrowly conceived national interest. No matter how unglamorous the real motives of national interest, interventions as tawdry as the Spanish–American War, our repeated involvement in Nicaragua, or the 1989 invasion of Panama have consistently been cloaked in high rhetoric and appeals to moral principle.

Rarely has American political discourse been content with forthrightly stating that the use of military force serves the sole purpose of advancing national economic and political interests. Instead, it has always tended to speak in universalizing terms of fighting wars to end all wars, advancing universal human rights and democratic political order, and opposing tyranny and despotism.

So the fact that our intervention in Kosovo (and Bosnia and Somalia) is described in terms of universalizing claims about the protection of the rights of individuals is not new. Yet it would be a mistake to interpret these interventions as merely additional instances of moral rhetoric to mask realpolitik. The end of the cold war has created, at least for this historical moment, a time and space for genuinely new forms of international relations. Whether those possibilities portend great moral progress in international affairs or will ultimately lead to disaster is yet to be determined.

It would be a mistake as well to read the present burst of enthusiasm for humanitarian interventions as merely a result of the end of the cold war. It is also the manifestation of a kind of idealism that has entered international law and—primarily through nongovernmental organizations—international politics. As Geoffrey Best wrote in *War and Law since 1945*:

> From 24 October 1945, the day the [UN] Charter entered into effect, it has had competition. Alongside it, and prefigured in the Charter itself, there ran a parallel legislative stream of humanitarian and human rights rules and standards which States undertook at least to take note of and which, if words mean anything, they should in some last resort be required to observe. . . . Members of the UN insist that they retain full sovereign rights, and nominally indeed they do so, yet they stand committed at the same time to a variety of human rights observances which in principle entitle their neighbours to complain in case of neglect.[2]

The expanding array of human rights commitments at the international level in the aftermath of World War II (perhaps best captured in the post-Holocaust motto Never Again!) created a legal framework and on-paper commitments by states to prevent gross violations of human rights. Much of the current confusion of U.S. foreign policy in these areas is the result of the fact that this humanitarian law was never well integrated with the older and more established state sovereignty law.[3] Although most sovereign states are committed in principle to universal and transnational humanitarian standards, the fact remains that any enforcement of those standards depends almost entirely on their voluntary efforts. Understandably, sovereign states are slow to commit blood and treasure to causes, no matter how noble, not demonstrably connected to vital national interests.

Further, the balance-of-power and proxy wars of the superpowers in the cold war served to ensure that only very rarely would a humanitarian crisis be far enough removed from superpower rivalry for the humanitarian impulse to be played out. Inevitably, claims to humanitarian concern as a basis for intervention would appear to be, and usually actually were, a kind of smokescreen behind which the major states jockeyed for cold war position. Equally inevitably, even the best-intentioned efforts at humanitarian intervention would almost always have secondary effects on the perceived interests of the superpowers.

The result of this combination of humanitarian legal development and superpower stalemate was that true humanitarian intervention was rare. The body of law that justified it in theory had little opportunity to generate precedents in practice and little practical need to be better reconciled with state sovereignty law.

The success at coalition building in the Gulf War at the very end of the cold war led U.S. president George H. W. Bush to imagine a New World Order. This would be an order, presumably, of united international support for universal values, led by the United States under the legal auspices of the United Nations.

It fell to Bill Clinton's administration to spell out the place of humanitarian intervention in the national military strategy of the United States in that new order. The first detailed articulation of this policy came in May 1994, with Presidential Decision Directive 25 (PDD-25), titled "The Clinton Administration's Policy on Reforming Multilateral Peace Operations." The directive notes that the cold war had severely hampered the ability of the United Nations to perform peace operations. However, "in the new strategic environment such operations can serve more often as a cost-effective tool to advance American as well as collective interests in maintaining peace in key regions and create global burden-sharing for peace."[4] At this juncture, I would simply note the ambiguity of linking peace operations to "American as well as collective interests" as if these were a single thing. Further, the term "collective" is itself ambiguous. Does it mean NATO? The United Nations? Coalitions of the willing that shift from crisis to crisis?

PDD-25 proceeds to lay out a number of criteria for U.S. participation in multilateral peace operations and to suggest internal reforms at the United Nations to enable future operations to be more professionally planned and executed from a military point of view. It notes that, as presently structured, the United Nations lacks competent command and control for complex military operations—not to mention common standards of training, interoperability of equipment, and so forth.

In May 1997, another presidential directive, known as PDD-56 and titled "White Paper: The Clinton Administration's Policy on Managing Complex Contingency Operations," was released. The background statement of this document begins:

In the wake of the Cold War, attention has focused on a rising number of territorial disputes, armed ethnic conflicts, and civil wars that pose a threat to regional and international peace and may be accompanied by natural or man-made disasters which precipitate massive human suffering. We have learned that effective responses to these situations may require multi-dimensional operations composed of such components as political, diplomatic, humanitarian, intelligence, economic development, and security; hence the term complex contingency operations.[5]

As examples of such operations, the directive cites Haiti, Somalia, northern Iraq, and the former Yugoslavia. The primary intent of the directive is to institutionalize lessons learned from those operations so as to enable various U.S. government agencies to better coordinate future operations. But it also notes that, very often, such contingency operations take place in complex coalitions as well, "either under the auspices of an international or regional organization or in ad hoc, temporary coalitions of like-minded states."[6]

This framing of international relations in terms of humanitarian interventions in the name of universal principles is not a uniquely American impulse. UN secretary-general Kofi Annan has again and again articulated his understanding of the central challenge of the international community in this generation. In his Annual Report to the General Assembly for 1999, he states: "The core challenge to the Security Council and to the United Nations as a whole in the next century [is] to forge unity behind the principle that massive and systematic violations of human rights—wherever they take place—should not be allowed to stand."[7]

Annan identifies the central issue posed by such an interventionist imperative: not only the idea of state sovereignty per se, but "the ways in which the Member States of the United Nations define their national interest in any given crisis." He continues:

A new, more broadly defined, more widely conceived definition of national interest in the new century would, I am convinced, induce States to find far greater unity in the pursuit of such basic Charter values as democracy, pluralism, human rights, and the rule of law.[8]

Annan's vision of an effective, consistent, and universal global commitment to the protection of individuals and their rights appeals to the deepest idealist impulses. The Clinton administration's policies attempted to go a long way in Annan's direction—while still operating with a less broadly conceived (but nonetheless quite broad) understanding of national interest than Annan's. But conceptions of national interest differ, and Annan's universalizing vision must be accomplished with the forces of sovereign states. Together, these conditions generate a competing imperative for U.S. participation in peacekeeping and peacemaking operations: that of force protection. This imperative arises not merely from political constraints but also from the moral contract between the nation, its citizens, and its military personnel.

## THE FORCE-PROTECTION IMPERATIVE

The dilemma of humanitarian intervention arises from some elementary facts. The international community has no army. The United Nations lacks an air force or navy. As Annan states the problem, "Unless the United Nations is given the means and support to succeed, not only the peace, but the war, too, will be lost."[9] But what would it entail to "give the means" to the United Nations?

One possibility is, of course, to give the United Nations its own organic military command and force structure. If one were convinced that universal, consistent, and prompt peace enforcement would then become the international norm, this would be the direction in which UN member states would have to move. But equally clearly, there is no political consensus in favor of a UN force—neither in the United States nor in the world generally. At most, PDD-25 calls for strengthening UN capabilities to exercise effective command and control over complex operations by creating a small standing military staff, a rapidly deployable headquarters, and prenegotiated contracts for airlift capability, among other things.[10]

Even though the Clinton administration went further than any previous U.S. administration in linking American strategy to participation in multinational operations, PDD-25 goes on to say:

> The President retains and will never relinquish command authority over U.S. forces. On a case by case basis, the President will consider placing appropriate U.S. forces under the operational control of a competent UN commander for specific UN operations authorized by the Security Council. The greater the U.S. military role, the less likely it will be that the U.S. will agree to have a UN commander exercise overall operational control over U.S. forces. Any large scale participation of U.S. forces in a major peace enforcement mission that is likely to involve combat should ordinarily be conducted under U.S. command and operational control or through competent regional organizations such as NATO or ad hoc coalitions.[11]

Although this paragraph is derived from U.S. policy documents, there can be little doubt that other sovereign states will and must think similar thoughts about putting their military personnel in harm's way.

Partly, this reluctance comes from a distrust of the competence and training level of commanders from other nations—even those in NATO, an organization with which the United States has worked and trained for fifty years. But if that were the only objection, it could be addressed by building up a professional officer corps, organic to the United Nations, and through frequent joint military exercises under UN command and control. Moreover, as is indicated above, PDD-25 calls for the development of just such a core competency in the United Nations itself, and it is an ability that Secretary-General Annan would clearly welcome.

But there is a larger moral question behind this jurisdictional and political struggle. It goes much deeper than practical questions about the ability of the United Nation to exercise competent and effective command and control over multinational forces. It also goes deeper than the longstanding tension between state sovereignty and effective international organization. At its root, I believe, it goes to the implicit moral contract between a nation and its soldiers. For the sake of brevity, I will not discuss the general question, but specifically the American case: What is the "deal" implicitly made between the U.S. all-volunteer professional military and national command authority?

Joining an all-volunteer military may usefully be construed as a kind of contract. There is, of course, the literal and legal contract, the stuff of recruiting, in which pay is stipulated and educational benefits are spelled out. But I mean to focus more on the implicit moral contract—the kind imagined in social contract theories of the state, such as those of Thomas Hobbes, John Locke, and John Rawls.

Like those social contracts, this one is constructed rather than literal. That is to say, just as there never was a real group of human beings in Rawls's original position, so there never was a moment when the national command authority of the United States convened a meeting with a group of soldiers and explained the terms of their relationship. But military service is, morally viewed, something more than a career choice.

Military personnel live in a unique moral world. They exist to serve the state. The essence and moral core of their service is to defend that state through the management and application of violence in defense of the territorial integrity, political sovereignty, and vital national interests of that state. Their contract has an "unlimited liability" clause—they accept (and in an all-volunteer force, unquestionably voluntarily accept) the obligation to put their lives at grave risk when ordered to do so. Their contract also requires them to kill other human beings and to destroy their property when given legal orders to do so.

The unlimited liability clause and the voluntary consent to kill and destroy make the soldier's contract a morally weighty one. No rational person would enter into such an agreement without morally serious reasons for doing so. Though it is true that one can cause the death of others or be harmed or killed in many other lines of work, in no other profession are such possible events integral to the enterprise itself. At every moment, the soldier's contract puts him or her at risk, if military power is misused, of committing murders or being maimed or killed in vain. Only if the soldier trusts that political authority will only call on military services for morally legitimate and weighty causes can the contract be entered into with confidence and moral security.

One might say, of course, that a military person's obligation is much simpler than this. All that is required is to follow every legal order. Political leaders, one might say, make the determination to use the military for whatever purposes they deem worthwhile and, as long as the orders are legal, those purposes are "above the pay grade" of the military person. Legally, this view is, of course, correct. But I believe that the legalist answer is superficial. The military contract obliges military personnel to run grave risks and to engage in morally and personally difficult actions. They do these things on the basis of the implicit promise that the circumstances under which they must act are grounded in political leadership's good faith judgment that the defense of the sovereignty and integrity of the nation (or, by careful extension, the nation's vital interests) requires their action. The farther a particular engagement or deployment departs from this clear contractual case, the more difficult it is for political leadership to offer moral and political justification for any killing and especially dying that their military forces experience.

The imperative for force protection when we use our forces in humanitarian interventions and peacekeeping and peacemaking operations is, of course, to a large degree political. It is difficult to maintain political support for operations, no matter how well intended, as the casualties mount and the body bags appear on the news. But I believe that this political problem has a deep moral root in the soldier's contract.

American military personnel are just that—American military personnel (the same qualification applies to the military of any other state). The contract they have accepted justifies the violent actions they perform and the risks they accept in the name of serving that state. When we use those forces in humanitarian causes distantly related to the terms of the contract, they and their fellow citizens may accept those deployments in the name of the ideals of international community, but only to a certain (and rather low) threshold of pain. The imperative for force protection in such deployments is only superficially an aversion to casualties induced by some type of Vietnam (and Somalia and Lebanon) syndrome. At a deeper level, it goes to the core of the moral meaning of military service to a sovereign state.[12] To such a use of American forces, the military person may say with moral seriousness, "This isn't what I signed up for"—and all the more if casualties mount, the length of the deployment drags on, and the probability of achieving the goal of the mission recedes.

Annan is correct when he suggests that building an effective international consensus to use military force consistently for humanitarian purposes would require a broader construal of national interest than has classically been the case. As PDD-25 argues, it would require considerable attention to internal UN mechanisms to authorize, command, and control such operations. Is the response to every legitimate moral reaction that "somebody should do something" about a given situation to be the effective and universal application of the political and, if necessary, military power of the international community? Such a program would require extensive, lengthy, and concentrated international attention to put in place political and military structures that could begin to meet the need.

But in the meantime, the use of American forces (and those of other nations) for purposes tangentially and marginally connected to defense and vital national interest will, inevitably, be filled with compromises. Even if the United Nations or other agencies of the international community could find the political and moral will to authorize such interventions consistently and according to uniform moral and political standards of judgment, such deployments would be problematic.

There will inevitably be more missions than willing forces. The will to support the use of national forces for them will be unreliable and easily dissipated. These political facts are grounded in the deeper moral issue of the contract implicitly made between the nation and its military. A consequence of this moral and political reality is that national forces will be used inconsistently in the full spectrum of peace operations, and that force protection will be among the highest priorities when they are so used.

Perhaps national interest may come to be defined as broadly as Annan advocates. The American public would need to embrace that redefinition with enthusiasm and deep acceptance of its consequences for the use of its forces—and be prepared to sacrifice significant blood and treasure in the pursuit of national interest, so defined. Or perhaps, in time, international organizations will be strengthened sufficiently so that they possess the organic capabilities to deploy in such circumstances. But until that happens, humanitarian intervention and peacekeeping operations will be piecemeal, inconsistent, and dependent on coalitions of the willing. They will be (and morally need to be) risk averse and highly focused on force protection.

The protection of innocent foreign nationals will be a priority as well—for the political reason that injured and killed civilians undermine the moral basis for humanitarian intervention, but also because of the moral concern with protection of innocent life. Yet even the concern with the protection of innocents will probably be secondary to the protection of a state's own forces, for the weighty moral reasons I have indicated.

## CONCLUSION

Can humanitarian interventions be supported and successfully executed under such constraints? The best answer we have at the moment is, I fear, *occasionally*. Traditional just war thinking places high regard on the lives of innocents in conflict and requires combatants to take measures, even at risk to themselves, to protect those lives. But in an operation such as Kosovo, where the moral basis of significant risk of loss by our own soldiers is dubious, there is an important and potentially troubling change to that traditional calculus. General Wesley Clark has written clearly about this:

> The minimization of civilian casualties and damage to civilian structures and property—whether Serb or Kosovar—was very high on our priority list. Any lack of discrimination between legitimate military targets and off-limits civilian areas would have undercut our efforts to explain what we were doing and maintain public support.[13]

There can be no doubt that NATO's bombing campaign strove mightily to meet this requirement. Even more than in the Gulf War, the weapons employed were precise, both because of technical improvements since 1991 and because an even higher percentage of all weapons used were precision munitions. More than 23,000 bombs and missiles were expended in this campaign, and a record 35 percent of them were smart weapons.[14]

Despite this emphasis on precision in an air campaign conducted at 15,000 feet, one cannot help but note that the precision would have been higher still had the aircraft operated at lower altitudes (and greater risk). Further, the decision to adopt (and announce in advance) an airpower-only campaign certainly lengthened the conflict and ensured that very little would be done in Kosovo to bring the atrocities that were the cause of the campaign itself to a halt. Because those small, dispersed units on the ground were the least susceptible to effective targeting given the chosen weapons platforms and tactics, unless Serbia capitulated quickly from the initial shock of the air campaign, NATO had implicitly embarked on a war of attrition of Serbian infrastructure. No matter how precise the weapons employed, the widespread destruction of national infrastructure is inherently an indiscriminate attack on the whole population. Thus no war can be truly immaculate.

Here we see the deep issue for further thought. No matter how idealistic the motives for humanitarian interventions, if force-protection considerations restrict the means to the point where the operation is unlikely to halt the atrocities in question and will have the foreseeable effect of widespread consequences for other innocent civilians, we must reassess the moral equation at the basis of the intervention. Certainly in the Kosovo case, it is worth considering what would have happened had Serbia not capitulated when it did. How widely would we let the target list expand? How far were we really prepared to go in destroying the Serbian economy, power grid, transportation system, and more, in the name of "precision" air war?

Even humanitarian operations that involve the possibility of real use of force are subject to one of the crucial tests of just war: a reasonable hope of success. Most dangerous of all is to follow the impulse to intervene, but to do so with such restraint and caution that we merely add damage to an already bad situation, with no reasonable hope of success in solving the underlying cause of the intervention.

In light of these considerations, Kosovo points to the profound need to rethink the moral contract between soldiers and their society. Further, we need to consider in hard practical terms the connection between the means we are really willing to use and the political and military ends we seek. Only if we can and do bring effective means to bear on those ends, within the constraints of the morally acceptable, can future humanitarian operations fulfill their missions with reasonable hope of success.

# NOTES

1. Harvey Sapolsky and Jeremy Shapiro, "Administration Deft to Predict Public Fatigue for a Longer War," *Army Times,* October 18, 1999, 78.
2. Geoffrey Best, *War and Law since 1945* (Oxford: Clarendon Press, 1994), 79.
3. Martin L. Cook, "Two Roads Diverged and We Took the One Less Traveled By," in *Kosovo: Contending Voices on Balkan Interventions,* ed. William Joseph Buckley (Grand Rapids, Mich.: Eerdmans, 2000).
4. "PDD-25 (Unclassified Version)," in *Legal Guide to Peace Operations,* ed. Glenn Bowens (Carlisle Barracks, Pa.: U.S. Army Peacekeeping Institute, 1998), 358.
5. "PDD-56 (Unclassified Version)," in *Legal Guide to Peace Operations,* 372.
6. "PDD-56 (Unclassified Version)," in *Legal Guide to Peace Operations,* 372.
7. UN Press Release SG/SM/7136, GA/95/96.
8. UN Press Release SG/SM/7136, GA/95/96.

 9. UN Press Release SG/SM/7136, GA/95/96.
10. "PDD-25," 363–64.
11. "PDD-25," 365.
12. Martin L. Cook, "Moral Foundations of Military Service," *Parameters* 29 (spring 2000): 117–29.
13. Wesley Clark, "The United States and NATO: The Way Ahead," *Parameters* 29 (winter 1999–2000): 2–14.
14. Earl H. Tilford Jr., "Operation Allied Force and the Role of Air Power," *Parameters* 29 (winter 1999–2000): 29.

NINE

# The Impact of Intervention on Local Human Rights Culture: A Kosovo Case Study

Julie Mertus

When and how does Western intervention positively nurture human rights norms? And when do these efforts have unintended negative consequences? This chapter explores these questions using a case study of western intervention in Kosovo.[1] In the first of two sections, the chapter introduces the terms "culture" and "human rights culture" and then discusses the nature of the human rights culture in Kosovar society[2] before the NATO bombing. I explain that although human rights norms were inculcated into Kosovar culture, Albanians' operational understanding of human rights was perilously incomplete.

Second, the chapter explores the impact of military and civil intervention on the human rights culture in Kosovo. In this section, I am interested in the effects of military intervention on human rights norms and the postagreement attempts to influence Kosovars' shared understanding of these norms. Given the paucity of research on the subject, I focus my discussion on the effects of nonmilitary, postagreement democratization efforts on Kosovo's human rights culture. My main finding is that the Western intervention in Kosovo, although undertaken with the purported aim of supporting human rights norms, has undermined efforts to build a sustainable human rights culture in Kosovo.

## EXAMINING THE HUMAN RIGHTS CULTURE IN KOSOVO

Culture is "the shared beliefs and understandings, mediated by and constituted by symbols and language, of a group or society."[3] As Renato Rosaldo succinctly explains, "[Culture] refers broadly to the forms through which people make sense of their lives."[4] Two dimensions of culture are particularly relevant to our discussion. First, cultures are not unidimensional and static; they are multidimensional and dynamic. Accordingly, this chapter examines dimensions of Kosovar culture that have been relevant to human rights during two periods, the pre-NATO bombing period of 1989 to early 1999, and the post-NATO bombing period of 2001, recognizing that culture is "interactive and process-like (rather than static and essence-like)."[5] Second, cultures are not primordially given. Rather, they are socially constructed according to an ideological and/or political purpose.[6] This insight reminds us that, although there is a specific content to "human rights" that shapes "human rights culture," human rights culture, like all cultures, is dynamic and socially constructed.

It is through human rights culture that human rights norms take root in and influence a population.[7] At the outset, human rights ideology stresses equality between human beings, asserting that each human being should be treated with dignity solely because he or she is human.[8] This conception of human rights supports not only the importance of individualism but also the centrality of community and communal responsibility. Jean Bethke Elshtain notes that "[rights] are woven into a concept of community" and "are intelligible only in terms of the obligations of individuals to other persons."[9] The Kosovar human rights movement illustrates this insight. Although Kosovars viewed themselves as being entitled to rights as individuals, they continually emphasized the communal nature of rights and individual obligations to community.[10]

In the post–cold war period,[11] state leaders also turn to human rights discourse to articulate "national interests" and assert moral superiority.[12] Virtually no state leader will acknowledge the state's human rights violations; instead, he or she will cling to the identity of human rights supporter.[13] Thus, state leaders seek legitimacy by claiming that human rights norms support their actions, whatever they may be.[14] In this sense, human rights norms served an enabling function for state actors wishing to intervene in Kosovo.[15] At the same time, however, human rights discourse was empowering for Kosovars. By framing their struggles in human rights terms, individuals and groups tap into a perceived moral consensus on universal rights and wrongs and, in so doing, claim the moral high ground.[16] Moreover, collectives and individuals wishing to promote change in existing national or international institutions, practices, or norms are more likely to gain an audience by framing their claims in human rights terms.[17]

By empowering individuals and groups to challenges patterns of domination of the powerful over the weak, the idea of human rights can be "a defense against the abuse of power everywhere."[18] Human rights ideology has long been viewed as limiting the power of the state over its citizens. More recently, human rights concepts have been applied to challenge abuses of power by nonstate actors as well.[19] In addition to placing a check on power, the notion of common humanity and human solidarity places responsibilities on state leaders and citizens to protect and assist all of humanity, regardless of state borders.[20] Human rights ideology also promotes a concept of "universal justice" that permits individuals to demand accountability for perpetrators of gross human rights abuses.[21]

Today, then, human rights norms can be said to have both "vertical" and "horizontal" significance in that, as Marie-Benedicte Dembour observes, "although human rights standards are primarily set to govern the relationship between the individual and the state ('vertical' significance), they also necessarily govern relations among individuals ('horizontal' significance) and in some cases this may well be their main significance."[22] This was indeed the case in Kosovar society where Albanians identified themselves as victims of human rights violations perpetuated by the state of Yugoslavia (or Serbia), by individual Serbians and also by collectives (of Serbians and their supporters).[23]

In Jack Donnelly's words, "human rights is the language of the victims and the dispossessed."[24] The disempowered turn to human rights discourse because it so "successfully manages to articulate (evolving) political claims."[25] As they shape human rights ideology and use it for their own goals, they exercise their moral agency. Just as groups are transformed by human rights discourse, the human rights claims are also "continually transformed as the result of struggles over political, symbolic, or economic resources within a state and transnational context."[26]

The adoption of human rights language is an essential step in building a human rights culture, but language alone is insufficient. Human rights concepts enter culture slowly as a population develops its own shared (yet contested) understanding of the prominence and importance of the norms. Incrementally, they become part of the "'frame' in which people derive a sense of who they are and where they are going."[27]

Central to this process is a population's own experiences of rights deprivation and rights affirmation, which often occurs through storytelling.[28] Human rights storytelling serves several functions. As Richard Rorty has suggested in his pragmatic argument for human rights, storytelling provides a "sentimental education" that generates the kind of sympathy necessary for the acceptance of human rights norms.[29] This is particularly important when the goal is to motivate a majority to accept the human rights of a minority. Human rights activists in Belgrade, for example, exposed stories about abuses against Albanians to garner the Serbs' sympathy.[30] Kosovars strongly believe that if not for the human rights storytelling, the NATO intervention never would have occurred.[31]

Human rights storytelling also facilitates a common understanding of experience, and in so doing it promotes group cohesion.[32] In Kosovo, the informal telling of stories in Kosovar family living rooms and the more formalized collection of stories by human rights groups served to strengthen Albanian solidarity as a united, oppressed people.[33] Similarly, Serbian stories about Albanians solidified their identity as victims at the hands of Albanians.[34] In this way, within one society, human rights storytelling was both unifying and fragmenting. Yet in neither the Serbian nor Albanian population did storytelling promote the central value of human rights: respect for each other.[35]

## THE HUMAN RIGHTS CULTURE IN KOSOVAR SOCIETY BEFORE 1999

As a form of resistance to Serbian rule and a method of survival in a time of oppression, Kosovar Albanians created their own "parallel society" in the early 1990s, complete with their own (illegal) government, schools, medical centers, and welfare system. To a great extent, the Kosovar parallel society stands as a paradigmatic example of the internalization of human rights norms by a people. It was through human rights claims that Kosovar Albanians expressed their demands for political rights[36]—autonomy within Yugoslavia and/or independence—and articulated their political aspirations for a more egalitarian society in which ethnic Serbs could not abuse and discriminate against ethnic Albanians.[37]

In making their arguments, Kosovars sought to take their claims about rights into the political arena.[38] The primary goal of Kosovar human rights activists was to influence, using some measure of justice, how the "international community" understood their behavior and, accordingly, the behavior of the Serbs.[39] A secondary goal was to create a local sensibility to human rights norms that would shape Kosovar collective life.[40] Just as the environmental movement in the West sought to get people to "think green," human rights activists in Kosovo sought to have their people "think human rights."

The degree to which local human rights groups influenced the cultural perceptions can be seen in the media, press statements of Kosovar politicians, publications of nongovernmental organizations (NGOs), the school curriculum, and the practice of family traditions. Attitudinal surveys and interviews on these same subjects over a period of time also provide evidence of changes in cultural perception.[41] According to these measures, human rights activists in Kosovo achieved some degree of success. Nearly every Kosovar had either personally, or through a close relative, experienced some form of state-sanctioned abuse that could be framed in human rights terms.

Throughout the 1990s, this frame was adapted by the independent Kosovar media, League for Democratic Kosovo press statements, and NGO press publications, which continually characterized the Kosovars' struggle in human rights terms. Moreover, human rights terminology was popularized through the Kosovar "parallel" school curriculum and through everyday family life, which emphasized the human rights deprivations that victims suffered. Kosovars decried the legitimacy of Serbia's constitution and instead looked to the UN Universal Declaration of Human Rights as a source of guiding principles for their lives.

The Kosovar human rights "sensibility" was tied to the Albanian political strategy of nonviolence.[42] Just as the Kosovar identity as nonviolent victim of human rights abuses was constructed against a violent, human rights abusing "other," their conception of human rights were framed in oppositional terms.[43] They did not really view individuals as possessing human rights had simply by virtue of their humanity. Rather, Kosovars perceived their own human rights in opposition to the human rights of other groups—that is, Albanians versus Serbs.[44] Given that Albanians no longer recognized the legitimacy of the state of Yugoslavia's rule over Kosovo, they looked not to their state for protection but to the international community; this community, they had no hesitancy in qualifying, meant the United States and, to a lesser extent, NATO.[45]

In the early 1990s, the practice of nonviolence and the emergence of a culture of human rights in Kosovo served several useful purposes. By casting their struggle in human rights terms, Kosovars gained legitimacy before many governments and nongovernmental organizations that showed concern about human rights. Their strategy of using the language of human rights helped them to gain entry into important international political forums. In addition, the language of human rights "served to validate the self-worth of Kosovars at a time when they were being vilified."[46] In this way, the language of human rights strengthened the nonviolent strategy by popularizing "patience in the face of aggression" and claiming the moral high ground.[47]

The nonviolent strategy, however, was built on a tenuous human rights foundation. Though Kosovars did have a strong human rights culture, it was incomplete. Howard Clark has observed that "the danger of deriving one's identity from a matrix of antagonisms is evident—a lack of flexibility, an inability to appreciate what is held in common . . . [and the acceptance of a] worldview where one is always the victim or martyr, the 'other' always the villain."[48] The notion of respect for the rights and positions of the "other" was "underdeveloped in Albanian self-understanding." John Paul Lederach reminds us that international mechanisms such as human rights are most useful for peace building if they "cut across lines of identity that mark the central divisions in society."[49] Instead of cutting across lines of identity in Kosovar society, the language of human rights served to cement lines of identity.

The challenge for the international community in responding to human rights violations in Kosovo was to support the development of the nascent Kosovar human rights culture. This aim would have best been served by encouraging Kosovars to mitigate the adversarial elements of the culture that undermined Serbs. As is explained more fully below, the international community offered no effective incentives for the development of a more inclusive discourse. Nor did the international community actively discourage Kosovar Albanians from tempering their hostile view of Serbs. Albanian leaders—not leaders of the international community—invoked the selective interpretation of human rights. To be sure, the international community cannot be blamed for the shortcomings in the Kosovar human rights culture. Moreover, mutual hostility can be viewed as both a cause and consequence of the incomplete human rights culture in Kosovo that existed before the NATO bombing. However, western powers could have done more to support local human rights culture.

# THE IMPACT OF MILITARY AND CIVIL INTERVENTION IN KOSOVO

The NATO bombing failed to vindicate the Kosovar struggle for human rights. Instead, the timing and method of intervention greatly compromised human rights interests in Kosovo. When Albanians returned to Kosovo after the bombing, few were thinking in human rights terms as they had in the past.[50] Returning refugees spoke about starting anew only in pragmatic and instrumentalist terms. Though some still framed the struggle for Albanian self-determination as a human rights concern, they recognized that the underlying decision on Albanian independence would be a political one, determined by the interests of the world powers, not by human rights norms. Kosovars' honor of the notion that one should recognize the human rights of all, particularly of the "other," had never been that strong; at that point, it reached a nadir. Though the vast majority of Kosovars did not condone revenge killings, as a community they were unable to prevent them or to punish the perpetrators.

There are several reasons why the international intervention in Kosovo, billed as a "human rights intervention," served to undercut Kosovar human rights culture.[51] Above all, the intervention came too late. The international community could have supported human rights groups in Kosovo and Serbia at a much earlier date. Although the Soros Foundation and other private organizations aided Albanian and Serbian media and other aspects of civil society throughout the former Yugoslavia beginning in the early 1990s, the United States and other major powers did not do all they could have to support civil society actors. They had the opportunity and means to offer financial and technical support to independent Serbian and Albanian journalists, opposition political parties, and civic organizations, from women's health groups to farmers' organizations.[52]

Civil society was perhaps the only sector that could have stemmed the violence or provided better grounds for conflict resolution or reconciliation. Though foreign governments have not traditionally engaged in such activities, they are beginning to do so as part of larger "peace-building" efforts; supporting civil society has emerged as a cost-effective alternative or addition to comparatively expensive military commitments. Most important, foreign governments had the opportunity to foster economic security by bolstering private businesses and offering potential funding for government projects as inducements to work on human rights issues. Instead, the United States imposed economic sanctions against Belgrade, a move that served to stoke Serbian feelings of victimization and ultimately enhanced Slobodan Milosevic's power.[53]

The failure of the international community to effectively support the Kosovars' nonviolent human rights struggle sent a clear message to Kosovars that world powers will respond to guns, not rights claims. Human rights reports on violations in Kosovo during the Albanian period of nonviolence (the early to middle 1990s) had little impact on decision making. Tim Judah observes: "Because there was no apparent urgency then and no all-important dead bodies on television to galvanize Western opinion, the very few diplomats who ventured down to Kosovo and who were beginning to realize that things were in fact changing found that their reports were having little impact."[54] In the face of international inaction, the human rights abuses in Kosovo continued and, indeed, worsened. As the Albanian nonviolent movement collapsed and the Kosovo Liberation Army (KLA) rose, the international community was finally prompted to pay more attention to the crisis.

The failure of the international community to respond early and consistently to human rights violations also fostered the belief that politically powerful countries see human rights merely as a bargaining chip to be used when their own interests are at stake and at their discretion. For years, NATO allies turned a blind eye to systemic human rights abuses in Kosovo, issuing only an occasional empty threat to the Milosevic regime. The United States and the other countries that belong to NATO decided to take up the human rights flag only after the emergence of the Albanian paramilitary organization, the KLA.[55]

Only at that point did the conflagration in Kosovo appear likely to result in a massive population displacement that would spill across national borders and disrupt trade and social relations among NATO countries. The resulting NATO bombing campaign expelled Yugoslav army and irregular Serb forces from Kosovo, but it did nothing to protect civilians from mass displacement, killing, and other abuses.[56] Realizing the self-serving nature of diplomatic human rights talk, Serbians and Albanians alike grew bitter toward the international community and cynical about the notion of universal human rights.

Although in part motivated by human rights considerations, Bill Clinton's administration refused to base its actions in Kosovo solely on human rights grounds.[57] The administration mixed human rights talk with the need for regional stabilization, national security concerns over a long war and a large refugee flow, the need to protect NATO's reputation, and America's interest in preserving prosperous and secure trade with Europe. Even though many of the interests identified were relevant to human rights, the administration chose instead to emphasize other justifications for the campaign. A case could be made for the legality of the air strikes under the UN Charter—specifically, by arguing that by committing gross human rights violations Serbia had waived its claim to sovereignty and that intervention was therefore needed under Articles 55 and 56 of the UN Charter to address human rights violations and restore the sovereignty of the people.[58]

However, no one in the U.S. administration was willing to articulate a legal basis for intervention on human rights grounds.[59] The ad hoc and extralegal justifications for the use of force appeared illegitimate, which undermined NATO's status and the legitimacy of the international human rights system.[60] This, in turn, served only to further the Serbs and Albanians' newfound belief that claims to human rights would not be universally enforced but, rather, used as another tool for powerful countries to wield as they saw fit.

## THE IMPACT OF POSTAGREEMENT EFFORTS

Following the Serbian acceptance of the Kosovo peace agreement,[61] the UN Security Council, acting under the authority of its Chapter VII powers, adopted a resolution setting forth the mandate of the international mission to rebuild peace in Kosovo.[62] Security Council Resolution 1244 directed the UN secretary general, in consultation with the council, to appoint a special representative "to control the implementation of the international civil presence."[63]

On July 2, 1999, the UN secretary-general appointed Bernard Kouchner as his special representative in Kosovo.[64] Kouchner moved quickly to solidify his power in Kosovo. Pursuant to the authority granted by Resolution 1244, he issued a regulation on July 25 that vested in the UN Interim Administration in Kosovo (UNMIK) all legislative and executive authority in Kosovo. Under UNMIK Regulation 1, this authority was "to be exercised by the Special Representative of the Secretary-General."[65] UNMIK Regulation 1 provides that the "Special Representative of the Secretary-General may appoint any person to perform functions in the civil administration in Kosovo, including the judiciary, or remove such person."[66] Moreover, "in the performance of the duties entrusted to the interim administration under United Nations Security Council Resolution 1244 (1999), UNMIK will, as necessary, issue legislative acts in the form of regulations."[67] Put thus, the authority of the Special Representative is virtually unlimited.[68]

UNMIK is unusual in that it encompasses the activities of three non-UN organizations under overall UN jurisdiction. UNMIK comprises five "pillars": (1) an interim civil administration (led by the United Nations); (2) humanitarian affairs (led by the Office of the UN High Commissioner for Refugees); (3) democratization and institution building (led by the Organization for Security and Economic Cooperation in Europe, or OSCE); (4) reconstruction (led by the European Union);[69] and (5) security, provided by the Kosovo Force, which is made up of 45,000 NATO-led troops. All five pillars have an interest in human rights. The interim administration, for example, has specific officers charged with overseeing human rights issues and OSCE offers training on democratization and human rights as part of its democratic institution building. This rush of activities focusing on human rights seemed destined to support a culture of human rights.

Despite its early promise, however, the postagreement intervention did not do much more than the NATO intervention to foster a human rights culture in Kosovo. A principled human rights culture failed to emerge, and is unlikely to, for life in Kosovo is now marked by cynical instrumentalism, in other words, a "whatever it takes" attitude. Principles, particularly those aimed at the greater good, were left behind and replaced by an attitude of "everyone for oneself and one's own family." Local human rights activists still persevere in Kosovo, but the new instrumentalist attitude hampers their ability to organize. Activists face great difficulty in garnering popular support for any project that entails long-term thinking and offers few tangible rewards in the short term. A human rights focus, which requires a commitment to principles, is a hard sell in Kosovo today.

The relationship between internationals and locals on human rights issues is fraught with difficulties. In Kosovo, as in many postagreement societies, international human rights workers tend to conduct their operations in a messianic fashion, believing that they are delivering human rights to the local people.[70] However, locals already have their own understandings of human rights, derived from earlier local adaptations of international human rights to suit local culture. As is explained above, the problem in Kosovo was not the complete absence of a human rights culture, but the underdevelopment of human rights ideas. The internationals working in Kosovo did not understand that in Kosovar society, human rights are adversarial and oppositional concepts; they do not form a common ground where different sides can agree on a foundation of mutual respect.

One of the international community's greatest mistakes with respect to human rights was in championing the Serbian Kosovar residents' rights to protection. Something had to be done to stop the revenge killings of Serbs, but this was the wrong tactic. "[The international community] came in saying, 'the Serbs, the Serbs, you must protect Serbs' human rights,' but all the time I wondered, 'what about our human rights?'" one Albanian student told me, echoing the sentiments of many Kosovars.[71] Albanians and Serbs alike saw themselves as victims. By focusing on justice and protection for all victims of violence, the internationals could have expanded each group's sensitivity about human rights so as to rid it of its adversarial nature.

Some internationals argue that they did in fact stress "the human rights of all people—Albanians, Serbs and everyone else."[72] But this is not what Albanians heard. They understood only that Serbs were the new victims and that Albanians were the new perpetrators. "It was like nothing every happened to *us*," one former KLA fighter complained, "and as if *we* were suddenly the bad guys."[73] The international approach did not just erase any acknowledgment of human rights abuses against Albanians; by only emphasizing the rights of Serbs, it also perpetuated the already prevalent notion in Kosovar society that human rights are "all about one group versus another—who abuses and who is abused."[74] Unwittingly, then, the international community perpetuated an incomplete, adversarial understanding of human rights.

Additional factors are related to the enormous power imbalance in favor of international actors. Internationals inevitably dominated the decision-making process during the transition period. UN administrators heralded the benefits of "localism," that is, the involvement of local experts and even direct grants to local NGOs,[75] but locals were often only granted token involvement. Vjosa Dobruna, a long-time human rights activist in Kosovo and former member of the joint interim administration in Kosovo, resigned from her post in the internationally sanctioned Kosovo government because internationals repeatedly disregarded the locals' concerns. The last straw for Dobruna was when UN administrators in Kosovo failed to hear and account for local experts' concerns over the new Kosovo constitution. The UN administration wanted to work with locals, but only insofar as they did not rock the boat on preordained UN plans.[76]

Failure to listen to local leaders and learn about the Kosovar parallel society has led internationals to overlook their potential as an efficient network for coordinating volunteer efforts, distributing public goods, and developing human rights values.[77] Instead of drawing from the existing civil society structures, internationals went to Kosovo with a template that did not fit. "The main problem," said Dobruna, "is that [the internationals] came and tried to do what they did in Bosnia here. But in Bosnia there was no alternative movement. In Kosovo, people were prepared for war. Maybe it wasn't a perfect 'civil society,' but there was a structure, a network of nongovernmental services, NGOs. Instead of making the old structure better, they went backward—as if nothing had ever been here." Whenever locals attempted to point to already existing structures and mechanisms, they were pushed aside. "That parallel government wasn't really a good model for democracy," explained one OSCE staff member.[78]

On one hand, good arguments exist for ignoring the parallel government and starting anew.[79] The international community's refusal to use existing civil society structures seems understandable if one considers them as contributing to furthering divisions in the community. It might seem that replacing rather than transforming the earlier structure might lead more quickly to more desirable results. On the other hand, the parallel government was rich in human resources and ideas that democracy builders could not afford to ignore. The parallel government reflected a participatory ethos. Efforts to build on it would have lent legitimacy and effectiveness to the international effort.

Failure to learn about Kosovar society has had another drawback. It has continually led the international community to favor the American style of advocacy NGOs even when other mechanisms may better promote a human rights culture. The attempt to transplant American-style advocacy NGOs to other countries is often unsuccessful, because advocacy NGOs are a product of the American experience and are completely alien to many sociopolitical cultures.[80] As Thomas Carothers has observed, American NGOs "have grown out of particular aspects of America's social makeup and history—whether the immigrant character of society, the 'frontier' mindset, the legacy of suspicion of central government authority, or the high degree of individualism."[81] The political culture in Kosovo arose out of a different historic and social context. Though advocacy NGOs could eventually work in Kosovo, they will be of a distinctly Kosovar flavor: one marked by a high degree of collectivism instead of individualism; single-issue campaigns (i.e., autonomy for Kosovar Albanians as the primary goal for all Albanian NGOs, from women's groups to sporting groups); and a tradition of working at the behest of some political leaders and against others (i.e., Albanian NGOs working closely with Albanian politicians and against Serbian ones).

The ability of advocacy NGOs in Kosovo to voice the varied concerns of the population is hindered by their evolution in emergency situations. The role of advocacy NGOs is to promote civic participation, general human rights norms, as well as more specific expressions of public interest. Yet, they often promote only the most popular (i.e., moneyed) causes, often at the expense of the real public interest. The problem is particularly acute in cases such as Kosovo, where totally new NGOs propped up by foreign dollars sprang up almost overnight. Though some of these NGOs perform admirable functions, their local public sees many of them as reflecting the values and interests of foreign governments and foreign NGOs and not the most pressing local concerns.[82] Because many of the newly created entities cease to exist when the internationals pull out their support, they have little impact on the development of local culture.

The structure of aid in Kosovo has encouraged people to create and operate through an NGO structure even when it would make more sense to work in some other manner, such as through an existing community network. Thus, donor dollars have unwittingly eroded and in some cases destroyed capable community structures and created tensions between the new "haves" and "have-nots." To complicate matters, local Kosovars who succeed in the new NGO world often are not the ones with the greatest experience, relevant skills, or legitimacy among their constituents. To be sure, some of the Kosovar NGOs are extremely capable and experienced, but many of the newly minted ones reflect an ability to respond to international demand more than local needs. Internationals reward the local NGOs that are willing to be cheap service providers for international programs. Such NGOs are staffed with those who are able and willing to use the rhetoric that donors want to hear and who can attend often useless and duplicative training sessions.[83]

After the war, for example, many of the donors that focused on women's issues relied on newly created local NGOs and women's sections of political parties instead of on the local women's projects that had existed throughout the 1990s. "They find us difficult to deal with," one long-time Kosovar women's rights activist explains, "because they want to *train us* and we don't want their training."[84] As another Kosovar women's rights activist explains, "I've been in Vienna [UN 1993 World Conference on Human Rights] and Beijing [UN 1995 World Conference on Women]. I *do* gender training, and [the internationals] try to tell me what gender is and why we need a gender focal point [a specific person in each organization focused on gender issues]."[85]

When women activists argued in favor of incorporating gender issues throughout the transitional Kosovo government, instead of creating a gender focal point to consider gender issues, the internationals "acted like [the local women] didn't understand."[86] After several disputes with the United Nations–appointed gender experts, the core group of local women's projects, the Kosovo Women's Network, refused to meet with the staff of the UN Office of Gender Affairs and eventually also barred this office's representatives from their meetings. The large amount of funding for gender-related projects, though well intentioned and, in some cases, well conceived, created conflict between locals and internationals as well as between various local representatives.

Internationals are seemingly unaware that international funding of advocacy groups often creates new cleavages and conflict-filled relationships within local power structures. "Aid providers treat political change in a pseudoscientific manner—as a clinical process to be guided by manuals, technical seminars, and flowcharts specifying the intended outputs and timeframes."[87] Such an approach inevitably dismisses other factors of political change that involve people, relationships, and power. When foreign governments and NGOs offer support to local leaders they alter existing relationships and power structures by choosing some people over others. The "newly anointed ones" may not in fact represent their purported constituency or be viewed as deserving and legitimate by their own people.[88] Thus, attention to NGOs may detract from other important voices such as official representatives and other community leaders who either have failed at attracting international support or who have chosen not to operate through an NGO.

Very few donors are cognizant of the potential and actual impact of aid on local conflicts. The U.S. Agency for International Development (USAID), the principal vehicle through which the United States directs assistance for democratization, does not routinely undertake conflict assessments before embarking on a new project. Although Andrew Natsios, the new head of USAID at the time of writing, announced that conflict prevention would become one of the four pillars of USAID's work, the decision has not yet been fully implemented.[89] Governments and organizations in fact chose many of their international representatives who build peace in Kosovo precisely because of their ignorance of Kosovar history and local power dynamics. "I don't understand it," said one British woman who had been working in Kosovo since 1993 and who found herself turned down for consultancy positions due to her "bias" toward locals. "If I were to team up with a career UN person, we would balance each other out. He would bring sensitivity about the international bureaucracy and I about the local. But no one sees his potential bias, only mine."[90]

The impact of the internationals on local culture has been largely negative. The flood of donor dollars into Kosovo has created an imbalance in the labor market and altered social values that once promoted community involvement. With the promise of making ten times the amount of their parents, young English-speaking students have abandoned their studies and accepted dead-end, short-term jobs with international agencies. With local government positions paying one-tenth the salary of parallel international positions, one-half the amount of a UN driver and one-third the amount of a translator, talented local professionals have little incentive to work in government.[91] The entry of international agencies into the provision of public services and the rise in the cost of living have killed any sense of volunteerism and reduced the Albanians' sense of group solidarity.[92] At the same time, the vast UN administration that replaced local government leaves little space for local accountability.[93]

Ironically, attempts to democratize Kosovo have had a particularly negative impact on human rights norms. In implementing democracy programs, internationals are seen as dictatorial and, in many cases, arbitrary, thereby raising the specter of a ruling elite. Through their projects, international donors attempt to reach out to and strengthen local leaders. But are they reaching the right leaders? In Kosovo, the UN administration guessed that the leaders who represented Kosovars at the Rambouillet and Kumanovo peace negotiations still spoke for the society in the post-conflict period. According to UNMIK civil administrator Thomas Koenig, "When it became clear that the United Nations needed to have some power sharing with local elites in running the place, we decided that these were the ones most likely to have legitimacy."[94]

Out of a set of bad choices, Koenig said, the United Nations attempted to make the best one. When it became clear that reliance on the Kosovar peace negotiators would in effect bar women and members of civil society from the transitional leadership, "an effort was made to include more representatives of civil society," according to Koenig.[95] Nonetheless, despite their active participation in civil society before the NATO bombing, women remained disproportionately underrepresented in the Kosovar Transitional Council and UNMIK joint civil administration.

Despite the values of participation and transparency preached by internationals, locals learned from the example set by the international effort in Kosovo that leadership in a democracy entails gaining power. Kosovars tend to understand their struggle for democracy as a struggle for "the right to rule."[96] Indeed, the language of democracy in the U.S. perpetuates this notion of a "ruling party"; much USAID and OSCE democracy assistance is designed to develop political parties' skills for participating in elections and competing for the right to rule.[97]

However, democracy should not be about "ruling," in the sense of absolute power to rule *over* the population and exercise political patronage.[98] Rather, democracy should be about good governance, which entails power-sharing among majority and minority voices, with ample protections for the human rights of ethnic, national, gender, and other minorities. Somehow the message on governance has been muted in the rush to fabricate other elements of popular democracy such as the formation of political parties and their operation in electoral politics.

Internationals not only convey misleading notions of ruling, they also send the wrong signals about the nature of institution building and norm formation. Somehow Kosovars have received the message that the international community will leave them with a democratic government that will resolve their conflict with Serbs.[99] But no democracy can claim that its institutions settle all public grievances. On the contrary, democratic institutions seek to create processes that will permit public debates to be heard in a civil fashion even when they arouse conflict or controversy.

To be sure, some norms are foundational for democracies, including fundamental human rights such as the right to life, freedom from torture, and freedom from discrimination on the bases of race, ethnicity, or gender. However, the outcomes of cases related to human rights are not determined according to a human rights framework. Instead, and most important, the democratic institutions shape the context for resolution. The notions of democratic processes and of leaders who govern instead of rule are alien to the political culture of Kosovo. But these are precisely the concepts that must be understood and embraced if a stronger human rights culture is to take root in Kosovo.

## CONCLUSION

In the summer of 2001, the civil administrator for Kosovo, Thomas Koenig, made a bold statement. He asserted that the success of the international administration in choosing and training future leaders and planting the seeds for democracy will be evaluated when locals begin to govern themselves with much less government assistance.[100] To some extent, he is correct. If a future government in Kosovo with Albanian leadership and Serbian proportional representation promotes stability and respect for human rights, this change will to some extent vindicate the international interventions in Kosovo.

But such a positive result may also reflect the reemergence of local human rights values and skills that existed *before* the international intervention and that survived *despite* international involvement. Although incomplete, a human rights culture existed in Kosovar society before the NATO bombing. The final verdict on the impact of international intervention on that culture will emerge in time.

## NOTES

The author expresses her gratitude to the U.S. Institute of Peace for its support; to her research assistants, Maryanne Yerkes and Ruth Reita; and to Janet Lord for her editorial and substantive suggestions. This chapter was presented at the American Political Science Association 2001 annual meeting in San Francisco.

1. My research was conducted in two distinct time periods. Before the NATO bombing in Kosovo and Serbia proper, in 1993–95 and 1998, I conducted extensive interviews throughout Kosovo on the nature of local understandings of human rights and the extent to which these understandings saturated political and social discourse. Also during this period, I engaged in "participatory" research, learning about the local human rights culture while conducting human rights education workshops in Kosovo and Serbia. Moreover, in 1999 and 2001, I conducted additional interviews with Kosovars on their self-understanding of human rights, on the impact of the NATO bombing on human rights culture, and on local experiences with officials of international organizations engaged in peace building. During this period, in Kosovo, Washington, D.C., and New York, I met with international government and nongovernment employees working on peace building in Kosovo. In the summer of 2001, I engaged in further participatory research when I taught a course on human rights and international law at the University of Pristina.

2. By "Kosovar" society, I refer to Albanian society in Kosovo.

3. Mayer Zaid, "Culture, Ideology and Strategic Framing," in *Comparative Perspectives on Social Movements: Political Opportunities, Mobilizing Structures, and Cultural Framings,* ed. Doug McAdam, John D. McCarthy, and Mayer N. Zald (Cambridge: Cambridge University Press, 1996), 262.

4. Renato Rosaldo, *Culture and Truth: The Remaking of Social Analysis* (Boston: Beacon Press, 1993), 26.

5. Yosef Lapid, "Culture's Ship: Returns and Departures in International Relations Theory," in *The Return of Culture in International Relations Theory,* ed. Yosef Lapid and Fredrich Kratochwil (Boulder, Colo.: Lynne Rienner, 1997), 8.

6. Richard Handlet, "Is 'Identity' a Useful Cross-Cultural Concept?" in *Commemorations,* ed. J. R. Gillis (Princeton, N.J.: Princeton University Press, 1994), 29.

7. John Witte, "A Dickensian Era of Religious Rights: An Update on Religious Human Rights in Global Perspective," *William and Mary Law Review,* 42 (2001): 707, 712. Witte states that human rights norms "need a human rights culture to be effective."

8. David P. Forsythe, *Human Rights in International Relations* (New York: Cambridge University Press, 2000), 3.

9. Jean Bethke Elshtain, *The Dignity of the Human Person and the Idea of Human Rights* (book review), *Journal of Law and Religion* 14 (1999–2000): 53, 57. See also Lisa Sowle

Cahill, "Toward a Christian Theory of Human Rights," *Journal of Religious Ethics* 9 (1980): 278.

10. E.g., when interviewed about being beaten by police, one man stated directly that the violation was against his people. Another man giving similar testimony also stressed his duty to his people to be strong in the face of human rights violations and to remain nonviolent. The interviews were conducted in Kosovo in March 1994.

11. Although ethical claims have long been made to support foreign intervention, what has changed since the end of the cold war is that Western powers have faced little opposition to their ability to define universal values and, in so doing, they have drawn on human rights ideology. What can explain this change? David Chandler offers two explanations. First, the demise of the Soviet Union has silenced many of those who previously supported anticolonialism and the possibility for independent economic and political development. This made room for states to use the international sphere to prompt ethical universals.

   Second, the turn toward reframing foreign policy in ethical terms has served the interests of domestic politicians who have sought to reach out to citizens who have grown alienated from party politics. As Chandler writes: "In these of increasing cynicism and doubt over government and politics at a domestic level, human rights promotion seems to be the one idea with the power to hold society together and point a way beyond the relativism and pessimism of our times." David Chandler, *From Kabul to Kosovo: Human Rights and International Intervention* (Sterling, Va.: Pluto Press, 2002), 63.

12. For an analysis of the impact of this shift toward human rights on U.S. foreign policy, see Steve Wagonseil, "Human Rights in U.S. Foreign Policy," *Journal of Intergroup Relations* 26 (1999): 30–31.

13. See, generally, David P. Forsythe, *Human Rights and Comparative Foreign Policy* (New York: United Nations University Press, 2000).

14. See Nicholas Wheeler, *Saving Strangers: Humanitarian Intervention in International Society* (New York: Oxford University Press, 2000), 285. Wheeler asserts that the international community is now more open to "solidarist themes."

15. Martha Finnemore, "Constructing Norms of Humanitarian Intervention," in *The Culture of National Security*, ed. Peter Katzenstein (New York: Columbia University Press, 1996), 159. See also Martha Finnemore and Kathryn Sikkink, "International Norm Dynamics and Political Change," *International Organization* 2(4) (1998): 895–905.

16. See Chandler, *From Kabul to Kosovo*, 4.

17. See, generally, Thomas Risse, Stephen C. Ropp, and Kathryn Sikkink, *The Power of Human Rights: International Norms and Domestic Change* (New York: Cambridge University Press, 1999).

18. David P. Forsythe, *Human Rights in International Relations* (New York: Cambridge University Press), 219.

19. For the evolution of the statist focus in human rights discourse and the increasing application of human rights ideology to nonstate actors, see Richard Falk, *Human Rights Horizons: The Pursuit of Justice in a Globalizing World* (New York: Routledge, 2000), and Mary Kaldor, "Transnational Civil Society," in *Human Rights in Global Politics*, ed. Timothy Dunne and Nicholas Wheeler (New York: Cambridge University Press, 1999), 223.

20. Nicholas Wheeler points out that this "notion of common humanity/human solidarity is diametrically opposed to the statist paradigm which is predicated on the contention that state leaders and citizens do not have moral responsibilities or obligations to aid those beyond their borders" (Wheeler, *Saving Strangers*, 10).

21. Michael Ignatieff, *Virtual War: Kosovo and Beyond* (New York: Metropolitan Books, 2000), 201.
22. Marie-Benedicte Dembour, "Human Rights Talk and Anthropological Ambivalence: The Particular Contexts of Universal Claims," in *Inside and Outside the Law: Anthropological Studies of Authority and Ambiguity*, ed. Olivia Harris (New York: Routledge, 1996).
23. See Julie Mertus, *Kosovo: How Myths and Truths Started a War* (Berkeley: University of California Press, 1999); Independent International Commission on Kosovo, *Kosovo Report* (New York: Oxford University Press, 2000).
24. Jack Donnelly, *International Human Rights*, 2d ed. (Boulder, Colo.: Westview Press, 1998), 20.
25. Dembour, "Human Rights Talk," 35.
26. Richard A. Wilson, *Human Rights, Culture and Context: Anthropological Perspectives* (London: Pluto Press, 1997).
27. Thomas Fitzgerald, *Metaphors of Identity* (Albany: State University of New York Press, 1993), 186.
28. For the importance of storytelling, see Julie Mertus, "Only a War Crimes Tribunal: Triumph of the International Community, Pain of Survivors," in *War Crime: The Legacy of Nuremberg*, ed. Belinda Cooper (New York: TV Books, 1999).
29. Richard Rorty, "Human Rights, Rationality and Sentimentality," in *On Human Rights: The Oxford Amnesty Lectures*, ed. Stephen Shute and Susan L. Hurley (New York: Basic Books, 1993), 114.
30. This is from the author's interview with Sonja Biserko, Helsinki Committee of Belgrade and senior fellow at the U.S. Institute of Peace, Washington, D.C., August 2001. Biserko stated that they were unsuccessful in persuading Serbs to be sympathetic to Albanians. "They [Serbs in Belgrade] never thought much about human rights until the economic situation in Serbia got oppressive and they started to think about deprivation of their own economic rights."
31. This is from the author's interviews conducted in July and August 2001 in Pristina and Prizren, Kosovo.
32. J. Senehi, "Language, Culture and Conflict: Storytelling as a Matter of Life and Death," *Mind and Human Interaction* 7(3) (1996): 150–64. See also K. Narayan, *Storytellers, Saints and Scoundrels: Folk Narrative in Hindu Religious Teachings* (Philadelphia: University of Pennsylvania Press, 1989).
33. This is from the author's interview with Sevdie Ahmeti, Kosovar human rights activist, co-head of the Center for the Protection of Women and Children, Pristina, August 2001.
34. See Mertus, *Kosovo*.
35. See Jean-Francois Lyotard, "The 'Other's' Rights," in *On Human Rights*, ed. S. Shute and S. Hurley, 135–48.
36. I disagree with David Chandler, who asserts that Albanians claimed "not human rights but political rights." Chandler, *From Kabul to Kosovo*, 108. Kosovar Albanians did in fact frame political rights as the human right to self-determination, the right to assembly and speech, the right to culture, and other specific human rights. See, e.g., various publications of Council for Defense of Human Rights, Pristina, 1993–99 (on file with the author).
37. The majority movement of Kosovars was less keen on other equality issues, e.g., the rights of women. "When we Albanians have our freedom, we [women] will have our freedom," women members of the League for Democratic Kosovo (the primary Albanian party in

the 1990s) used to say. See Julie Mertus, *War's Offensive on Women: The Humanitarian Challenge in Bosnia, Kosovo, and Afghanistan* (Bloomfield, Conn.: Kumarian, 2000) and Julie Mertus, "Contested Terrains: National Identities' Role in Shaping and Challenging Gender Identity: Women in Kosovo," in *Women, Society, and Politics in Yugoslavia and the Yugoslav Successor States*, ed. Sabrina P. Ramet (University Park: Pennsylvania State University Press, 1999).

38. This case runs contrary to David Chandler's argument that human rights activists seek to be empowered through the "legal process" and, thus, are forced to "play the role of supplicant to the human rights judges who will listen and decide" (Chandler, *From Kabul to Kosovo*, 230). My experience with Kosovar human rights activists during the past twelve years has led me to understand how deeply they mistrust all courts and how their adoption of human rights discourse is both willing and knowing.

39. Kosovar Albanians usually imagined "international community" in an instrumental manner, that is, being composed of the most influential Western nations who could respond to their plight.

40. Paul Wapner, "Politics Beyond the State: Environmental Activism and World Civic Politics," in *Green Planet Blues*, 2d edition, ed. Ken Conca and Geoffrey D. Dabelko (Boulder, Colo.: Westview Press, 1998), 118, 121.

41. For an example as to how these techniques can be employed see Mertus, *Kosovo*.

42. Paul Wapner helpfully describes a growing "environmental sensibility." I am indebted to him for his insight on the ways in which changes initiated by transnational (and local) activists occur independently of state policies. See Paul Wapner, "Politics Beyond the State: Environmental Activism and World Civic Politics," *World Politics* 47 (1995): 311–40.

43. Shkelzen Maliqi, *Kosovo: Separate Worlds: Reflections and Analyses, 1989–1998* (Pristina: MM Society, Dukagjini, 1998), 101–4.

44. Sometimes the opposing view of human rights was stated bluntly, e.g., when asked in 2001 whether human rights mattered, an Albanian working with a women's humanitarian assistance project asked, "By which group against which group?" This is from the author's interview in Prizren, Kosovo, August 2001.

45. This is from the author's interviews in Kosovo in 1994 and 1995. Albanians continually stated that it would be up to the United States to protect their human rights and, some also said, NATO with the United States in command.

46. Howard Clark, *Civil Resistance in Kosovo* (London: Pluto Press, 2000).

47. This is how Ibrahim Rugova described his nonviolent strategy to me in March 1994.

48. This is from the author's interview with Ibrahim Rugova, March 1994.

49. John Paul Lederach, *Building Peace* (Washington, D.C.: U.S. Institute of Peace, 1997), 142.

50. This is from the author's interviews with returning refugees in Albania, June 1999.

51. See Adam Roberts, "NATO's 'Humanitarian War' over Kosovo," *Survival* 41(3) (1999): 102–23.

52. Clark, *Civil Resistance*.

53. For an argument that sanctions more closely targeting Milosevic and his supporters would be more effective at promoting democratic change in Serbia, see Independent International Commission, *Kosovo Report*, 234–35.

54. Tim Judah, *Kosovo: War and Revenge* (New Haven, Conn.: Yale University Press, 2000), 119.

55. For general agreement with this proposition, see Independent International Commission, *Kosovo Report*.

56. Noam Chomsky makes this point. See Noam Chomsky, *A New Generation Draws the Line: Kosovo, East Timor and the Standards of the West* (New York: Verso, 2000), 42.

57. See Stephen M. Walt, "Two Cheers for Clinton's Foreign Policy," *Foreign Affairs* 79(2) (2000): 63–79. Walt identifies one of Clinton's four goals to be "build[ing] a world order compatible with basic American values by encouraging the growth of democracy and by using military force against major human rights abuses" (p. 67). See also, Editors, "Clinton's Foreign Policy," *Foreign Policy* 79 (November–December 2000): 18–28. They argue that the so-called Clinton Doctrine included a strong human rights component, although it was inconsistently and opportunistically applied.

58. I develop both of these theories in Julie Mertus, "Reconsidering the Legality of Humanitarian Intervention: Lessons from Kosovo," *William and Mary Law Review* 41(5) (2000): 1743–87. See also Michael Reisman, "Sovereignty and Human Rights in Contemporary International Law," *American Journal of International Law* 84 (1990): 866–76.

59. This is from the author's interview with Mike Matheson, July 2001, Washington, D.C. I interviewed seven additional legal advisors on Balkan issues in the Clinton administration and all of them said that the administration had been unwilling to come up with a clear legal definition.

60. This is the main thrust of much of the criticism in Tariq Ali, ed., *Masters of the Universe? NATO's Balkan Crusade* (New York: Verso, 2000).

61. General principles on a political solution to the Kosovo crisis were adopted on May 6, 1999, S/1999/516, Annex 1 to UN Security Council Resolution 1244. The Federal Republic of Yugoslavia indicated its acceptance in a paper presented in Belgrade on June 2, 1999, S/1999/649, Annex 2 to UN Security Council Resolution 1244.

62. UN Security Council, S/RES/1244 (1999); www.un.org/docs/scres/1999/99sc1244.htm.

63. UN Security Council, S/RES/1244 (1999), para. 6.

64. Chronology, UN Interim Administration in Kosovo (UNMIK); www.un.org/peace/kosovo/news/kos30day.htm.

65. UN Interim Administration in Kosovo, UNMIK/REG/1999/1, section 1(1), "On the Authority of the Interim Administration in Kosovo," July 25, 1999; www.un.org/peace/kosovo/pages/regulations/reg1.html.

66. UN Interim Administration in Kosovo, UNMIK/REG/1999/1, section 1(2).

67. UN Interim Administration in Kosovo, UNMIK/REG/1999/1, section 4. Section 4 further provides that "such regulations will remain in force until repealed by UNMIK or superseded by such rules as are subsequently issued by the institutions established under a political settlement, as provided in United Nations Security Council Resolution 1244."

68. In examining similarly expansive powers granted to UN administrators in Bosnia, Christine Bell astutely remarks: "It appears that the price of democracy is democracy" (Christine Bell, *Peace Agreements and Human Rights* [Oxford: Oxford University Press, 2000], 180).

69. Chronology, UN Interim Administration in Kosovo; www.un.org/peace/kosovo/news/kos30day.htm.

70. Michael Barnett and Martha Finnemore have called international organizations the modern missionaries of our time. See Michael Barnett and Martha Finnemore, "The Politics, Power and Pathologies of International Organizations," *International Organization* 53(4) (1999): 699–734.

71. This is from the author's interview with a student in Pristina, August 2001.

72. This is from the author's interview with an OSCE staff member in Pristina, August 2001.

73. This is from the author's interview with a former KLA fighter in Pristina, August 2001.
74. This is from a statement made by a Kosovar law student, Pristina, August 2001.
75. Thomas Carothers, *The Learning Curve* (Washington, D.C.: Carnegie Endowment for International Peace, 1999), 339.
76. This is from the author's interview with Shkelzen Maliqi, Pristina, August 1991.
77. I discuss the importance of such networks further in Julie Mertus, "Human Rights and the Promise of Transnational Civil Society," in *The Future of International Human Rights*, ed. Burns Weston and Stephen P. Marks (The Hague: Kluwer, 1999).
78. This is from the author's interview with an OSCE staff member, Pristina, August 1991.
79. I am grateful to Stefan Wolff for encouraging me to address this argument.
80. See, generally, Julie Mertus, "The Liberal State and the Liberal Soul: Rule of Law Projects in Societies in Transition," *Social & Legal Studies* 8(1) (1999; and Julie Mertus, "Mapping Civil Society Transplants: A Preliminary Comparison of Eastern Europe and Latin America," *University of Miami Law Review*, 53 (1999): 921.
81. Carothers, *Learning Curve*, 98.
82. Carothers, *Learning Curve*, 212.
83. See Mertus, *War's Offensive on Women*.
84. This is from an interview by the author, August 2001, Pristina.
85. This is from an interview by the author, August 2001, Pristina.
86. This is from an interview by the author, August 2001, Pristina.
87. Carothers, *Learning Curve*, 98.
88. This is a quotation from a member of a Kosovar NGO group, in an interview with the author, August 2001, Pristina.
89. This is from the author's interviews with Dayton Maxwell, USAID, July 2001, and with Dick McCall, USAID, Washington, D.C., August 2001.
90. This is from an interview by the author in Pristina, August 2001.
91. This is from the author's interview with Vetton Surroi in Pristina, August 1991.
92. This is from the author's interview with Urim Ahmeti in Pristina, August 1991. Ian Guest has made this point as well. See Ian Guest, "Misplaced Charity Undermines Kosovo's Self-Reliance," *Viewpoint* (Overseas Development Council), February 2000.
93. Chandler makes this observation as well in *From Kabul to Kosovo*, 203–94.
94. This is from an interview by the author in Pristina, August 2001.
95. This is from an interview by the author in Pristina, August 2001.
96. This is from the author's interview with a Kosovar university student, August 2001.
97. USAID and OSCE may not speak of "the right to rule," but this is how election assistance is understood by locals.
98. I am grateful to Thomas Koenig for this point; this is from an interview by the author in Kosovo, August 2001.
99. For the vast majority of Albanians, this means independence from Serbia and integration into Europe.
100. This is from an interview by the author in Kosovo, August 2001.

## TEN

# Bureaucratizing the Duty to Aid: The United Nations and Rwandan Genocide

### Michael Barnett

Discussions of humanitarian intervention invariably invoke a duty to aid. To claim that the international community can legitimately intervene in the affairs of another state because a certain "threshold" of suffering has been, or will be, crossed is to claim that the international community has a moral obligation to assist those in need.

Yet at what point does the international community have a duty to aid? Scholars and policymakers who champion some form of humanitarian intervention attempt to set the bar high enough to mitigate the dangers of abusing what many assert should be an exception to sovereignty's principle of noninterference, but not so high that it becomes an impregnable obstacle to action.[1] Because many advocates find it exceedingly difficult to establish universal criteria, they understandably create broad boundary conditions that are dependent on the (collective) eye of the beholder. Michael Walzer, for instance, argues that the crimes committed must have reached a level that they shock the conscience of the international community.[2] The Kosovo Commission concluded that humanitarian intervention is warranted when there is the "suffering of civilians owing to severe patterns of human rights violations or the breakdown of a government, the overriding commitment to the direct protection of the civilian population, and the calculation that intervention has a reasonable chance of ending the humanitarian catastrophe."[3]

Rwanda is the most straightforward case for humanitarian intervention and a duty to aid. Between April 6 and July 19, 1994, roughly 800,000 individuals were murdered. A Genocide Convention enjoined states to do something. At the beginning of the genocide there were 2,500 UN peacekeepers on the ground. Soon after the killing began, the UN force commander, Canadian general Romeo Dallaire, pleaded for a well-equipped battalion to stop the slaughter. Even those who worry that the great powers abuse the principle of humanitarian intervention concede that there was a moral imperative to stop the bloodletting; UN forces on the ground should have been allowed to protect civilians, and the United Nations should have authorized a humanitarian intervention.

Yet, for the first several weeks of the killing, the UN Security Council and Secretary-General Boutros Boutros-Ghali did not push for a humanitarian intervention or invoke a duty to aid. The council not only failed to authorize an intervention, it actually reduced the UN presence from 2,500 to 270 peacekeepers. Though these actions occurred before the United Nations might have been able to recognize the genocide for what it was, they knew that tens of thousands of individuals had perished and that tens of thousands more were in grave danger. What sets the Rwandan genocide apart from all other genocides is that the international community could have intervened at a relatively low cost before its effects were fully realized. It is this extraordinary gap between the demonic violence in Rwanda and the glacial response at the United Nations that has led many analysts to conclude that only an indifferent United Nations, comprising self-absorbed states, could have ignored such an unambiguous moral imperative and duty to aid.[4]

Beneath the surface of this tale of amoral indifference is a more complicated and troubling story that raises important questions regarding the relationship among humanitarian intervention, humanitarian organizations, and the bureaucratization of the duty to aid. In this chapter, I adopt an interpretivist approach to explain how the duty to aid was understood by those at UN headquarters; how the United Nations used the rules of peacekeeping to conclude in the first weeks that no such duty existed by attributing the killings to the more causally prominent civil war; and how the United Nations began to feel that duty only after the genocide became undeniable in late April.[5] In essence, I am attempting to discern how the participants understood and gave meaning to their actions, which were significantly shaped by the social and bureaucratic rules that defined what they believed was appropriate and proper. Doing so allows us to recognize that what scholars and observers might (falsely) conclude was UN behavior driven by the lack of ethical scruples was, in fact, behavior that those in New York considered ethical and legitimate.

This interpretivist approach involves two central assertions. First, we need a better understanding of how the duty to aid is manufactured and lived by those individuals who are charged with enacting that duty. Said otherwise, we need an ethnography of institutional ethics to understand the ethical reasons individuals use to guide and legitimate their actions. Most postmortem assessments of the Rwandan genocide proceed on the assumption that the United Nations had a duty to aid from the very moment that the violence first erupted on April 6, and from that assumption, attempt to investigate why it failed to execute that duty. In doing so, these analyses fail to ask how those in New York constructed their duty to aid and how the conceptualization of that duty was reflected in the assessment and actions of the United Nations. States, international organizations, and nongovernmental organizations are expected to develop thresholds regarding when there is a duty to aid. These thresholds evolve in relationship to organizationally situated reflections on the past and pressing imperatives of the present.

My second central assertion is that the thresholds organizations use to determine when there is a duty to aid are likely to be bureaucratized, that is, transformed into rules that policymakers subsequently use to guide their response to events. Policymakers and UN officials draw on formal and informal rules to determine when a humanitarian intervention is warranted. These rules, in short, are intended to rationalize and systematize their decisions. This is one of the virtues of a bureaucratic ethos: It establishes objective criteria to ensure that decisions are made in an impartial—and not in a politically driven—way. In the context of humanitarian intervention, developing such rules helps to ensure that states are less likely to dress their invasions in humanitarian discourse and that those humanitarian nightmares that do not have a great-power sponsor are not forsaken.[6] Yet these rules invariably evolve in practice, as actors interpret them in ways that depart from their original ethical positions. We need to understand how bureaucratization is a process and not a structure as we investigate the duty to aid.

The chapter is organized in two sections. It opens with an exploration of the rules of peacekeeping during the cold war; how the end of the cold war led those in New York to relax these rules in ways that expanded the obligations of the United Nations; how this expansion led to a situation of near moral and organizational overload; how headquarters tightened the rules of peacekeeping to save the United Nations from exploitation and ensure that the United Nations was "effective when selective"; and how the United Nations, by tightening the conditions for an intervention, recalibrated its duty to aid.

I then focus on the failure of the United Nations to recommend a humanitarian intervention during the first weeks of the Rwandan genocide and hone in on the reasons connected to the rules of peacekeeping that led it to conclude that there was no duty to aid. Specifically, once headquarters attributed the killings to the (preexisting) civil war, it concluded that there was no basis for an intervention. This determination was present not only in the Security Council but also among the very UN staff who are presumed to espouse humanitarian principles and therefore were most likely to feel the weight of a duty to aid in the presence of such killings.[7] I conclude by raising the general themes of the bureaucratization of the duty to aid and the logics that can unfold when searching for rules of humanitarian intervention.

## PEACEKEEPING RULES AND THE DUTY TO AID

Although the UN Security Council was initially envisioned as a forum to foster international peace and security, the cold war quickly crippled all of the security instruments contained in the UN Charter. As is well known, it took an extraordinary situation, the Suez crisis of 1956, for the United Nations to invent peacekeeping, a concept that did not exist in the charter. Peacekeeping quickly became the most robust UN tool. During the next forty-three years, the circumstances surrounding the Suez crisis and subsequent operations shaped the development of some rules of peacekeeping. Consent, neutrality, and impartiality were the core rules. Peacekeeping operations were to be deployed with the consent of the parties involved. The operations were to be impartial and function without prejudice to any side. Operation forces were to be lightly armed and thus rely on their moral authority and persuasion to influence parties and use force only in self-defense.[8]

These practices grew out of the strategic and political environments in which peacekeepers were deployed and the function that they were supposed to serve. Peacekeepers—rarely deployed in ongoing conflicts and never expected to enforce a peace—would only be expected to monitor cease-fires or peace agreements. There were occasional and highly controversial departures from these rules, most notably in the Congo operation, but these exceptions only reinforced the desirability of these rules.[9] In general, these rules shaped how UN officials understood the very identity of the organization, represented the source of UN influence in world politics, and affected how peacekeepers operated in the field.

These rules inscribed a very limited duty to aid for UN peacekeeping. Simply put, a direct line could be drawn between traditional conceptions of state sovereignty, peacekeeping, and the organization's operational translation of a duty to aid. Throughout much of the cold war, the United Nations operated with a highly traditional notion of state sovereignty, honored the principle of noninterference, and rarely, if ever, became involved in human rights abuses or the domestic affairs of states. Certainly, member states were reluctant to give the global organization a precedent that it might use to encroach on the state's sovereign prerogatives. But UN officials also were self-censoring, reluctant to encroach on the internal affairs of states lest they be punished by powerful states or find themselves being accused of being "political."

This traditional notion of sovereignty shaped peacekeeping patterns during the cold war.[10] Peacekeepers were largely deployed to oversee a cease-fire between two or more states. As signaled by the rules of peacekeeping, the UN "duty to aid" was evoked only under the highly restrictive condition that there was, at the very least, a cease-fire between two combatant states and the consent of the parties. There was thus very little consideration of whether peacekeepers might be deployed to aid peoples that were threatened by their governments or whose states had failed them. Although there were several moments when UN staff wanted to become involved in "humanitarian" emergencies, most famously in Bangladesh in the early 1970s, there is little evidence that they sought a peacekeeping operation for a humanitarian intervention.[11]

The end of the cold war breathed new life into the United Nations, left the Security Council busier than ever with an increasingly expanding security agenda, and saw peacekeepers deployed in record numbers. These developments affected and were affected by an expanding definition of "threats to international peace and security." Article 24 of the UN Charter hands the Security Council the "primary responsibility for the maintenance of international peace and security." Yet because the charter does not define such a threat, the council has some discretion over its meaning.[12] Whereas the council limited the definition to interstate disputes during the cold war,[13] afterward it began expanding the definition to include domestic conflict and humanitarian emergencies. Through practice and declarations, it demonstrated the view that it had a legitimate right to intervene in domestic space in intrastate disputes with regional security consequences and that it had a moral obligation to respond to humanitarian tragedies.

The growth of peacekeeping operations was the most visible indicator of increased UN activism in international and domestic security. Between 1989 and 1994, the Security Council authorized twenty-six operations across the globe, doubling in five years the number of operations it had authorized in the previous forty. The growing number of operations was impressive, as was their shifting purpose. Certainly, many of these post-1989 operations resembled the "classical" prototype. But a growing number were situated in unstable environments, where a cease-fire was barely in place if at all, governmental institutions were frayed, and rag-tag armies posed threats but were not parties to the agreement. In these settings, the United Nations was charged with multidimensional and complex tasks that were designed to repair deeply divided societies marked by a humanitarian imperative.

There were strong murmurs of a duty to aid in these developments. Specifically, the growing sense was that the "international community," that is, the United Nations, had an obligation to help those peoples and states that could not help themselves. Certainly, the Security Council used the claim of "threats to international peace and security" to justify its growing involvement in the domestic affairs of states. The council frequently observed that there was an intimate link between domestic and international security and asserted the need to help those states attempting to move from civil war to peace.

Yet the language of moral obligation also was present in UN resolutions and declarations. There was a growing sentiment that the international community should not be a bystander to those acts that shock the conscience and that sovereignty should no longer be an excuse by UN member states to commit murder. Likewise, it was felt that the international community should not stand aside and allow such acts to be labeled "private" affairs, and that it was unconscionable for the United Nations to sit idly by when doing a little might have a miraculous payoff.[14] The United Nations began to deploy peacekeepers to more situations that differed dramatically from classical peacekeeping. The organization also began to insinuate with greater frequency that it had a duty to aid and to articulate the philosophical maxim that those who can, ought.

The insertion of peacekeepers into more complex and unstable environments and growing humanitarian sentiments triggered a debate over what the rules of peacekeeping should be. Three issues were at the center of this debate: (1) when is peacekeeping a proper and effective instrument for international peace and security; (2) whether or not enforcement operations are desirable; and (3) what is the meaning of UN neutrality and impartiality. From 1990 through 1993, the United Nations drifted from the rules that had guided classical peacekeeping in all three areas. It was presumed that new conflict environments required new rules, as sticking to the old rules under new circumstances, where the lives of innocents were at stake, would be nothing short of moral turpitude.

Although the United Nations still desired the consent of the parties before authorizing a peacekeeping operation, it decided that in places like Somalia, where there was no recognized party, it must still intervene—especially when lives were at stake. Beginning with the Gulf War, the Security Council entered a new stage of peace enforcement and authorized several Chapter VII operations. The foray by the United Nations into civil wars and humanitarian assistance challenged the meaning of impartiality. How would the United Nations construe impartiality and neutrality in the face of human rights abuses, crimes against humanity, or active obstruction by the parties to the implementation of the mandate? Impartiality and neutrality became a dysfunctional shield that nearly transformed the United Nations into an unwitting accomplice to highly undesirable outcomes. The alternative, however, was to try to enforce the mandate without parties' consent, which would make the operation a party to war and compromise its credibility. The United Nations began to debate and experiment with these rules.

The sheer number of operations and the expansion of the rules of peacekeeping had two painful results. One was moral overload. The United Nations had jumped onto a slippery slope without much consideration of how to arrest its possible descent. Specifically, it became increasingly responsive to the idea that it had a duty to help those who could not help themselves, but the implication was to open itself up to more suffering than it could possibly assuage. In the aftermath of the cold war and the disintegration of the Soviet Union, there were more humanitarian nightmares than ever before (or at least the major powers opened their eyes to the steady stream that had always been present), which meant that there were many opportunities to try to rescue millions of people.

The United Nations, financially strapped, bureaucratically challenged, and comprised of self-absorbed states, did not have the political, logistical, or financial resources to accept all the opportunities and invitations. Consequently, it had to ask tough questions about who would receive its scarce resources. It began to develop rules that were supported by ethical considerations to make this determination. Headquarters started to ask whether an operation had a reasonable degree of safety and chance of success. As the secretary general, Kofi Annan, observed: "One can ask whether it is ethically sound for the international community to expend resources and political will coaxing recalcitrant parties into negotiations, or becoming involved prematurely on the ground, where there is little chance of compliance and prospects for success somewhere else are not as daunting."[15] In other words, helping those who could not help themselves could suffocate the organization. Thus the United Nations—stretched thin and facing a nearly inexhaustible number of potential crises—had to make tough choices regarding who deserved its attention. One reasonable criterion was the active support of those whom it is helping.

A related development was the UN authorization of more peacekeeping operations than it could reasonably handle, and one result was "failures" in the field. Though there was a general consensus that member states could be blamed for many of the perceived stumbles, there was also a general concern that the United Nations was engaging in its own version of "imperial overstretch." There were also fears that such commitments were putting strain on the capacity of the United Nations, thereby reducing its effectiveness in any single operation. These failures were costing the organization political capital and goodwill. Indeed, there were those in Washington who seemed to take perverse pleasure in the foibles of the United Nations, using every misstep to pump up their criticism and demand a miniaturized and tamed United Nations. Those in New York began to worry that unforgiving great powers were primed to use every setback as just cause to reduce the stature of the United Nations. These fears were already palpable by early 1993, but they became consuming after the October events in Somalia. Officials in and around the United Nations began to take greater care to protect the organization's interests, reputation, and future.

Because of the threat of moral overload and the danger to the organization's survival, the consensus at headquarters was that the United Nations had to establish more discriminating criteria for when peacekeepers were deployed and how they operated in the field. As the Secretariat and Security Council reflected on the "lessons learned," they retraced their steps back to a classic interpretation of consent, impartiality, and neutrality in peacekeeping.[16] UN staff were on board with this conception. An assistant to Kofi Annan, Sashi Tharoor, said that "this department is not in a hurry to recommend . . . any operation that would call for peace enforcement. . . . The moment we become party to a conflict, as happened in Somalia, we lose our capacity to fulfill other tasks."[17] Boutros-Ghali, who once was an enforcement enthusiast, tempered his initial zeal because of Somalia and Bosnia: "The United Nations is not able to do a huge peace-enforcement operation. This is the lesson of the last two years."[18] At another moment, he insisted: "The United Nations cannot impose peace; the role of the United Nations is to maintain peace."[19] This, he publicized, was the new "UN mentality."[20] Annan summarized the lessons he learned from recent experiences: "Peacekeeping works when you have a clear mandate, a will on the part of the people to make peace. The inspiration for acceptable and viable peace can only spring from the leaders and the people in the country."[21] Boutros-Ghali "used to say that the United Nations, like a good doctor, could not say No when asked to intervene. He has now amended this. It will intervene, but only when the patient takes its advice."[22]

While the Security Council had been employing heuristics to determine whether or not to authorize an operation, the sheer number of operations it had authorized, coupled with the failures in the field, led it to construct more rational, objective criteria that could become the focal point for future discussions and introduce more discriminating criteria. These broad sentiments were already in place and being acted upon before the October events in Somalia, but from then on, the council became more scrupulous in making consistent its use of discriminating rules.

These rules were in operation for several months before they were formalized on May 3, 1994, in a Security Council resolution, which stated that an operation would be authorized (1) when there is a genuine threat to peace and security, (2) when regional or subregional organizations can assist in resolving the situation, (3) when a cease-fire exists and the parties have committed themselves to a peace process, (4) when a clear political goal exists and is present in the mandate, (5) when a precise mandate can be formulated, and (6) when the safety of UN personnel can be reasonably assured.[23] Although the Security Council (and others) understood that it had not magically rationalized and depoliticized its decision process, it was viewed as a step forward.

By getting "back to basics" and employing more discriminating peacekeeping criteria, headquarters felt better able to protect the organization from mismanagement and misappropriation, to ensure that its peacekeepers are effective when selected, and to protect its standing in world politics. Those in New York could justify this development as not only a pragmatic recognition of the possible but also a principled defense of the United Nations.

The adoption of these rules also constricted the UN duty to aid. The Security Council was much less likely to inject peacekeepers into humanitarian crises where there was no "peace to keep," and the United Nations could not count on the parties on the ground for assistance and cooperation.[24] UN staff were largely supportive of this constriction, for they lived in constant fear that any more perceived failures would lead to the demise of the organization; reducing its exposure would increase its durability. The important point here is that the contraction of the UN duty to aid was no accident, even if the implications were not completely understood or well thought out. After all, it was because of such humanitarian nightmares as Bosnia and Somalia that New York became interested in limiting the exposure of the United Nations, determining that one condition for success was the existence of a "peace to keep."

In many respects, headquarters was attempting to locate a compromise between moral overload and moral insularity, to recognize the limited resources available to the United Nations, and to reserve it for those moments when the conditions were ripe. Nevertheless, there were strong overtones of organizational survival in the willingness of the United Nations to abstain from humanitarian crises. The organization now judged operations depending on whether they were, as one observer noted, "good for the UN or bad for the UN, a determination that hinged partly on the level of stability on the ground at these places. Simply put, the UN was as interested in its own security as in human security. The Security Council's response to Burundi in late October 1993, when tens of thousands died in ethnic violence, was partly driven by these considerations."[25] Those who opposed intervention contended that because such crises are by-products of wars marked by instability, the United Nations should require, as a precondition for effective peacekeeping, a modicum of stability. Headquarters now read all operations—including Rwanda—through these rules of peacekeeping.

## RWANDA AND THE DUTY TO STAND ASIDE

When the possibility of a UN operation in Rwanda was first formally considered by the Security Council in August, 1993, it sought answers to some of the criteria outlined in the May 3, 1994, resolution.[26] Specifically, it wanted evidence of a cease-fire; a commitment by the parties to a peaceful resolution of their conflict; a formal, negotiated peace agreement; a schedule that laid out the steps in the peace process and the endpoint of the UN involvement; and a reasonably precise mandate that spelled out UN financial, political, and security responsibilities.

The United Nations received reassuring answers to these questions. The Rwandan Patriotic Front and the Rwandan government had established a cease-fire and brokered a far-ranging political agreement, the Arusha Accords. The accords appeared to possess the ingredients required to settle the ethnic conflict and civil war. They contained provisions for attaining a multiethnic and multiparty democracy, democratic elections, the demilitarization and recreation of a national army, reform of public security apparatus, and the reintegration of the refugees.

The contribution of the United Nations to the peace process also was identified in sufficient detail. Specifically, the force was to contribute to the establishment of a weapons-free zone in Kigali; monitor the cease-fire and the security situation, assist with de-mining and refugee repatriation; investigate accusations of noncompliance with the agreement by the parties; help coordinate humanitarian affairs, and investigate reports on the police and *gendarmerie*. The Security Council limited the force to 2,548 personnel, which was only half of the planning team's recommended number. The council did this because a Chapter VI operation to oversee a peace process required the support of the parties, and because the United States and other council members became less interested in the operation as it became more expensive. To monitor all of Rwanda, the force had to be spread thin, which was not a major worry because this was to be a monitoring operation done with the consent of the parties.[27]

The Security Council believed that an operation was warranted because all the major criteria on the peacekeeping checklist were met. New York also concluded from its checklist that it would be an "easy" operation. This was a relief in two important ways. The United Nations hardly wanted to take on another troubled operation at this moment. Indeed, during its debate over the Rwandan operation, on October 3 eighteen American soldiers died in Mogadishu, giving the United Nations a major black eye. The United Nations, which was debating the Rwandan operation at the time of the Mogadishu incident, was convinced that, unlike Somalia, Rwanda passed all inspection tests. Second, the United Nations saw in Rwanda an "easy operation" but also one that would show the world that it could still make an important contribution to international peace and security. For an organization that was desperately searching for some good news, Rwanda might become the poster child for UN success. Reassured and relieved, on October 5, 1993, the Security Council authorized a new operation in Rwanda, the United Nations Assistance Missions in Rwanda (UNAMIR).

What the United Nations predicted would be an "easy" operation rapidly begged for reclassification. There were two immediate issues. The parties agreed to establish immediately a broadly based transitional government, but opposition to the Arusha Accords from the extreme right blocked the implementation of this key provision. The result was that a cornerstone to the accords was perpetually delayed by ongoing efforts by Juvenal Habyarimana's government to co-opt the extremists, who viewed any sort of power-sharing arrangement with the much-hated Tutsis and the Rwanda Patriotic Front (RPF) as tantamount to political suicide. The security situation, moreover, was becoming increasingly tense, with flashes of lethal violence. For many onlookers, there was a strong connection between the paralysis in the peace process and the deteriorating security environment. The general view from New York was that the failure to establish the transitional government was contributing to the deteriorating security environment, which was in turn frustrating the establishment of the transitional government. The only way to escape this downward spiral was to impel the creation of the transitional government.[28]

A major debate among UN officials concerned the proper role of force in providing the security required to push the peace process forward. This debate flared at those moments when either violence flashed or was predicted. The most famous moment came on January 11, 1993, when Dallaire sent a cable to UN headquarters. The cable contained an insider's account of how the extremists were planning ethnic killings to scuttle the Arusha Accords and notified headquarters of his plan to seize the weapons before they could be distributed. His view was that UNAMIR was being asked to help provide the security needed to implement the accords. If this meant using force to enforce the mandate, then force would have to be applied; the judicious use of force would keep the extremists off balance and give the moderates the assurances they needed to take the political leap forward.

The Secretariat opposed any measures that potentially violate the rules of consent and impartiality. Dallaire's recommendations were coming on the heels of a major defeat in Somalia. There, a very well armed American-led UN force suffered a major hit from extremists, which injured the U.S. position as well as that of the United Nations. At that point, Dallaire was proposing a similar operation but without the military or political support afforded by the UN Operations in Somalia (UNOSOM) operation. UN staff insisted that UNAMIR remain impartial and operate with the consent of the parties and try to use diplomatic and political means to get the parties to fulfill their agreements. This was post-Somalia peacekeeping, classical-style.

On April 6, President Habyarimana flew back from Dar es Salaam, where he was rumored to have overcome the remaining objections to the transitional government. His plane was shot down as it approached the Kigali airport, killing him and the president of Burundi. After the crash, the Rwandan military and the Interhamwe (a paramilitary force in Rwanda) erected roadblocks around the city and began to murder Tutsi politicians and moderate Hutus. Although there was considerable confusion over the extremists' objectives—was this a military coup, a return to civil war, or something else?—there was no mistaking the resumption of violence and the probable end of the Arusha Accords.

With only 2,500 lightly armed peacekeepers scattered throughout Rwanda, UNAMIR was confronted by two, increasingly untenable, tasks: protecting the lives of civilians and defending themselves. The tension between these two goals became immediately apparent when ten Belgian peacekeepers were brutally murdered while protecting a moderate politician on April 7. Headquarters feared that the entire operation was in danger. The remaining Belgian troops were running dangerously low on basic provisions and appeared marked for assassination. Moreover, resupplying or rescuing the troops was becoming increasingly difficult as the airport became a major battleground. Furthermore, the civil war between the RPF and the Rwandan government appeared likely to reignite within hours. Thus, an emaciated UN force was about to confront a terror campaign and a civil war.

The Security Council broke into two camps regarding UNAMIR's future: those favoring intervention, guided by Nigeria, New Zealand, and the Czech Republic; and those insisting on withdrawal, led by the United States and the United Kingdom. Although those in the council found ways to interject their national interests, the council's discussions were guided by the rules of peacekeeping.

Those opposing intervention had the upper hand during the entire debate; the United States and others persuasively argued that by the council's own criteria, which were intended to rationalize its decisions, there was no basis for an intervention and the peacekeepers should be withdrawn. The parties had never showed a commitment to the peace process. Arusha was on the books, but the mandate was over. A cease-fire did not exist. UNAMIR was unable to impose a cease-fire, and the RPF, fearing that France would use the United Nations to intervene on behalf of its Rwandan allies, had warned the United Nations that it might treat any intervention as a hostile act. The council, therefore, had to worry that the United Nations would become an unwitting and outgunned combatant. Indeed, this discussion was taking place against the backdrop of Gorazde, the safe haven in Bosnia where peacekeepers hardly provided a physical shield for the individuals they were sent to protect. The example from Gorazde only served to reinforce the view that putting peacekeepers into conflict situations was irresponsible.

Furthermore, the situation in Rwanda was a civil war, and peacekeepers had not proven effective under such conditions. There is considerable debate regarding why the United Nations focused on the civil war, an issue that I cannot take up here.[29] It was a fact that a civil war was taking place. The council tended to associate the obscenely high civilian death toll with that war because of a prior understanding of the nature of the Rwandan conflict and the assumption that this presumed past could be mapped directly onto current circumstances. Many argued that because the council framed Rwanda as a civil war with horrendous civilian casualties, the peacekeepers, at the very least, had to try to negotiate a cease-fire between the RPF and the Rwandan forces. There was little else for the United Nations to do. In other words, those in New York grabbed the UN rulebook and concluded that if these civilian deaths were related to the civil war, then the appropriate and best available response was to arrange a cease-fire. After assigning the cease-fire as UNAMIR's chief task, they then decided that a handful of UN personnel could do the job.

Those in the council who opposed intervention identified other barriers to action. First, there were no other troops ready to reinforce UNAMIR or to provide a realistic basis for an intervention. No member state said that it was ready to dig deeper into its reserves and contribute soldiers to an ill-defined operation in the middle of a bloodbath. Moreover, any chance for an intervention virtually disintegrated on April 10, when Brussels indicated it would almost certainly withdraw its troops in the immediate future.[30] Belgium was UNAMIR's backbone. No governments volunteered to reinforce or offered to replace UNAMIR's troops, because Belgium was already a fixture on the ground. And the peacekeepers were in mortal danger. Ten peacekeepers had been brutally murdered. The Secretariat was providing graphic depictions of a UNAMIR consumed by self-protection tasks. The Secretariat concluded that if there were no troops to reinforce UNAMIR, then it should be withdrawn immediately; any delays only increased the risk to UN personnel.

There also was the future of peacekeeping to consider. Peacekeeping depends on the willingness of member states to provide troops. If member states believed that the council was unable to take reasonable measures to protect their soldiers, then they would be reluctant to provide such forces in the future. Peacekeepers, unprotected and exposed, could do little good for those on the ground and much harm to the reputation and longevity of the United Nations. The organization had learned a valuable lesson the hard way; that is, inserting peacekeepers, who were at best only a symbol of the international community's concern, helped no one on the ground, transformed peacekeepers into sacrificial lambs, and damaged the health of the organization.

In general, those in the council that opposed intervention pointed to the rules of peacekeeping to argue that the conditions were not ripe for an intervention; the existence of the civil war meant that UN obligations were attenuated, and that, though tragic, there was very little that the international community could do when ethnic groups were determined to kill each other. By these standards, there was no duty to aid the Rwandans.

Those in the council who favored intervention could not demonstrate how Rwanda fulfilled the minimal conditions for a peacekeeping operation, which crippled their cause. They could point to the massacres, but they could not credibly claim that the killings posed a threat to international peace and security. They could not point to any volunteers among the international troops, to a viable peace process, or to a cease-fire. In short, they could not point to the essentials. The rules of peacekeeping were an impregnable barrier to action.

By the beginning of the second week of debate, the council ceased to consider intervention and decided to maintain a semblance of a force in Kigali. It did so for several reasons. The council thought Dallaire should be given the chance to arrange a cease-fire. Peacekeepers were protecting thousands in various sites in Kigali. Even a stripped-down force could provide the platform for a future intervention. It wanted to maintain appearances and avoid the image of abandoning "Africa" in its hour of need. Guided by the rules of peacekeeping and confronting the cold realities as they saw them on April 21, the council members voted by consensus on Resolution 912, which reduced UNAMIR to 250 troops and restricted its mandate to the negotiation of a cease fire between the Rwandan military and the RPF.

The council was not alone in using the rules of peacekeeping to determine that there was no duty to aid, for the evidence suggests that the Secretariat used a similar path to arrive at the same conclusion. During this entire two-week period, there was not a single, concerted statement by the secretary general arguing that there was a duty to aid and favoring intervention. Moreover, there is no evidence that the Secretariat held its tongue because it feared that the council would reject a plea for an intervention. Instead, the compelling evidence suggests that it used these same rules to determine that there was no basis for peacekeeping; that the return of civil war meant that UN responsibilities were lessened; that it was quite likely that even if the troops could be found they would meet failure in the field; and that in this post-Somalia moment, such a failure might very well spell the end of the United Nations. The Secretariat also concluded that there was no duty to aid the Rwandans—and if a duty existed, it would be to the survival of the organization.

Those at UN headquarters used the rules of peacekeeping to prioritize UN commitments and to generate their duty to aid. Especially robust was the linkage between the civil war and the propriety of withdrawal. The return of civil war fed into a contractual view of responsibility that had begun to take root. An emerging proposition held that the United Nations was obligated to help those who could help themselves, and that the failure of the parties to fulfill their responsibilities lessened the obligations of the United Nations to them. This shifted the locus of responsibility. It also signaled that the limited resources of the United Nations would be distributed to those who demonstrated a willingness to abide by agreements. For instance, in the months immediately before the genocide, the Security Council and the secretary general told the Rwandans that if they did not establish the transitional institutions, the United Nations would close down the operation; this created, in essence, a quid pro quo. The United States exploited this contractarian approach in its case against intervention. It argued, in effect, that the Rwanda mandate was an implied contract between voluntary parties, in this case between the United Nations and the Rwandan signatories to the Arusha Accords. Because the Rwandan parties had broken the contract, the mandate was null and void.

This contractual discourse was intertwined with rules of peacekeeping that arranged UN obligations in such a manner that the United Nations was elevated over Rwanda. All were aware of the thousands dead and the thousands more at risk. But as long as the dead were associated with a civil war, UN duties remained limited to trying to find a cease-fire. More caustically, as long as the number of dead was kept below a certain threshold (e.g., 100,000) and was not convincingly connected to a premeditated campaign of extermination, then many in New York could conclude that UN duties should remain limited. This conclusion was not precedent setting but consistent with recent practices and as designed by the rules. The rules of peacekeeping functioned as intended, limiting the conditions for a duty to aid and creating an ethic of indifference.

## CONCLUSION

The relative indifference of those in the organization has been more unsettling than anything because of our expectations about their professional roles and normative commitments. This raises the central issue of why individuals embrace a different moral yardstick once they are cradled inside an organization. Perhaps because one's contribution is relatively small, one cannot relate it to the larger outcome of the institution's decisions. Perhaps the sheer physical, psychological, and social distance between officeholder and subject make it more difficult to fully comprehend the effects of one's actions. Perhaps the absence of dissident voices and a normal fear of being ostracized and ridiculed lead to a normalization of complacency. Perhaps the bureaucratic appeal to broad rules reduces concern for the particular and makes it more difficult to see and to act in extreme and extenuating circumstances. Perhaps Western culture has become rule governed and legalized to the point that legalities and rules become a substitute for private morality. Perhaps blind ambition plays a part in the belief that one's career prospects are best served by ignoring ethical dilemmas.[31] All of these factors surfaced at various moments during the involvement of the United Nations in Rwanda and shaped the moral terrain and the meaning and practice of duty.

The patterns of moral differentiation were many, but it is difficult to escape the totemic importance of bureaucratic rules. The rules were constructed to determine when peacekeeping would be an efficient instrument of international peace and security. The presumed virtue of these rules was that they would go some distance in creating benchmarks that could be applied across a range of cases. Such a move would help to depoliticize and rationalize the Security Council's discussions. No one held the illusion that the mere articulation of these criteria would magically expunge power politics, but there was considerable consensus that these rules would help bring greater rigor to discussions.

However, it was not only the desire to be more efficient and rational that produced these rules; also prominent was the logic of organizational survival. Those in New York worried that the very absence of sufficiently restrictive rules was doing grave damage to the organization. They hoped that with more restrictive rules, the United Nations would be better buffered against the elements. To be sure, this meant that UN engagement would only be appropriate when there was a "peace to keep." Indeed, past failures in the field clearly demonstrated that the United Nations was the "right tool for the job" only when there was a peace to keep, and that deploying the United Nations under any other circumstances does little good on the ground and exposes the organization to much harm.

These rules, once established, served to channel arguments and provide templates for reasons that had a dramatic impact on how those in New York conceptualized their responsibilities toward human suffering and during moments of humanitarian catastrophes. The rules, in effect, condensed how those in New York looked upon their responsibilities; if the United Nations is effective only under conditions of stability and a working cease-fire, then it is not obligated to intervene in all humanitarian nightmares. The rules differentiated subjects of concern from subjects of neglect, those to whom responsibilities were unmediated, and those to whom they were abridged. This rule-guided development, moreover, dug a moat around the United Nations. Its overdeveloped sense of responsibility was creating moral overload and proving to be self-destructive. Acting responsibly, the United Nations recognized, also included a duty to safeguard the organization's health. It was Rwanda's misfortune to be the first explicit applications of these rules.

The UN decisions that led it to be a virtual bystander to genocide did not come to pass because it had lost its ethical scruples. It believed that by standing aside, it was doing the right thing. The rule-driven morality of the United Nations, argumentatively put, had driven out the private morality of those in New York, leading them to adopt an ethical position that made turning away from crimes against humanity not merely pragmatic but also principled. The rules of peacekeeping had reconstructed the moral compass, pointing the needle north toward New York and away from Kigali. Those at the United Nations believed that they had a duty to aid—just not then.

## NOTES

1. For discussions regarding the conditions governing a humanitarian intervention, see Henry Shue, "Let Whatever Is Smouldering Erupt? Conditional Sovereignty, Reviewable Intervention and Rwanda 1994," in *Between Sovereignty and Global Governance: The United Nations, the State, and Civil Society*, ed. Albert J. Paolini, Anthony P. Jarvis, and Christian Reus-Smit (New York: Saint Martin's Press, 1998); J. Bryan Hehir, "Intervention: From Theories to Cases," *Ethics & International Affairs* 9 (1995): 1–13; Michael Smith, "Humanitarian Intervention: An Overview of Ethical Issues," *Ethics & International Affairs* 12 (1998): 63–80; Dan Smith and Mona Fixdal, "Humanitarian Intervention and Just War," *Mershon International Studies Review* 42(2) (1998): 283–312; and Terry Nardin, "The Moral Basis of Humanitarian Intervention," *Ethics & International Affairs* 16(1) (2002): 57–70. For a terrific overview of the issues, see Nicholas Wheeler, *Saving Strangers* (New York: Cambridge University Press, 2000), chap. 1.
2. See Michael Walzer, "Politics of Rescue," *Dissent* 42 (winter 1995): 35–41.
3. The Ottawa Roundtable for the International Commission on Intervention and State Sovereignty Report from the Ottawa Roundtable, International Commission on Intervention and State Sovereignty, essentially adopted the criteria from the Kosovo Report. For the Ottawa Roundtable findings, see Canadian Center for Foreign Policy Development, January 15, 2001; http://web.gc.cuny.edu/icissresearch/ottawa%20independent%20report.htm. For the Kosovo Report, see Independent International Commission on Kosovo, Kosovo Report, December 20, 2001; www.kosovocommission.org/reports/1-summary.html. Also see Sean Murphy, *Humanitarian Intervention: The United Nations in an Evolving World Order* (Philadelphia: University of Pennsylvania Press, 1996), 294–97.
4. The literature on the United Nations and Rwanda is quite voluminous. See Samantha Power, *A Problem from Hell: American in the Age of Genocide* (New York: W. W. Norton, 2002); Carol Off, *The Lion, the Fox, and the Eagle: A Story of Generals and Justice in*

*Rwanda and Yugoslavia* (Canada: Random House, 2001); Arthur Jay Klinghoffer, *The International Dimension of Genocide in Rwanda* (New York: New York University Press, 1998); Bruce Jones, *Peacemaking in Rwanda: The Dynamics of Failure* (Boulder, Colo.: Lynne Reinner, 2001); Alan Kuperman, *The Limits of Humanitarian Intervention* (Washington, D.C.: Brookings Institution Press, 2001); Boutros Boutros-Ghali, *The United Nations and Rwanda, 1993–1996* (New York: United Nations Press, 1996); *The International Response to Conflict and Genocide: Lessons from the Rwanda Experience* (Copenhagen: Joint Evaluation of Emergency Assistance to Rwanda, March 1996); Philip Gourevitch, "The Genocide Fax," *New Yorker*, May 11, 1998, 42–46; UN Department of Peacekeeping Operations (DPKO), *Comprehensive Report on Lessons Learned from United Nations Assistance Mission for Rwanda* (UNAMIR) (New York: United Nations, 1996); United Nations, *Final Report of the International Commission of Inquiry* (Rwanda) (New York: United Nations, 1999); Senate of Belgium, *Parliamentary Commission of Inquiry Concerning Rwanda* (December 1997); Howard Adelman and Astri Suhrke, eds., *The Path of a Genocide: The Rwanda Crisis from Uganda to Zaire* (New Brunswick, N.J.: Transaction Publishers, 1999); and Organization of African Unity, *Report on the UN and Genocide in Rwanda*, May 2000.

5. The themes developed in this essay derive from Michael Barnett, *Eyewitness to a Genocide: The United Nations and Rwanda* (Ithaca, N.Y.: Cornell University Press, 2002).

6. For the importance of impartiality as a principle of justice, see Thomas Nagel, *The View from Nowhere* (New York: Oxford University Press, 1986). Advocates of humanitarian intervention also have been attentive to impartiality, but they have tended to focus less on the rules determining whether a humanitarian intervention is warranted and more on the body that makes this determination. See Shue, "Let Whatever Is Smouldering Erupt?" and Hehir, "Intervention."

7. Although the United States and other member states were reluctant to undertake an intervention because it did not coincide with their "national interests" at this moment, in the council the debate over intervention was fought over application of generalized rules and not over particularistic interests. I also find no compelling evidence that the Secretariat determined that because the council was not going to intervene it decided to avoid recommending a policy that it knew would be rejected. See Barnett, *Eyewitness to a Genocide*, chap. 4.

8. See Marrack Goulding, "The Evolution of United Nations Peacekeeping," *International Affairs* 69(3) (1993): 453–55.

9. For a brief overview of the development of these rules, see Rod Paschall, "U.N. Peacekeeping Tactics: The Impartial Buffer," in *Soldiers for Peace*, ed. Barbara Benton (New York: Facts on File, 1996); and I. Rikhye, M. Harbottle, and B. Egge, *The Thin Blue Line: International Peacekeeping and Its Future* (New Haven, Conn.: Yale University Press, 1974), chap. 2.

10. Michael Barnett, "The New U.N. Politics of Peace: From Juridical Sovereignty to Empirical Sovereignty," *Global Governance* 1(1) (winter 1995): 79–97.

11. Brian Urquhart, *A Life in Peace and War* (New York: W. W. Norton, 1987), 221–22.

12. Hans Kelsen, *The Law of the United Nations: A Critical Analysis of Its Fundamental Problems* (New York: Praeger, 1950), 727; and Rosalyn Higgins, *The Development of International Law Through the Political Organs of the United Nations* (New York: Oxford University Press, 1963), 266.

13. Michael Howard, "The Historical Development of the UN's Role in International Security," in *United Nations, Divided World: The UN's Roles in International Relations*, ed. A.

Roberts and B. Kingsbury (New York: Oxford University Press, 1993), 69–70. In 1961, the Security Council declared the situation in Congo a threat to peace and security; in 1966 it made a similar determination in the case of Rhodesia, and again in 1977 it did so in South Africa. But these were notable exceptions to the general rule.

14. There is a debate about whether the United Nations and/or the Security Council is the agent of the "international community." See, e.g., Chris Brown, "Moral Agency and International Society," *Ethics & International Affairs* 15(2) (2001): 87–98. I argue that the Security Council views itself as the representative of the international community in "The Politics of Indifference at the United Nations: The Security Council, Peacekeeping, and Genocide in Rwanda," *Cultural Anthropology* 12(1) (1997): 551–78.

15. Kofi Annan, "Peacekeeping, Military Intervention, and National Sovereignty in Internal Armed Conflict," in *Hard Choices: Moral Dilemmas in Humanitarian Intervention*, ed. Jonathan Moore (New York: Rowman & Littlefield, 1998), 64–65.

16. The U.S. assistant secretary of state for international organizations, Douglas Bennet, remarked, "Call it lessons learned. What's been happening is a pretty steep learning curve on which we have discovered some of the strengths and weaknesses of collective peacekeeping" (Jon Stewart, "U.N. Learns Hard Lessons on Peacekeeping," *San Francisco Chronicle*, March 28, 1995, A1).

17. Stewart, "U.N. Learns Hard Lessons."

18. Julia Preston, "Vision of a More Aggressive UN Is Diminishing," *Washington Post*, January 4, 1994, A24. Also see Georgie Anne Geyer, "The World as Viewed from the U.N. Helm," *Washington Times*, April 3, 1994, B4; Barbara Crossette, "U.N. Leader to Call for Changes in Peacekeeping," *New York Times*, January 3, 1995, A3.

19. Julia Preston, "U.N. Officials Scale Back Peacemaking Ambitions; Planned U.S. Withdrawal from Somalia Demonstrates Limitations," *Washington Post*, October 28, 1993, A40.

20. Geyer, "World as Viewed from U.N."

21. Barbara Crossette, "U.N. Falters in Post-Cold-War Peacekeeping, But Sees Role as Essential," *New York Times*, December 5, 1994, A12.

22. "Trotting to the Rescue," *Economist*, June 25, 1994, 22.

23. UN Security Council Presidential Statement, May 3, 1994, *Statement on the Conditions for the Deployment and Renewal of Peacekeeping Operations* (S/PRST/1994/22). This proposal was seen as a natural follow-on to previous resolutions, including that of May 28, 1993 (S/25859).

24. See, e.g., U.N. Security Council Resolution, May 31, 1994, *Renewal of the Mandate of the UNOSOM and the Process of National Reconciliation* (S/Res/923).

25. Alan Ferguson, "U.N. to Reject Burundi's Plea for Peacekeepers," *Toronto Star*, November 3, 1993, A17. Also see Julia Preston, "No Mission to Burundi, U.N. Says; Peace Deployments Apparently on Hold," *Washington Post*, November 2, 1993, A10.

26. For overviews of Rwanda, see Mahmood Mamdami, *When Victims Become Killers: Colonialism, Nativism, and the Genocide in Rwanda* (Princeton, N.J.: Princeton University Press, 2001); Human Rights Watch, *Leave None to Tell the Story: Genocide in Rwanda* (New York: Human Rights Watch, 1999); Gerard Prunier, *The Rwanda Crisis: History of a Genocide*, 2d ed. (New York: Columbia University Press, 1999); Catharine Newbury, *The Cohesion of Oppression: Clientship and Ethnicity in Rwanda, 1860–1960* (New York : Columbia University Press, 1988); and Rene Lemarchand, *Rwanda and Burundi* (New York: Praeger Press, 1970).

27. Astri Suhrke, "Dilemmas of Protection: The Log of the Kigali Battalion," in *The Path of a Genocide*, ed. H. Adelman and A. Suhrke (New Brunswick, N.J.: Transaction Publishers, 1999), 257.

28. "Second Progress Report of the Secretary-General on the United Nations Assistance Mission for Rwanda," S/1994/360.

29. See Barnett, *Eyewitness to a Genocide*, chap. 4.

30. Human Rights Watch, *Leave None to Tell the Story*, 619.

31. Mark Bovens, *The Quest for Responsibility: Accountability and Citizenship in Complex Organizations* (New York: Cambridge University Press, 1998), 128–30.

ELEVEN

# Humanitarian Intervention after September 11, 2001

## Nicholas J. Wheeler

What impact will September 11, 2001, have on the future of humanitarian intervention? For liberals like Michael Ignatieff, the worry is that the "war against terrorism" is trumping human rights concerns in U.S. foreign policy.[1] Rather than promoting human rights, the United States is aligning itself with repressive governments that support its counterterrorist policies. This strategy is a twenty-first–century replay of the cold war, when the need to secure allies against Soviet communism led the United States to support dictators all around the world. The considerable softening of the American position on Russia's human rights violations in Chechyna in return for its support in the war against terrorism is one of the many examples of this shift in priorities.[2]

The marginal role accorded human rights under U.S. president George W. Bush is a disturbing development, but it would be wrong to imply that this marks a decisive break with past American policy. Whatever the rhetoric of Bill Clinton's administration, it did not strongly advance human rights and humanitarian intervention in its foreign policy. Indeed, what is striking in the area of humanitarian intervention is the similarity between the position taken by Clinton and his successor. During the election campaign, Bush and his Democratic challenger Albert Gore publicly endorsed Clinton's decision not to send U.S. troops to Rwanda to stop the genocide in 1994.[3] It is virtually inconceivable that the Bush administration would risk U.S. forces to save strangers in peril after having declared a state of national emergency following the attacks on September 11. The president likened the threat posed by al Qaeda to the United States to that of Nazism.[4]

This privileging of national interest over an ethic of human solidarity continues the trend in U.S. and Western policy during the past decade. In the 1990s, the humanitarian impulse was not the dominating factor in any cases of armed intervention that placed the lives of military personnel at significant risk.[5] There was considerable debate among academics and practitioners in the 1990s as to whether there is, or should be, a legal right of humanitarian intervention for individual states. But the barrier to protecting endangered citizens in Rwanda and Bosnia was not the constraint of sovereignty and the norm of nonintervention. It was the reluctance of states, in the words of UN secretary-general Kofi A. Annan, to "pay the human costs of intervention" when they believed they had no significant interests at stake.[6] Based on this reading, September 11 merely serves to accentuate the political constraints on humanitarian intervention established in the last decade.

The war against terrorism opens up an alternative moral possibility: Military interventions could be used to promote both counterterrorist and humanitarian objectives. If what was lacking in the 1990s was a compelling security interest to motivate intervention in situations of humanitarian emergency, then does the threat posed by global terrorism supply the missing ingredient? The case of al Qaeda's relationship with the Taliban in Afghanistan suggests that terrorists will find secure havens in "failed states." Such states are defined by a collapse of the civil government, an absence of law and order, gross and systematic human rights abuses, massive violations of international humanitarian law, and private militias and factions controlling the means of violence.[7] Could military intervention aimed at wiping out terrorist groups in failed states also contribute to protecting their endangered populations? To explore this question, this chapter focuses on the U.S. intervention in Afghanistan. Bush claimed that humanitarian goals would be accomplished at the same time as the defeat of al Qaeda and the Taliban when he launched Operation Enduring Freedom (OEF) on October 7, 2001.

There is considerable controversy over the legality and the legitimacy of the U.S. use of force in response to the attacks of September 11. It is not my intention here to enter into this debate.[8] Rather, my purpose is to show the contradictions between U.S. humanitarian claims and the conduct of its intervention in Afghanistan. Crucially, I argue that there were (and are) alternative policies available that would have satisfied U.S. security interests while also protecting Afghan civilians from starvation and lawlessness. The first section of the chapter considers which criteria should be met for an intervention to count as humanitarian. This revolves around the complex relationship among motives, justifications, means, and outcomes. This framework is then applied to the case of Afghanistan.

The second section of the chapter exposes the discrepancy between the altruistic protestations of the Bush administration and the moral consequences of its military and political strategy. There is disagreement over how far intervenors should take on a long-term responsibility for rebuilding failed states. What is significant in this case is that the administration acknowledged an obligation to help the Afghan people rebuild a viable government. Living up to this pledge requires a prolonged political, economic, and military commitment. The third section of the chapter argues that although the United States and the wider international community have committed economic aid for general reconstruction, there has been a failure to provide the military forces necessary for the effective security of the Afghan people.

## WHAT COUNTS AS A LEGITIMATE HUMANITARIAN INTERVENTION?

The generally accepted understanding of humanitarian intervention is defined by Wil Verwey as "the threat or use of force by a state or states . . . *for the sole purpose of preventing or putting a halt to a serious violation of fundamental human rights.*"[9] Similarly, Bhikhu Parekh considers humanitarian intervention as an act "wholly or primarily guided by the sentiment of humanity, compassion or fellow feeling, and in that sense disinterested."[10] Intervention of this character is thus viewed as an act of great kindness in which a particular political community places the lives of its nationals at risk to save noncitizens in danger. Richard Miller pushes this logic to its extreme when he suggests that it is "a form of altruism writ large, a kind of self-sacrificial love"[11] that expresses our common humanity. Outsiders should be totally regarding of others in their actions, to the point of giving up their lives to protect fellow humans in need.

Few versions of humanitarian intervention would establish such a demanding requirement. In effect, Miller's position requires soldiers to place the protection of civilians before any concerns about their own survival. A more modest ethic would require soldiers to accept considerable risks to save noncitizens but still maintain the right to protect themselves. Even this concession to a cosmopolitan morality challenges head-on the realist or statist conviction that military humanitarian intervention violates the compact between state and citizen; states have a primary obligation to protect their citizens from danger, including those who serve in the armed forces.[12]

Some realists would rule out any military humanitarian intervention on these grounds. Others would accept that there is a responsibility to help those in need, subject to this not challenging core security interests or imposing overly high costs on the intervening state's military personnel. This concern with reducing the risks faced by soldiers sits very uneasily with Miller's notion that humanitarian intervention is an act of self-sacrifice. Faced with these two extreme positions on the balance to be struck between self and other-regarding actions, the challenge is to find a strategy that protects civilians without exposing military personnel to excessive dangers. Western states failed to achieve this balancing act in the 1990s. It was the value of "force protection" that dominated the conduct of Western intervention, leading to a failure to act when civilians were at risk as in Bosnia and, most shockingly, in Rwanda, where more than 800,000 people perished in the genocide.

The West's failure to satisfy an ethic of humanitarianism in its interventions fueled the long-standing suspicion of the doctrine of humanitarian intervention on the part of many states in the developing world. In debates on the legitimacy of humanitarian intervention, spokespersons for governments of developing countries stress the importance of disinterestedness in a state's actions. Soliman Awaad, Egyptian assistant foreign minister for multilateral affairs, maintains that the legitimacy of intervention depends upon "norms and criteria of humanitarian intervention . . . [being] indiscriminately applied to all cases without double standards or politicization."[13]

Requiring an intervention to be exclusively motivated by ethical values sets too high a moral standard, and no action will satisfy such an ambition. It is hardly surprising, then, that we find this position advanced by those governments that are opposed to legitimating a doctrine of humanitarian intervention. Moreover, it begs the question of how to judge whether an intervention is motivated purely by this consideration. Individuals are often blind to the multiplicity of reasons that inform their actions. Why should it be assumed that governments are any different? Judging the publicly professed reasons against a state's subsequent actions is one test for gauging the validity of the rationales invoked for an action. However, even if there is no discrepancy, this does not rule out the presence of other nonhumanitarian motives.

A less stringent requirement is that humanitarian motives be the primary but not exclusive reason for intervention. This position was adopted in the 2001 report of the International Commission on Intervention and State Sovereignty (ICISS), which declares: "The primary purpose of the intervention, whatever other motives intervening states may have, must be to halt or avert human suffering."[14] This viewpoint presupposes the legitimacy of nonhumanitarian reasons when the moral imperative to rescue is the driving force behind action. The ICISS suggests three possible subtests for assessing whether this criterion has been satisfied: The operation should be multilateral in character; it should have the support of other states in the region, and the intervention should be welcomed by those whom it is intended to help.[15] The difficulty with this formulation is that it provides no basis for distinguishing between strong and weak humanitarian motives. Comparing the gap between justifications and subsequent actions might alleviate the problem, for if the humanitarian motive is weak or even nonexistent, it might be expected that the demonstrated commitment to defending humanitarian values would be very limited.

Making the primacy of motives the defining test of a legitimate humanitarian intervention excludes cases in which states act for nonhumanitarian reasons but produce a positive humanitarian outcome. The best examples of this are India's intervention in East Pakistan in 1971, Vietnam's intervention in Cambodia in December 1978, and Tanzania's intervention in Uganda in 1979.[16] In each case, the use of force motivated primarily by concerns of self-defense led to the ending of human rights emergencies. This leads Michael Walzer to argue "mixed motives are a practical advantage";[17] in the absence of important security interests, neither India nor Tanzania (he does not mention Vietnam) would have intervened. The ICISS argues that a good test of a state's humanitarian bona fides is the degree to which the victims welcome the intervention.

This argument breaks down in the case of Vietnam's intervention in Cambodia, because the available evidence suggests that humanitarian concerns played little or no part in Vietnam's decision to intervene.[18] Yet the Cambodian people initially viewed the action as one of liberation, for it rescued them from the brutality of the Khmer Rouge.[19] This was a case in which self-defense was compatible with the rescue of the Cambodian people from what Bouhdiba, chair of the UN

Subcommission on Prevention and Discrimination and Protection of Minorities, described as nothing less than "auto-genocide."[20] The humanitarian credentials of the Vietnamese action were tarnished by the subsequent human rights abuses of the government it installed to replace the Khmer Rouge. But this does not alter the fact that Vietnam's actions in removing the Pol Pot regime provided an important measure of protection for the Cambodian people compared with the horrors through which they had just lived.

This case lends support to those like Fernando Tesón who argue that the prominence accorded the motives of the intervenor is based on a flawed methodology. He writes that unless the nonhumanitarian reasons behind an action "have resulted in further oppression by the intervenors . . . they do not necessarily count against the morality of the intervention. The true test is whether the intervention has put an end to human rights deprivations. That is sufficient to meet the requirement of disinterestedness, even if there are other, nonhumanitarian reasons behind the intervention."[21] This argument is supported by Gary Klintworth, who argues that Vietnam's toppling of Pol Pot met "the criteria for an excusable humanitarian intervention, because 'the net result of [the intervention] was to interrupt the killing that was underway inside Cambodia.'"[22]

Building on Tesón's work, I argued in *Saving Strangers* that motives should only disqualify an intervention as humanitarian if it could be shown that they had undermined the humanitarian success of the operation. To satisfy the minimum or threshold requirements of a legitimate intervention, four criteria must be met. First, there must be a supreme emergency, which I defined following Walzer as an act that "shock[s] the moral conscience of mankind." Second, all credible avenues of peaceful redress must have been exhausted (the principle of last resort, in the just war tradition). Third, the military means employed must be proportionate to the gravity of the human rights violations. And fourth, there must be a positive humanitarian outcome, which is defined as both short-term *rescue* (i.e., ending the humanitarian emergency) and long-term *protection* (i.e., addressing the underlying political causes of the abuse of human rights).

The fourth requirement is particularly controversial. Parekh argues that humanitarian intervention should be distinguished from the delivery of aid to those in need. The latter, he argues, is only concerned to relieve suffering; it does not address its underlying causes. It might be argued that satisfying this requirement establishes too demanding a test of humanitarian intervention. Moreover, if this standard were widely accepted, it could have the effect of inhibiting states from engaging in such open-ended commitments.

This concern is reinforced by the worry that ambitious experiments in "nation building" aimed at addressing the root causes of gross human rights abuses would end in failure and a humiliating exit. Are outsiders engaging in a dangerous kind of moral hubris in believing they can solve the problems of troubled war-torn societies such as Afghanistan, Kosovo, and Somalia? Without ignoring the force of these arguments, or denying that armed rescue to end genocide or mass murder is morally preferable to inaction, this short-term conception of intervention is fatally flawed.

The problem is that once the intervening forces pull out, there would be little to prevent a return to conflict and violence within the society. The challenge facing intervening states is to relieve the immediate suffering while taking on a long-term political, economic, social, and military commitment to help local actors create a new polity governed by law. The ICISS called this the "responsibility to rebuild," arguing that the long-term aim of "international actors . . . [is] "to do themselves out of a job" by handing back responsibility to local elites.[23]

To avoid the danger of intervention turning into a new imperialism or neocolonialism, outside actors must, according to Parekh, "ensure that the structure [new government] is evolved by or in cooperation with the affected parties and not externally imposed."[24] The question that he does not answer is how intervenors should respond if the dominant power holders within the society forcibly resist the creation of new structures of legitimate authority that seek to marginalize their influence.

Although Vietnam's intervention in Cambodia was widely condemned at the time as a breach of the sovereignty principle, I argued in *Saving Strangers* that it counts as humanitarian because there was a happy—if purely inadvertent—coincidence among motives, means, and a positive humanitarian outcome.[25] Vietnam did not consciously tailor its intervention to meet the goals of proportionality and long-term protection of human rights, and in this sense, its ending of "auto-genocide" inside Cambodia is best labeled a case of "inadvertent humanitarian intervention."[26]

This can be contrasted with cases in which an actor justifies the use of force by invoking humanitarian claims. States that seek to occupy the moral high ground risk being exposed as hypocritical if they fail to meet this standard of behavior. American intervention in Afghanistan poses some difficult conceptual issues in this regard, because there was no attempt by the Bush administration to argue at the outset that it was motivated primarily by humanitarian reasons. Nevertheless, there was a clear intention on the part of the administration to buttress political support for the action by partly defending the operation in these terms. The remainder of the chapter examines how well U.S. political and military leaders lived up to these humanitarian claims.

## HUMANITARIAN MOTIVES AND MEANS IN OPERATION ENDURING FREEDOM

The plight of the Afghan people in the 1980s and 1990s is well documented. Twenty years of civil war had destroyed any semblance of legitimate state institutions, with warlords ruling different parts of the country.[27] Throughout the 1990s, there was a growing toll of civilian casualties as a result of armed conflicts between the rival factions, and all parties to the civil war were responsible for gross violations of human rights. Faced with such a desperate situation, 2.3 million people had sought refuge in neighboring Iran since the early 1980s.[28] In 2000, international nongovernmental organizations (NGOs) concerned with human rights and UN humanitarian relief agencies predicted an impending humanitarian catastrophe, exacerbated by the worst drought in thirty years, placing 1.5 million Afghans at risk. The Taliban's own brand of fanatical Islam compounded the suffering of women, who found themselves virtually enslaved; they were denied basic education, an authoritarian dress code was imposed, and their access to medical care was restricted.[29]

The humanitarian emergency inside Afghanistan in 2000–1 raises the question whether armed intervention was justified to protect a population in danger. The Clinton administration never seriously considered using U.S. forces to remove the Taliban. Instead, it restricted itself to nonmilitary coercive pressures by supporting the imposition of sanctions in the hope that this would induce the Kabul government to stop providing a safe haven for al Qaeda. At the same time, the administration delivered humanitarian aid to alleviate the suffering of the Afghan people. Indeed, the United States was the largest supplier of humanitarian aid to Afghanistan in 2001.

The atrocities inflicted on U.S. citizens by al Qaeda on September 11, 2001, fundamentally changed calculations on intervention in Afghanistan. Bush declared the following objectives in launching OEF on October 7, 2001: to attack al Qaeda terrorist training camps and military installations of the Taliban regime; to bring al Qaeda's leaders—crucially Osama bin Laden—to justice; and to send a signal to other states that those harboring terrorist groups risk similar attacks being visited on them.[30] Yet from the outset of the campaign, the president also felt it necessary to justify the action in humanitarian terms. He declared:

> The oppressed people of Afghanistan will know the generosity of America and its allies. As we strike military targets, we'll also drop food, medicine and supplies to the starving and suffering men and women and children of Afghanistan.[31]

Given President Bush's publicly stated opposition to using the U.S. military for "soft" humanitarian purposes, the depth of his moral commitment should be called into question. Conversely, it could be argued that the commitment to deliver humanitarian aid as part of the operation against al Qaeda and the Taliban was a logical development of the administration's prewar role as the major aid donor to Afghanistan.[32] Trying to demonstrate Bush's sincerity—or lack of it—demonstrates the limits of relying solely on motives as the defining yardstick of legitimate intervention. What matters is that the president felt it was necessary to publicly defend the action in humanitarian terms, an implicit admission that this justification was a necessary enabling condition of the action. The president recognized the importance of being seen to address the humanitarian crisis in bolstering international support for U.S. action, especially among public opinion in the Islamic world.

Six weeks into the war, U.S. deputy assistant secretary of defense for peacekeeping and humanitarian affairs Joseph J. Collins repeated Bush's pledge that humanitarian assistance was an integral part of the Pentagon's military strategy. He stated that "military actions have not slowed humanitarian assistance but rather . . . [it has been] possible to both fight successfully and to accelerate humanitarian assistance at the same time."[33] Collins pointed to UN World Food Program deliveries of aid, which reached record levels in October and November.

Before OEF, at least 1.5 million Afghans were at risk from starvation. Speaking at a State Department briefing on January 3, 2002, Andrew S. Natsios, administrator of the U.S. Agency for International Development (USAID), declared that this number had received assistance. In reply to a question regarding the impact of the military operation on the delivery of aid, he claimed that the defeat of the Taliban in November had "made it possible for [humanitarian] operations to get back up [leading to] the success, the rapid success."[34] The extent to which the need to publicly legitimate military operations as a contribution to relief efforts had become part of the language of U.S. military leaders can be seen in remarks given by the chief of the U.S. Central Command, General Tommy Franks, at a press conference on January 18, 2002. He claimed that the attack against the Taliban had gone hand-in-hand with a humanitarian relief operation that had saved thousands of lives and that this was something of which Americans should be proud.[35]

This rosy picture of the humanitarian consequences of OEF differed sharply from the story told by the NGOs concerned with relief that were operating inside the country. The president of Médécins Sans Frontières, Jean-Herve Bradol, reiterated the organization's long-standing view that there was a fundamental contradiction between "shooting with one hand while offering aid with the other."[36] If aid is not perceived as entirely neutral, then there is a risk that those delivering it will be viewed as partisan and hence legitimate targets of war. Ian Wallace, operations director of the U.K. relief organization Tearfund, endorsed this view. He stated that, "Food should not be used as a weapon of war . . . there is an inevitable conflict of interest between the political objectives of Operation Enduring Freedom and the humanitarian principles of impartiality and neutrality."[37] The United States dropped hundreds of thousands of packets of food aid from airplanes, but aid workers dismissed this as a propaganda stunt. The action was aimed at winning the favor of the Afghan people, which aid agencies recognized as a political, and not a humanitarian, objective. Médécins Sans Frontières officials contended that the food drops were so minor and poorly targeted in relation to the needs of the people that they were far outweighed by the negative effects of the bombing.[38]

Moreover, there is evidence that the aid packets had adverse humanitarian consequences. Civilians were killed on occasions when packages hit them or their homes; the vulnerable and weak were the least able to take advantage of such drops; and many Afghans were afraid to approach the rations packets, which were the same color as the U.S. Air Force's cluster bomb casings.[39] Those humanitarian NGOs that opposed the U.S. military intervention called upon all sides in the conflict to create a neutral humanitarian space within which the UN World Food Program and relief organizations could safely deliver food. Exposing the "humanitarian cover" employed by the United States as a sham, the president of Médécins de Monde, Claude Moncorgé, argued that this "humanitarian label" should not be given "to strategies, interests . . . and options decided by a military staff in function of the interests of the state that employs them."[40] These views reflect the strong antipathy among many aid agencies to the idea that force can support humanitarian objectives.

The NGOs' prescription to create a neutral humanitarian space overlooked the fact that it was the difficulty of securing consent from the warring parties that had contributed to a worsening of the humanitarian situation in 2001–2002. Moreover, the criticism that association with the U.S. military would compromise humanitarian relief efforts was founded on a misunderstanding of the role that the military was playing. Because of concerns that relief convoys with U.S. military protection would become targets, USAID had recommended that the military not be used for the specific delivery of aid. This decision was justified on the basis of U.S. experience in Bosnia, where "the convoys that had no military protection had a higher delivery rate than those with military protection."[41] This decision makes an important concession to those in the humanitarian aid community who worry that military intervention jeopardizes their neutrality while also recognizing that force is sometimes necessary to create a secure environment in which such operations can take place.

Although the available evidence points to a significant increase in humanitarian aid reaching Afghans by January 2002, the short-term effect of the bombing campaign was to significantly undermine existing relief efforts. It was not until late November that adequate supplies of relief aid were reaching the country, with the fall of the Taliban and Bush's decision to give a further $325 million in aid being key factors in this improvement. With the demise of the Taliban, UN international staff and NGO staff who had left the country owing to the lack of security returned, and local drivers were now prepared to deliver aid to areas where previously there had been fighting. Nevertheless, it took a couple of months to reach most of those who needed help. It is estimated that during this period there was a 40 percent reduction in aid deliveries.[42]

Carl Conetta, who has undertaken an authoritative study of the humanitarian consequences of the U.S. bombing campaign, estimates that the number of internally displaced persons increased by approximately 360,000; 200,000 Afghans fled to Pakistan and Iran, and a minimum of 3,000 Afghans died as a result of the disruption to aid deliveries.[43] The latter could be a conservative figure, for much depends upon how the disruption of aid affected already very high mortality rates in central, northern, and western Afghanistan. On a worst-case basis, Conetta estimates that it could have been as many as 20,000, whereas Jonathan Steel suggests that the figure could have been as high as 49,600.[44] These estimates are, of course, counterfactual, because no one knows how many Afghans would have died had the bombing not taken place.[45]

Any assessment of the humanitarian results of OEF has to take into account not only the indirect effects of the bombing but also its direct impact on Afghan civilians. The Pentagon has released no official figures for civilian casualties, but Conetta claims in a separate study that the bombing killed 1,000 to 3,000 innocent Afghans.[46] The Pentagon made considerable efforts to avoid civilian casualties, and U.S. Secretary of Defense Donald Rumsfeld declared, "I can't imagine there's been a conflict in history where there has been less collateral damage, less unintended consequences."[47] There is evidence that air strikes were called off due to concerns about civilian casualties. Nevertheless, there are also grounds for arguing that the United States did not exercise sufficient care in targeting residential areas where it suspected al Qaeda and Taliban personnel were hiding.

Likewise, it can be argued that the United States did not make sufficient effort to ensure that the intelligence it received from local regional commanders was accurate before launching air strikes. The inadvertent but foreseeable killing of Afghan civilians as a consequence of U.S. strikes rested very uneasily with Bush's claim that the use of force was aimed at the Taliban and al Qaeda and not at the Afghan people.[48] As one anti-Taliban commander, whose forces were central to the battle in December against al Qaeda in the Tora Bora Mountains, lamented: "Why are they hitting civilians? This is very bad. Hundreds have been killed and injured. It is like a crime against humanity. Aren't we human?"[49] One of the horrific realities of war is that it is impossible to provide total immunity to civilians. The ethical question raised by the U.S. conduct of OEF is whether American military personnel should have accepted greater risks to better protect innocent civilians.

Was there a more humane means of intervention that would also have met the vital U.S. security interest in defeating al Qaeda? Conneta argues that OEF should not have been launched until the regional military commanders had reached a firm consensus on the political framework for a post-Taliban government.[50] The United Front, which included the Tajik based "Northern Alliance" (dominated by the Panshiri faction of the Shura-i-Nazar) and the Uzbek forces of General Abdul Rashid Dostrum, was the backbone of the anti-Taliban resistance. Any new political order had to accommodate this grouping, but the key to building a new legitimate government depended upon ensuring that other ethnic groups—crucially, the majority Pashtun community—were also brought into the governing process. The best means of achieving this would have been the rapid deployment of a force of at least 30,000 troops to come in behind the United Front as it routed Taliban forces.[51]

Such a force, mandated under Chapter VII of the UN Charter, could have facilitated humanitarian relief efforts, reduced the risks of banditry, disarmed any warlords who challenged the agreed structure of political authority, and helped train a new national army and police force. Even in the absence of an agreement on a new political framework, the deployment of a robust international force would have facilitated relief efforts and helped establish a secure environment.[52] This operation would not have precluded U.S. Special Forces attacks against al Qaeda and Taliban personnel, including the use of limited air power.[53] However, it would have reduced the number of direct and indirect civilian casualties that occurred as a consequence of the bombing campaign. The Bush administration opposed such a deployment for three reasons. First, it viewed this type of operation as a distraction from the central task of defeating the Taliban and al Qaeda. Second, it worried that its forces would suffer higher casualties than would be the case with an air campaign. And third, it did not want to get sucked into a protracted ground commitment.

The bombing campaign clearly exacerbated the humanitarian crisis in the short term. Nevertheless, it could be argued that in removing the Taliban from power, the

United States opened the door to the possibility of a new and more humane order in Afghanistan.[54] The key issue is whether the United States and the wider international community are exploiting this new opportunity to improve human rights or whether Afghanistan is slipping off the map of moral concern, as happened after the withdrawal of Soviet forces in the late 1980s.

## THE "RESPONSIBILITY TO REBUILD"

Having started down the path of intervention in Afghanistan and having confined the humanitarian component to the delivery of aid, the Bush administration found that it was not so easy to limit U.S. humanitarian responsibilities. In several speeches during 2002, administration officials expanded the moral justifications behind their intervention to encompass the rebuilding of Afghanistan as a law-governed state.[55] In an interview with the *Daily Telegraph* in February 2002, Rumsfeld asserted in response to a question of what had been won through the war: "Well, I think . . . number one [is] the fact that the Taliban no longer are the governing factor in that country. And in that sense, the people of Afghanistan have, in a significant way, been liberated from the policies and the repressive actions of the Taliban government."[56]

U.S. officials were quick to point to expressions of this "liberation," such as the freedom of women not to wear the traditional *burqa* (though many are continuing to do so) and the return of girls and women to education. Speaking on April 17, 2002, at the Virginia Military Institute, the president emphasized the U.S. responsibility to help the people of Afghanistan. Invoking the vision of George Marshall and his successful plan that rebuilt Western Europe, Bush stated: "We know that true peace will only be achieved when we give the Afghan people the means to achieve their own aspirations . . . peace will be achieved by helping Afghanistan develop its own stable government. . . . By helping to build an Afghanistan that is free from this evil [the Taliban] and is a better place in which to live."[57]

Although it was a very small sum in comparison with the $3.8 billion spent on the war against al Qaeda and the Taliban, the United States committed $297 million as part of a three-year, $4.5 billion package of international aid agreed on at the Afghan donor conference in Tokyo in January 2002. Two months later, the House International Relations Committee voted to approve further American aid through a package of $1,100 million over a four-year period.[58] In addition, the United States continues to be the highest donor of emergency aid to Afghanistan. This is a vital contribution, given the UN estimate in March 2002 that "millions of people will need food aid to survive until mid-2003."[59]

There was (and is) a fundamental flaw in the Bush administration's thinking about rebuilding Afghanistan. It has not recognized that long-term success depends upon a robust international military commitment to establishing peace and security. Without a replacement of "rule by Kalashnikov"[60] with the rule of law, there is no prospect of long-term security for Afghans. Representatives of the different factions met in Bonn in December 2001 and agreed to establish an interim central government headed by Hamid Karzai. They also agreed as part of the negotiations to the deployment of an International Security Assistance Force (ISAF) to help stabilize the situation. The UN Security Council adopted Resolution 1386 on December 20, 2001, establishing under Chapter VII a seventeen-nation force led by the United Kingdom and consisting of 4,500 troops. Its mandate was to assist the interim government in the maintenance of security in Kabul and its surrounding areas. The force is not charged with a peacekeeping role in the classic sense of the term, because it has the authority "to take all necessary measures to fulfil its mandate."[61]

Central authority in Afghanistan is very weak, and Karzai's writ barely extends beyond Kabul, where ISAF protects him and his administration.[62] The dominant political force in the government is the Tajiks, who control the Defense and Interior Ministries. The Pashtuns resent the influence wielded by the Tajiks, as do the Uzbek and Hazara militias that dominate the northeast. A major flash point occurred in the summer of 2002, when the Tajik general Ostad Atta Muhammed clashed with the Uzbek commander Dostrum over control of Mazar-i-Sharif.[63] This pattern of regional military commanders competing for power and influence is repeated across large parts of the country.[64]

Recognizing that his authority depended upon an expansion of ISAF nationwide, Karzai requested this in January 2002.[65] UN officials from the secretary general on down supported such a development. On March 27, Kamal Hossain, the UN special representative on human rights in Afghanistan, in his report to the Human Rights Commission, stated: "The first priority in restoring human rights is security . . . how do you start the rule of law after the rule of the gun for so many years?"[66] In calling for the deployment of more troops across Afghanistan, Hossain reflected that "never has so much been at stake if a modest request for 10,000 to 20,000 international security forces is not urgently and immediately made available."[67] The United States–based NGO Human Rights Watch (HRW) supported this pessimistic evaluation. On the basis of fieldwork in the country, it produced a report on May 6, 2002, that documented a climate of chronic insecurity in which ethnic minorities and women were especially vulnerable.[68] In a press release issued a day later, Kenneth Roth, HRW's executive director, declared, "If the international community doesn't take more effective steps immediately to establish security throughout Afghanistan, the country is likely to return to the rampant human rights abuses and warlordism that characterized the last decade."[69] The disparity between Bush's promise to help Afghan civilians live in dignity and the cruelty and abuses depicted by HRW could not be starker.

The United States is not oblivious to the need to provide security, but there was a debate within the administration during 2002 over how best to do this. On one side of the argument were the civilian leaders in the Pentagon, who argued strongly against any direct participation of U.S. forces in ISAF or any expansion of the force beyond Kabul, for four reasons. They argued, first, that America contributes logistic and intelligence support, and is committed to helping evacuate ISAF in the event of an emergency. A key reason for their opposition to an expansion of ISAF is that this would make any such operation far more dangerous.

Second, it was believed by the civilian leaders in the Pentagon that an enlargement of ISAF would impair U.S. search-and-destroy operations against residual al Qaeda forces. Third, an ISAF with a mandate to protect civilians would have to be prepared to challenge the power of the regional warlords, and the secretary of defense was not persuaded that this was a mission for which it was worth risking the lives of U.S. soldiers. Fourth, Rumsfeld had his eye on the larger war against terrorism and did not want U.S. forces tied up in Afghanistan when they could be needed to fight Iraq. Set against this position was the State Department, which argued that without an expansion of ISAF, there would be no long-term stability in Afghanistan.

Rumsfeld wanted the Afghans to take responsibility for their own security, and this position prevailed within the administration. The U.S. commitment to restoring law and order consisted of providing funds for the training of a new national army and police force.[70] And in the interim, while this is being created, the administration has assigned small teams of Special Forces to keep the peace between the regional commanders and build up support for the central government. The problem is that the United States relies on local warlords to provide the intelligence to track down residual pockets of al Qaeda, and in exchange for this help, these warlords want weapons and money. However, strengthening the warlords in the southern and eastern parts of the country is inimical to the task of building new state institutions, because these Pashtun commanders resent the influence wielded by the Tajiks in the new government.[71]

The contradiction at the heart of U.S. postwar planning is that given the discontent felt by Pashtuns towards the central government, it is going to be very difficult to create a multiethnic national army. The defense minister, General Mohammed Fahim (leader of the Northern Alliance), is viewed with great suspicion by the other military commanders, who perceive his plans to build a national army as a cover for consolidating the power of the Tajiks in government. And though the other warlords feel threatened by Fahim, they are unlikely to agree to demobilize their forces.[72]

The Bush administration's decision to accommodate the regional warlords rather than contribute to an expanded ISAF stemmed from fears of becoming trapped in an Afghan quagmire. It also rested on a profound misunderstanding of what went wrong in Somalia. The belief is that Operation Restore Hope, initiated by George H. W. Bush in December 1992, succeeded because the United States worked with the militia leaders. Conversely, the UN operation that replaced the United States–led force failed because it embarked on the process of disarmament with disastrous results. This interpretation overlooks the fact that the mandate given by the Security Council to UN Operations in Somalia (UNOSOM II) in March 1993 was crucial because it aimed to strip the militias of their power and create the space for a civilian leadership to emerge.[73] The problem was that the UN force that replaced the Americans was too weak to challenge the power of the warlords. What U.S. officials have failed to see is that the initial intervention was flawed because it did not put in place structures for the long-term maintenance of the rule of law in Somali society.

It is ironic that the current administration is repeating exactly the same error in Afghanistan.[74]

To succeed in Afghanistan where the United Nations failed in Somalia, it is vital that ISAF be expanded to the major cities, display a readiness to use force against any factions violently opposing its mission, and be equipped for combat operations with effective air support. Also, the process of disarmament needs to be applied in an impartial manner, any use of force must respect the laws of war, ISAF must have the widest possible backing among the different ethnic groups in Afghan society, ISAF operations must exhibit cultural sensitivity; and the intervenors must not exit at the first sign of serious trouble.

By the late summer of 2002, it was apparent that opposition to a limited expansion of ISAF was softening among Pentagon hard-liners. As the security situation in Afghanistan deteriorated, and pressure mounted within Congress for a stronger international security presence, the administration indicated that it was prepared to support a modest expansion of the international force. Joseph Biden and Richard Lugar of the Senate Foreign Relations Committee spearheaded a bipartisan effort in early August 2002 that resulted in a bill urging Bush to expand ISAF, authorizing $1 billion to this end.[75]

The concern among members of the Senate Foreign Relations Committee was that a failure by the United States to provide effective security could lead to a renewal of civil war, necessitating a more costly American intervention to rectify the situation. In an interview with the *Daily Telegraph* on August 21, 2002, Paul Wolfowitz, the deputy secretary of defense, gave voice to the shift in administration thinking: "I think there are some benefits that could come from using ISAF in ways outside of the capital, not necessarily as a permanent presence but as a way of providing some transitional security in places where it's needed."[76] Some ideas being considered involved creating a mobile group of peacekeepers that could deployed to trouble spots and placing forces in cities where there are tensions between rival warlords, as in Mazar-i-Sharif.[77] One important motivation behind the change of heart on the part of senior Pentagon officials was that improved security might allow U.S. troops to be redeployed if needed against Iraq.[78]

The extent of this shift should not be exaggerated, because there was still no question of American troops being committed to ISAF. And in the absence of this, it is extremely unlikely that other states will be prepared to volunteer the necessary forces. The continuing reluctance of the Bush administration to join ISAF is crippling efforts at rebuilding a viable civic authority in Afghanistan. U.S. officials have expressed frustration at the slowness with which the $4.5 billion in aid pledged at the Tokyo conference has been reaching Afghans. Aid is significant in boosting the authority of the central government, and in providing combatants with incentives to lay down their arms and return to civilian life.

Indeed, economic development offers the best long-term hope of persuading people to abandon the patronage of the warlords. However, as many critics of the administration have pointed out, the prerequisite for this process of political and economic reconstruction is greater security. In the absence of this, as Mike Jendrzejczyk of HRW points out, there will be no "re-emergence of Afghan civil society, and [no establishment of the] legal and administrative institutions to protect the rights of all Afghans."[79] This is why a major expansion of ISAF led by the United States remains crucial if Bush is to live up to his promise to leave Afghanistan better than he found it. [80]

In addition to its moral responsibilities to the Afghan people, the United States has a compelling security interest in making Afghanistan a success. In response to the charge that U.S. policies risk a return to civil war—with the possibility that a new hostile government could come to power—supporters of the administration reply that no future Afghan government would defy the United States after having seen what its military power did to the Taliban.[81] If this viewpoint describes official thinking, then it highlights the marginal role that humanitarian concerns play in administration policy. But even on its own terms, this conception of security is myopic and self-defeating; it fails to locate the war in Afghanistan as part of a larger struggle for hearts and minds in the Islamic world.

After promising to help Afghans live in dignity, the United States will further erode what support it enjoys among Muslims if it is perceived as merely seeking its own interests in Afghanistan—the effect will be to further radicalize Muslim opinion against U.S. interests and values.[82] The problem is that this threat to U.S. security is intangible to policymakers in comparison with the immediate costs and hazards of taking on a robust peace enforcement role inside Afghanistan.

## CONCLUSION

Just as Vietnam would not have launched its intervention in Cambodia without a compelling threat to national security, the United States only used force against the Taliban because of the attacks on September 11. Yet the fact that the U.S. national interest was the primary motivating factor should not automatically disqualify Operation Enduring Freedom as a humanitarian intervention.

As I argued in relation to the Vietnamese action in Cambodia, the key test is whether nonhumanitarian motives prevent an intervention from satisfying—however accidentally—the criteria of proportionality and a positive humanitarian outcome (presupposing that the other two criteria I identified have also been satisfied). Endorsement of OEF as a case of "inadvertent humanitarian intervention" has come from Michael Walzer, a prominent member of the liberal left in U.S. politics. He suggests that "the Taliban regime had been the biggest obstacle to any serious effort to address the looming humanitarian crisis, and it was the American war that removed the obstacle. It looked (almost) like a war of liberation, a humanitarian intervention."[83]

There are two basic problems with this position. First, it exaggerates the success of OEF in humanitarian terms. Second, it overlooks the fact that U.S. policymakers explicitly defended the use of force on humanitarian grounds. It is important to differentiate between cases where a humanitarian outcome is an unintended by-product of an intervention (Vietnam's intervention in Cambodia) and those in which governments publicly establish a normative benchmark with which to judge the results of an intervention. By laying claim to the moral high ground in the hope of winning over domestic and world public opinion, the Bush administration exposed itself to such an assessment. I have argued that measured against this yardstick, the U.S. action fails as a humanitarian intervention. The administration's refusal to take the lead on ISAF expansion is the best example of its failure to match words with deeds.

The reluctance of the United States to accept the risks to its military personnel that would be required by a long-term commitment to protect Afghans is indicative of the minor role that humanitarian considerations played in the decision to act. This supports Roberto Belloni's contention that "if motives are largely non-humanitarian, then it is unlikely that the intervening states would be involved in any way in a post-war transition, because the principles that led to the intervention are only superficially altruistic."[84] The implication of this is that if humanitarian intervention is defined—as I have argued it should be—in terms of a "responsibility to rebuild," it will be rare to find a correspondence between nonhumanitarian motives and a positive humanitarian outcome.

The U.S. intervention in Afghanistan, like that of the Vietnamese in Cambodia, was primarily justified as self-defense. But the fundamental change in legitimating principles in international society in the intervening two decades also enabled the United States to utilize humanitarian arguments. During the cold war, this line of defense had not been available to policymakers, because human rights imperatives were firmly subordinated to the principles of sovereignty, nonintervention, and the nonuse of force. The best example of a state being constrained from raising humanitarian claims during the cold war was Tanzania's intervention to topple the government of Idi Amin in 1979. Despite being moved to act by humanitarian concerns, there is every reason to think that without the earlier Ugandan attack against Tanzanian territory, President Julius Nyerere would not have acted. He acknowledged in several speeches at the time that humanitarian intervention was not a legitimate basis for the use of force against another sovereign state.[85]

However, as a consequence of the inroads that human rights made into the principle of sovereignty during the 1990s, a new norm of intervention has developed that supports the use of force to protect civilians from genocide, mass murder, and ethnic cleansing. This norm is strongest in Western states, which were the key players throughout the 1990s in establishing this new principle in international society. The extent to which the language of humanitarianism has become a legitimating ground for U.S. intervention can be seen in the fact that despite being primarily motivated by vital security interests, the administration felt the need to invoke a humanitarian rationale alongside that of self-defense.

There are two opposing interpretations of this increasing reliance on humanitarian justifications. One is that if governments are required to defend the use of force on these grounds, this will inhibit them from acting in ways that directly contradict the stated moral purposes. The argument for this "constraining effect" is that governments—even the most powerful—do not want to be exposed as hypocrites. This creates a need to ensure conformity between legitimating reasons and subsequent actions. Alternatively, there are those who argue that this belief in the power of norms underestimates the capacity of states to manipulate the discourse of humanitarianism to serve their own ends.[86]

The case of American intervention in Afghanistan suggests that the critics are right to caution against investing too much confidence in the constraining effect of humanitarian norms. Before September 11, opponents of U.S. foreign policy were anxious that the discourse of humanitarianism would enable the United States to intervene at will. American policy in Afghanistan will have done nothing to mollify this concern.[87] Although there has been criticism of U.S. policy from members of Congress, the media, academics, and the wider human rights community, an effective opposition capable of holding the administration accountable for its actions has not developed.

Does this mean that humanitarian norms cannot function to inhibit the single superpower? Such a conclusion is too sweeping, because two contextual factors might be adduced as to why this constraint failed to exert much influence in this case. The first is that most Americans were fixated on the atrocities committed by al Qaeda and the continuing threat posed by terrorism. As a result, they did not feel a strong sense of solidarity with the plight of Afghan strangers. The second explanation is that public opinion simply did not recognize an inconsistency between the administration's words and deeds. Walzer suggests that effective opposition to U.S. policy has been "politically disarmed" by "pictures of [Afghan] women showing their smiling faces to the world, of men shaving their beards, of girls in school."[88]

As I have argued, these manifestations of progressive change are predominantly restricted to Kabul, where ISAF operates. For many Afghan civilians, their daily lot remains one of fear, insecurity, and a struggle for survival. Unfortunately, this picture of Afghan life painted by human rights NGOs and other informed commentators have failed to capture the moral imagination of millions of Americans. Strengthening the inhibiting effect of humanitarian norms on future U.S. policy depends upon establishing a public sphere in which American citizens are mobilized to demand the inclusion of humanitarian values in foreign policy. In the absence of this, the danger is that U.S. policymakers will come to believe that they can use force without legal or moral censure—as long as they couple force with a token humanitarianism that will nullify dissent at home.[89]

There are two fundamentally different ways to view the relationship between humanitarian intervention and self-defense in the war against terrorism. The first is the model of "direct self-defense," whereby military strategy is aimed at defeating the capabilities of selected terrorist groups or states that sponsor and/or perpetrate terrorism. The motivation for intervention would be to protect vital national interests, and the threat of danger is both compelling and immediate. The challenge facing those committed to human rights is to mobilize domestic and international public opinion to ensure that humanitarian aims are factored into military planning. The Bush administration did not deny this responsibility in relation to Afghanistan, but it failed to back up its moral claims with an effective strategy for civilian protection. An important task for those who believe that violent humanitarianism is not a contradiction in terms is to show that there were alternative military strategies that could have met both counterterrorist and humanitarian goals.

Even if future operations of direct defense are conducted with greater regard for their humanitarian impact, the nexus between human rights and self-defense offers no prospect of humanitarian intervention for cases in which there is no direct threat to national security. It was the lack of a compelling security rationale that led UN member states to abandon the people of Rwanda to their fate in 1994. Unless a future genocide posed a clear threat to prospective intervenors, reliance on direct defense would provide no basis for rescue.

Direct defense can be contrasted with the second way to view the relationship between humanitarian intervention and self-defense, what Richard Miller calls "indirect self-defense," whereby states recognize a general interest in preventing the spread of violence and oppression on a global scale.[90] In this view, although the danger to a nation's security is not immediate, as in the case of direct defense, allowing injustice and violence to flourish in distant places will cause an erosion of restraints against violence everywhere. Had such an argument shaped Western policy toward Afghanistan in the early 1990s, the country might never have become a sanctuary for bin Laden and al Qaeda. What September 11 showed was not only the terrible moral consequences that can flow from allowing states to collapse into violence and disorder but also the indivisibility of security on a global scale. Writing before the terrorist attacks against New York and Washington, Miller contended that indirect self-defense was flawed as a motivation for humanitarian intervention because states that are less vulnerable to the effects of distant violence have no incentive to act. Conversely, those that have most to gain from containing the escalation of conflict might be least capable of acting.[91]

Miller is right that indirect self-defense has not served to persuade citizens of Western countries to sacrifice for strangers, but it does not follow from this that it is flawed as a moral basis for humanitarian intervention. The thrust behind indirect defense is that the price of inaction only manifests itself over the long term. This is the argument that Western governments should have made to their publics when confronted with the genocide in Rwanda.

In his speech to the British Labour Party conference in October 2001, Tony Blair asserted that the international community would have a compelling "moral duty" to stop another genocide like the Rwandan one.[92] He was keen to identify his support for Bush's war against terrorism as part of a wider moral agenda of internationalism. But his promise that future genocides would not be ignored begs the question of whether an ethic of human solidarity can be developed to realize this project. The story of humanitarian intervention in the 1990s points to the triumph of particularist moral attachments over universalist ones. Western publics have sympathized with those in need, and they have often been quite generous in donating aid. But their governments have steadfastly refused to pay the human costs necessary for effective intervention. The failure of Western states—crucially the United States—to take a leadership role in ISAF expansion in Afghanistan does nothing to suggest that this basic moral proclivity has changed.

The Bush administration failed to seize the opportunity in Afghanistan, but September 11 opens the door to interventions that protect both U.S. security and humanitarian values. Yet at a deeper level, the war against terrorism has not affected the struggle between a realistic ethic that seeks to limit risks to intervenors and one of common humanity that believes military personnel should be placed in danger to protect fellow humans in peril. It is the outcome of this moral battle and not September 11 that will determine the future of humanitarian intervention.

## NOTES

The author thanks Alex Bellamy, Jean-Marc Coicaud, Tim Dunne, Toni Erskine, Anne Harris, Anthony Lang, Colin McInnes, Patricia Owens, Robert Patman, and Tom Weiss for their many helpful comments on earlier versions of this chapter. He is also grateful to William Maley and Amin Saikal for sharing their considerable knowledge of Afghan politics with him.

1. Michael Ignatieff, "Is the Human Rights Era Ending?" *New York Times*, February 5, 2002. For a less pessimistic view, see Tim Dunne, "After 9/11: What Next for Human Rights," *International Journal of Human Rights* 6, no. 2 (summer 2002).
2. For a further discussion see Dunne, "After 9/11."
3. Quoted in Cori E. Dauber, "Implications of the Weinberger Doctrine for American Military Intervention in a Post-Desert Storm Age," in *Dimensions of Western Military Intervention*, ed. Colin McInnes and Nicholas J. Wheeler (London: Frank Cass, 2001), 80. The furthest Bush would go was to state that were another Rwanda to occur when he was President, he would seek to "encourage [the United Nations] to move." Quoted in Tom Farer, "Humanitarian Intervention after 9/11: Legality and Legitimacy," in *Humanitarian Intervention: Legal, Political and Ethical Perspectives*, ed. Jeff Holzgreffe and Robert Keohane (Cambridge: Cambridge University Press, 2002).
4. See the text of Bush's speech to Congress, *Los Angeles Times*, September 20, 2001; www.latimes.com (downloaded November 4, 2001).
5. This argument is made in Nicholas J. Wheeler, *Saving Strangers: Humanitarian Intervention in International Society* (Oxford: Oxford University Press, 2000).
6. Kofi A. Annan, *Preventing War and Disaster: A Growing Global Challenge*, 1999 Annual Report on the Works of the Organization (New York: United Nations, 1999), 21.
7. U.K. Ministry of Defense's *Peace Support Operations Joint Warfare Publication*, JWP 3-50 (London: Joint Warfare Publications and Ministry of Defense), para 205.
8. For a good overview see Michael Byers, "Terror and the Future of International Law," in *Worlds in Collision: Terror and the Future of Global Order*, ed. Ken Booth and Tim Dunne (London: Palgrave Macmillan, 2002), 118–28.
9. Quoted in Oliver Ramsbotham and Tom Woodhouse, *Humanitarian Intervention in Contemporary Conflict* (Cambridge: Polity Press, 1996), 43 (emphasis added).
10. Bhikhu Parekh, "Rethinking Humanitarian Intervention," *International Political Science Review* 18, no. 1 (January 1997): 54.
11. Richard B. Miller, "Humanitarian Intervention, Altruism, and the Limits of Casuistry," *Journal of Religious Ethics* 28, no. 1 (spring 2000): 17.
12. For an exploration of how humanitarian intervention challenges the postulates of the statist paradigm, see Parekh, "Rethinking Humanitarian Intervention."

13. Soliman Awaad, "Sovereignty and Intervention: The Legal Aspects," paper presented at the Conference on State Sovereignty in the Twenty-First Century: Concept, Relevance, and Limits, New Delhi, July 23–24, 2001, 4.

14. *The Responsibility to Protect*, report of the International Commission on Intervention and State Sovereignty (Ottawa: International Development Research Center, 2001), xii.

15. *Responsibility to Protect*, 36.

16. The three cases are discussed in detail in Wheeler, *Saving Strangers*, 55–139.

17. Michael Walzer, "The Argument about Humanitarian Intervention," *Dissent*, vol. 49, no. 1 (winter 2002): 6; www.dissentmagazine.org/archive (downloaded March 7, 2002).

18. A humanitarian justification was explicitly rejected by the Vietnamese foreign finister as a legitimate basis for the use of force. Foreign Minister Nguyen Co Thach told Congressman Stephen Solarz that "human rights was not a question; that was their problem. . . . We were concerned only with security" (quoted in Stephen A. Garrett, *Doing Good and Doing Well: An Examination of Humanitarian Intervention* [Westport, Conn.: Praeger, 1999], 120). For a detailed discussion of the Vietnamese intervention, see Gary Klintworth, *Vietnam's Intervention in Cambodia in International Law* (Canberra: Australian National University, 1984).

19. On the basis of interviews with survivors of the Pol Pot regime, William Shawcross concluded that "the Vietnamese intervention had been a true liberation" (quoted in Klintworth, *Vietnam's Intervention in International Law*, 65). Further evidence for this claim is provided by Prince Sihanouk, who said that the Cambodian people welcomed the Vietnamese as "saviours" (*Cambodian Information Office Newsletter*, May 1997, 19, quoted in Klintworth, *Vietnam's Intervention in International Law*, 65). As a seasoned observer of the region, Nayan Chanda, reflected: "In hundreds of Cambodian villages, the Vietnamese invasion was greeted with joy and disbelief. The Khmer Rouge cadres and militia were gone. People were free again to live as families, to go to bed without fearing the next day . . . it was as if salvation had come. . . . One refrain that I heard constantly from the survivors was 'If the Vietnamese hadn't come, we'd all be dead'" (Nayan Chanda, *Brother Enemy the War after the War* [New York: Collier, 1986], 370).

20. Quoted in Klintworth, *Vietnam's Intervention in International Law*, 62.

21. Fernando Tesón, *Humanitarian Intervention: An Inquiry into Law and Morality* (Dobbs Ferry, N.Y.: Transnational Publishers, 1998), 106–7.

22. Klintworth, *Vietnam's Intervention in International Law*, 76.

23. *Responsibility to Protect*, 45.

24. Parekh, "Rethinking Humanitarian Intervention," 55–56. This definition of a successful humanitarian intervention is also encapsulated in Tesón's test as to whether it has "rescued the victims of oppression, and whether human rights have subsequently been restored." See Tesón, *Humanitarian Intervention*, 106.

25. This occurred in the Cambodian case because Vietnam's toppling of Pol Pot for exclusively national security reasons ended the tyranny of the Khmer Rouge over the Cambodian people. Such a fortuitous result cannot be guaranteed in other cases. I am grateful to Jack Donnelly for alerting me to the significance of this latter point.

26. I am grateful to Colin McInnes for suggesting this term. The moral philosopher Peter French refers to cases where actions motivated by other reasons accidentally lead to good ends as "unintended good Samaritanship" (Peter French, ed., *A World Without Responsibility* [New York: Saint Martin's Press, 1991], 5). I am grateful to Toni Erskine for bringing French's work to my attention.

27. The term warlord is popularly evoked to describe the political makeup of failed states. I am following the New Oxford Dictionary of English, which defines a warlord as "a military commander, especially an aggressive regional commander with individual autonomy."

28. Briefing by the American Red Cross, October 8, 2001; www.redcross.org/news/ds/0109wtc/011008afghanaid.html (downloaded March 17, 2002).

29. The litany of abuses is set out in the State Department's Report, "The Taliban's War Against Women," U.S. Department of State International Information Programs, November 17, 2001; www.usinfo.state.gov/topical/rights/women/01111702.htm (downloaded March 16, 2002).

30. "President Bush Announces Military Strikes in Afghanistan," October 7, 2001, U.S. Department of State International Information Programs; www.usinfo.state.gov/regional/eur/terrorism/bush1007.htm (downloaded March 16, 2002).

31. "President Bush Announces Military Strikes in Afghanistan," October 7, 2001, U.S. Department of State International Information Programs; www.usinfo.state.gov/regional/eur/terrorism/bush1007.htm (downloaded March 16, 2002).

32. British prime minister Tony Blair reportedly had stressed to Bush his firm belief that counterterrorist goals should be pursued in conjunction with relief efforts. Michael Evans, "Airstrikes May Have to Wait for Aid Airlift," the *Times* (London); www.thetimes.co.uk (downloaded May 20, 2002).

33. Joseph J. Collins, "Special Briefing on Humanitarian Assistance for Afghanistan"; www.centcom.mil/news/press_briefings/Franks_18jan.htm (downloaded March 19, 2002).

34. Andrew S. Natsios, "Special Press Briefing on Humanitarian Assistance to Afghanistan," U.S. Department of State, January 3, 2002; www.state.gov/p/sa/ris/rm/7027.htm (downloaded May 20, 2002).

35. Jim Garamone, "Humanitarian Success Story in Afghanistan"; www.militarylifestyle.com/home/ (downloaded June 19, 2002).

36. Quoted in Jonathan Chait, "Look Who's Against Dropping Food," *New Republic*, November 5, 2001; www.thenewrepublic.com/110501/chait110501.html (downloaded March 23, 2002).

37. Quoted in Keith Ewing, "Tearfund: Safe Areas for Afghanistan Better than Air-Drops," *Reuters*, October 12, 2001; www.alertnet.org/thenews/fromthefield/300678 (downloaded March 20, 2002.

38. See interview with Austen Davis, general director of MSF Holland, October 15, 2001; www.msf.org/countries/page.cfm?articleid=6305a703-eb70-4f41-8a0e25ed5f24969e (downloaded March 22, 2002).

39. Stephen Castle, "Humanitarian Air Drops Criticised after US Aid Kills Woman in Her Home," the *Independent*, November 30, 2001; www.independent.co.uk (downloaded May 20, 2002). Nathan Ford, "Afghanistan: Humanitarian Aid and Military Intervention Don't Mix," Médécins Sans Frontières website, November 7, 2001; http://www.msf.org/countries/page.cfm?articleid=6a534f6c-233b-46ae-83bbef2580a86ad4 (downloaded March 22, 2002.

40. Claude Moncorgé, "Humanitarianism Doesn't Rhyme with Military," *Liberation*; www.perso.fraise.net/compose/liberation-foodbombs.html (downloaded March 22, 2002).

41. Andrew S. Natsios, "Special Press Briefing on Humanitarian Assistance to Afghanistan," U.S. Department of State, January 3, 2002; www.state.gov/p/sa/ris/rm/7027.htm (downloaded May 20, 2002).

42. Jonathan Steele, "Forgotten Victims," the *Guardian*, May 20, 2002.

43. Carl Conetta, "Strange Victory: A Critical Appraisal of Operation Enduring Freedom and the Afghanistan War," Project on Defense Alternatives, January 30, 2002; www.comw.org/pda/0201strangevic.html (downloaded March 7, 2002).

44. These figures are arrived at by estimating the mortality rate among internally displaced persons based on a comparable figure with the death rate in the refugee camps. This in turn is contrasted with the mortality rate before the bombing took place. For a fuller discussion, see Conetta, "Strange Victory," and Steele, "Forgotten Victims."

45. Steele, "Forgotten Victims."

46. Carl Conetta, "Operation Enduring Freedom: Why a Higher Rate of Civilian Bombing Casualties," Project on Defense Alternatives, Briefing Report 11, January 24, 2002; www.comw.org/pda/0201oef.html (downloaded January 25, 2002). The most controversial assessment of the number of civilian casualties was provided by Marc W. Herold in December 2001. See Herold, "Afghan Killing Fields," letter to the *Guardian*, February 13, 2002. For his full report, see Herold, "A Dossier on Civilian Victims of United States' Aerial Bombing of Afghanistan: A Comprehensive Accounting" (unpublished manuscript), December 3, 2001. A report by Associated Press dated February 11, 2002, and based on eyewitness accounts claimed that the casualty figure did not exceed a 1,000. See Deb Riechmann, "Hundreds Lost, Not Thousands," Associated Press, February 11, 2002; www.msnbc.com/news/704903.asp?cp1=1 (downloaded May 15, 2002).

47. Cited in William Arkin, "Fear of Civilian Deaths May Have Undermined Effort," *Los Angeles Times*, January 16, 2002; www.latimes.com (downloaded January 16, 2002).

48. For a discussion of the ethical issues raised by U.S. targeting policy, see Nicholas J. Wheeler, "Dying for 'Enduring Freedom': Accepting Responsibility for Civilian Casualties in the War against Terrorism," *International Relations* 16, no. 2 (2002): 205–25.

49. Quoted in Conetta, "Strange Victory," 21.

50. Conetta, "Strange Victory," 27–31.

51. I am grateful to Amin Saikal for suggesting this point to me.

52. Conetta, "Strange Victory," 15.

53. Conetta, "Strange Victory," 6.

54. Chait, "Look Who's Against Dropping Food." Also see Michael Walzer, "Can There Be a Decent Left," *Dissent*, spring 2002; www.dissentmagazine.org/editors/index_editors.htm (downloaded July 4, 2002).

55. Simon Chesterman, "Humanitarian Intervention and Afghanistan," in *Humanitarian Intervention and International Relations*, ed. Jennifer Welsh (Oxford: Oxford University Press, forthcoming).

56. "You Can Only Defend by Finding Terrorists and Rooting Them Out," interview with U.S. secretary of defense, February 25, 2002; www.telegraph.co.uk/ (downloaded March 16, 2002).

57. "President Outlines War Effort, Remarks by the president to the George C. Marshall ROTC Award Seminar on National Security," April 17, 2002; www.whitehouse.gov/news/releases/2002 (downloaded May 20, 2002).

58. "Powell Calls for Reconstruction in Afghanistan," International Information Programs, April 24, 2002; www.usinfo.gov/regional/nea/sasia/afghan/text/0424pwl.htm (downloaded May 25, 2002). Also see "Congressional Report: Afghan Aid Package Approved," International Information Programs, www.usinfo.gov/regional/nea/sasia/afghan/text/0321aid.htm (downloaded May 25, 2002).

59. "Afghanistan: US$1.18 Billion Still Needed for Recovery Aid in 2002, UN Says," UN News Center, March 3, 2002.

60. The phrase is Conetta's.
61. UN Security Council Resolution 1386, December 20, 2002.
62. After the assassination of one of the five newly appointed vice presidents, Karzai relied on American bodyguards to protect him. His own vulnerability was graphically underlined on September 5, 2002, when he narrowly escaped assassination during a visit to Herat.
63. Michael Ignatieff, "Nation-Building Lite," *New York Times*, July 28, 2002; www.nytimes.com/2002/07/28/magazine/28nation (downloaded July 29, 2002).
64. "The Loya Jirga: One Small Step Forward," Afghanistan Briefing, International Crisis Group, May 16, 2002, 2–3.
65. Elizabeth Olson, "U.N. Official Calls for a Larger International Force in Afghanistan," *New York Times*, March 28, 2002, A14.
66. Olson, "U.N. Official Calls for a Larger International Force."
67. Olson, "U.N. Official Calls for a Larger International Force." This was also the urgent recommendation of the International Crisis Group. In *Securing Afghanistan: The Need for More International Action*, a report published in March 2002, the International Crisis Group called for the immediate expansion of the force from 4,500 to upward of 25,000 with a mandate to provide security in the major cities and secure the main transport routes.
68. "Afghanistan: International Community Urged to Improve Security;" letter from Kenneth Roth, executive director of Human Rights Watch to the president of the Security Council, May 6, 2002; www.hw.org/press/2002/05/afghanlet/050702.htm (downloaded May 25, 2002). Peter Bouckaert and Saman Zia-zarafi in an op-ed piece for the *Washington Post* on March 20 had pointed out that factional leaders were carving up the country and that the Tajik, Uzbek, and Hazara leaders who controlled northern Afghanistan were responsible for human rights abuses against Pashtun civilians in the north. They cite one old man in an abandoned village who pleaded, "If the foreigners don't help us, we won't be alive." Peter Bouckaert and Saman Zia-Zarifi, "For the Sins of the Taliban," *Washington Post*, March 20, 2002, A33.
69. "Afghanistan: Rise in Factional Fighting Threatens Fragile Peace," press release by Human Rights Watch, May 7, 2002.
70. Gary J. Gilmore, "U.S. Military Will Help Train Afghan Army," American Force Press Service, March 25, 2002; www.ntcgl.navy.mil/bulletin/operation.html (downloaded March 28, 2002). Also Ann Scott Tyson, "Pentagon Challenge: Build an Afghan Army," www.globalpolicy.org/security/peacekpg/training/0411afg.htm, April 11, 2002 (downloaded on June 13, 2002).
71. Ignatieff, "Nation-Building Lite."
72. Ahmed Rashid, "Afghanistan Still Waiting to be Rescued," *Far Eastern Economic Review*, March 14, 2002; www.e-ariana.com/articles/artic225.htm (downloaded June 14, 2002). In a speech to the Senate Foreign Relations Committee on March 21, 2002, Senator Joseph Biden noted that "Gen. McColl's [British Commander of ISAF] planners has worked up a detailed strategy for creating an Afghan army and taking at least the heavy weaponry away from local warlords. "US Must Stay the Course in Afghanistan, Biden Says," International Information Programs; www.usinfo.state.gov/regional/nea/sasia/afghan/ (downloaded May 21, 2002).
73. For a longer discussion of this argument, see Wheeler, *Saving Strangers,* 188–200.
74. A similar view is taken by Sarah Sewall, who writes that "President George W. Bush is effectively setting up the UN to fail in Afghanistan, much as his Father's policies sowed the seeds for failure in Somalia." Sarah Sewall, "Confronting the Warlord Culture," *Boston*

*Globe*, June 6, 2002; www.globalpolicy.org/security/issues/afghan/2002/0606warlords. htm (downloaded June 9, 2002). Walter Clarke (who was deputy chief of mission at the UN embassy in Somalia during Operation Restore Hope) and Jeffrey Herbst argue that the failure to disarm the Somali warlords was a "tragic mistake" and that the United States "simply postponed the problems that logically followed from the intervention." Walter Clarke and Jeffrey Herbst, "Somalia and the Future of Humanitarian Intervention," *Foreign Affairs*, vol. 75, no. 2 (1996): 74–75.

75. Glenn Kessler, "U.S. Fears Grow over Turmoil in Afghanistan," *Washington Post*, August 8, 2002; www.washingtonpost.com/a57194-2002aug7?language=printe (downloaded September 10, 2002).

76. U.S. Deputy Secretary of Defense Paul Wolfowitz, interview with Ahmed Rashid, *Daily Telegraph*, August 21, 2002; available at Defense Link, U.S. Department of Defense, www.defenselink.mil/news/aug2002/t08292002_t0821.html (downloaded September 6, 2002). General Tommy Franks, speaking at Bagram Air Force base north of Kabul in late August, stated: "There are in fact views and a number of places that would indicate the desirability of expanding the International Security Assistance Force" (quoted in Michael R. Gordon, "U.S. Backs Increase in Peacekeepers for Afghanistan," *New York Times*, August 30, 2002; www.nytimes.com/30afgh.html?tntemail0=&pagewanted= print&position=to [downloaded August 31, 2002]).

77. Michael R. Gordon, "U.S. Backs Increase in Peacekeepers for Afghanistan," *New York Times*, August 30, 2002; www.nytimes.com/30AFGH.html?tntemail0=&pagewanted= print&position=to (downloaded August 31, 2002). Some of the ideas under consideration in the administration such as an air and land mobile armored unit for deployment to trouble spots was first suggested by William Durch in his "A Realistic Plan to Save Afghanistan," *Washington Post*, August 30, 2002; www.washingtonpost.com/a18564-2002jul29?language=printe (downloaded September 10, 2002).

78. Michael R. Gordon, "U.S. Backs Increase in Peacekeepers for Afghanistan," *New York Times*, August 30, 2002; www.nytimes.com/30afgh.html?tntemail0=&pagewanted= print&position=to (downloaded August 31, 2002).

79. Mike Jendrzejczyk, "A Major U-Turn in U.S. Policy on Peacekeeping," *International Herald Tribune*, September 6, 2002; www.iht.com/ihtsearch.php?id=69895&owner= (IHT)&date=20020909155211 (downloaded September 10, 2002).

80. This was the view of Senator Biden, whose preference was for other states to contribute the bulk of an enlarged ISAF, but he was emphatic that the U.S. should commit "to insuring the mission's success [and] . . . if the deployment of American troops as part of an international force is deemed necessary, we should certainly step up to the plate" (quoted in "U.S. Must Stay the Course in Afghanistan, Biden Says"). U.S. forces in Afghanistan are committed to providing logistic support, communications, and military assistance to ISAF.

81. See comments by Ted Galen Carpenter, "After Afghanistan: The Future of Intervention and Nation Building," Cato Institute Policy Forum, Washington, D.C., December 12, 2001.

82. Fred Hiatt, "Underachieving Afghanistan," May 20, 2002, *Washington Post*; www.washingtonpost.com/ac2/wp-dyn/A42742 (downloaded May 20, 2002).

83. Walzer, "Can There Be a Decent Left." This claim also finds endorsement from Martin Woollacott, who writes, "But a new interventionism governed by the drive against terrorism is not primarily about rescuing 'them' but about rescuing 'us.' Tony Blair finds it possible to sit these two things side by side, presenting Afghanistan as both a pre-emption

of terror and a *humanitarian intervention. Of course this is correct, but we know which came first*" ("Peacekeeping Is No Longer about Helping 'Them' but 'Us,'" *The Guardian*, July 5, 2002 [emphasis added]).

84. Roberto Belloni, "Kosovo and Beyond: Is Humanitarian Intervention Transforming International Society," *Human Rights and Human Welfare*, vol. 2, no. 1 (winter 2002): 38.

85. This case is discussed in detail in Wheeler, *Saving Strangers*, 111–39.

86. An exponent of this view is Noam Chomsky. See Chomsky, *The New Military Humanism: Lessons from Kosovo* (Monroe, Maine: Common Courage Press, 1999).

87. Noam Chomsky, *9-11* (New York: Seven Stories Press, 2001).

88. Walzer, "Can There Be a Decent Left."

89. I owe this point to Patricia Owens.

90. Miller, "Humanitarian Intervention," 17. Miller identifies Walzer's writings as indicative of this position. He cites Walzer's claim that "all states have an interest in global stability [because] "Uncivilized behaviour . . . tends to spread, to be imitated and reiterated . . . [leading to] turmoil and lawlessness nearer home (quoted in Miller, "Humanitarian Intervention," 17).

91. Miller, "Humanitarian Intervention," 17–18. He might have cited the case of Rwanda in support of his argument: those African states that had the will to act lacked the means, and those Western states that had the means to act lacked the will.

92. Tony Blair, speech to the Labour Party Conference, October 2, 2001; www.cnn.com/2001/world/europe/10/02/ret.blair.address (downloaded July 4, 2002).

# Contributors

**Michael Barnett** is a professor of political science and director of the International Studies Program at the University of Wisconsin. His teaching and research interests are in the areas of international relations, international organizations, and Middle Eastern politics. His most recent books are *Identity and Foreign Policy in the Middle East*, coedited with Shibley Telhami (2002), and *Eyewitness to a Genocide: The United Nations and Rwanda* (2002).

**Richard Caplan** is a research fellow at the Center for International Studies, Oxford University, and a lecturer in politics and international relations at the University of Reading. His writings on international organizations and conflict management have appeared in *International Affairs, International Peacekeeping, Survival, Diplomacy & Statecraft, Nations and Nationalism*, the *Journal of Strategic Studies*, and *Forced Migration Review*, among other publications. He is the author, most recently, of *A New Trusteeship? The International Administration of War-Torn Territories* (2002).

**Simon Chesterman** is a senior associate at the International Peace Academy, where he directs the Project on Transitional Administrations. Before joining the International Peace Academy, he worked at the International Criminal Tribunal for Rwanda and with the Office for the Coordination of Humanitarian Affairs in the Federal Republic of Yugoslavia. He is the author of *Just War or Just Peace? Humanitarian Intervention and International Law* (2001) and the editor of *Civilians in War* (2001).

**Martin L. Cook** is a professor of philosophy at the U.S. Air Force Academy. He is the former Elihu Root Professor of Military Studies and professor of ethics at the United States Army War College. Before joining the War College faculty in 1998, he was a tenured faculty member at Santa Clara University. He has also taught at the College of William and Mary, Saint John's College, and Gustavus Adolphus College.

**Sohail H. Hashmi** is Alumnae Foundation Associate Professor of International Relations at Mount Holyoke College. He is the author of numerous articles on Islamic ethics and international relations and the editor or coeditor of five books, including *Islamic Political Ethics: Civil Society, Pluralism, and Conflict* (2002). He is currently completing a book on the Islamic ethics of war and peace.

**Anthony F. Lang Jr.** teaches political science at Albright College. He previously served as a program officer at the Carnegie Council on Ethics and International Affairs, directing the council's work with faculty in higher education to incorporate ethics into their teaching and research and the council's Studies Program on Ethics and the Use of Force. Before joining the council, he was an assistant professor of political science at the American University in Cairo. He is the author of *Agency and Ethics: The Politics of Humanitarian Intervention* (2002) and the coeditor, with Albert Pierce and Joel Rosenthal, of *Ethics and the Future of Conflict* (2003).

**Julie Mertus** is an assistant professor in the School of International Service at American University. She was formerly a senior fellow at the United States Institute of Peace, a Harvard Law School human rights fellow, a MacArthur Foundation fellow, a Fulbright fellow (Romania), and counsel to Human Rights Watch. She is the author or editor of more than three dozen academic articles and five books, including *Kosovo: How Myths and Truths Started a War* (1999), *The Suitcase: Refugees' Voices from Bosnia and Croatia* (1997), and *War's Offensive Against Women: The Humanitarian Challenge in Bosnia* (2000).

**Terry Nardin** is a professor of political science at the University of Wisconsin–Milwaukee. His authored or edited books include *Law, Morality, and the Relations of States* (1983), *Traditions of International Ethics* (1992), *The Ethics of War and Peace* (1996), *The Philosophy of Michael Oakeshott* (2001), and *International Relations in Political Thought* (2002).

**Nicholas Onuf** is a professor of international relations at Florida International University and the author of *World of Our Making: Rules and Rule in Social Theory and International Relations* (1989), *The Republican Legacy of International Thought* (1998), among others. He is currently writing a book with his brother, Peter Onuf, *Liberal Histories, Nation Making, and the Coming of the Civil War*.

**Amir Pasic** is currently the director of corporate and foundation relations at the Paul H. Nitze School of Advanced International Studies of Johns Hopkins University. He was previously foundation specialist at the Library of Congress and deputy director of the Rockefeller Brothers Fund Project on World Security. He was formerly a fellow and visiting scholar at Brown University's Thomas J. Watson Institute for International Studies.

**Thomas G. Weiss** is presidential professor at the Graduate Center of the City University of New York and director of the Ralph Bunche Institute for International Studies, where he is also codirector of the United Nations Intellectual History Project and editor of *Global Governance.* His recent books include *Military–Civilian Interactions: Intervening in Humanitarian Crises* (1999); *Humanitarian Challenges and Intervention,* 2d edition (2000); *The United Nations and Changing World Politics,* 3d edition (2001); *Ahead of the Curve? UN Ideas and Global Challenges* (2001); and *The Responsibility to Protect: Research, Bibliography, and Background* (2001). He is currently working on several books, including two edited volumes on terrorism and on human rights.

**Nicholas J. Wheeler** is a senior lecture in international politics and director of graduate studies at the University of Wales. He previously taught at the University of Hull and King's College London. His research interests include humanitarian intervention, human rights, and normative international relations theory with special reference to international society. He is the author, with Ian Clark, of *The British Origins of Nuclear Strategy, 1945–55* (1989), and of numerous chapters in edited volumes and books, and he is the coeditor, with Timothy Dunne, of *Human Rights in Global Politics.*

# Index